A Political Economy of Africa

Claude Ake

Longman

Longman Group Limited,
Longman House, Burnt Mill,
Harlow, Essex CM20 2JE

Published in Nigeria by Longman Nigeria Limited
and in the United States by Longman Inc.

Associated companies, branches and representatives
throughout the world

First published 1981

ISBN 0 582 64374 0 (Cased)
     0 582 64370 8 (Paper)

Printed and bound in Great Britain by
William Clowes (Beccles) Limited, Beccles and London

Contents

List of tables

Preface

I have written this book in the hope that it will advance the study and understanding of contemporary Africa. In particular it is intended to shed light on the salient features of contemporary Africa, how they have come to be, and how they might change. Throughout this work the emphasis is on how to approach the study of Africa so that we can better understand how things are and why. In so far as I have taken an interest in how Africa might change, this interest has generally taken the form of examining and following the logic and dynamics of events to see where they might lead, rather than trying to bring Africa around to a particular state of being, however desirable. That is not to say that I do not appreciate the necessity for change in Africa. I believe I do. But I also believe that the conventional wisdom about the necessity of understanding society in order to change it should be taken more seriously. Many well-meaning attempts to change things in Africa have come to grief for lack of understanding, and the quest for understanding Africa has all too often been ambushed and thwarted by our fixation on what ought to be.

This book is not so much a study of the African economy as of the total society. That is not to say the title is misleading. On the contrary. The title properly draws attention to the approach of this book, and to where its real potential for advancing the study of Africa lies. This method, based on dialectical materialism, assumes that material conditions, particularly the economic system, are the decisive formative influences on social life, and constitute the essential point of departure for discovering the laws of motion of a society and for explaining it. If I devote a great deal of attention to the economic system it is not on account of a narrow interest in economics but because of the pervasive influence of the economic system in society. In fact the approach of this work essentially rejects the idea of specialised disciplines, such as economics, in favour of a composite social science using material conditions as its focal point and proceeding dialectically.

The organisation of the work reflects its method. The exposition has been organised in such a way as to bring into clear relief the logical and historical development of the salient features of contemporary Africa. I have tried to avoid treating the present reality as a fossilised determination but rather as something which is in process, something which has become, and will pass away. This is all the more necessary because we do not really understand a society until we can account for how it came to be what it is, until we can articulate its laws of motion. I am by no means claiming to have discovered the laws of motion of Africa. The best that can be claimed for this work is that it tries to clarify some problems, to show how we might profitably proceed in our study of Africa, and why.

I have had to treat Africa in an undifferentiated manner. It could hardly be otherwise given the fact that I am mainly interested in how to approach the study of Africa so as to discover the logic of its movement. I am sure that there are aspects of Africa for which the analytical tools offered here are not so suitable, and that some of my generalisations may well be irrelevant or even misleading in some instances. Even with these weaknesses, if this work advances the study of Africa, its purpose will have been well served.

Claude Ake
Faculty of Social Sciences
University of Port Harcourt
Nigeria

1 Methodology and theoretical foundations

Methodology

A very important feature of this book is its method of analysis, which is based on dialectical materialism. It is therefore necessary to begin with an explanation of what this method is and why it is desirable to use it. What are its characteristics?

1 The primacy of material conditions

First it is a method which gives primacy to material conditions, particularly economic factors, in the explanation of social life. The justification for giving economic factors such primacy should become clearer as the book progresses. But a brief discussion is in order here. To begin with, economic need is man's most fundamental need. Unless man is able to meet this need he cannot exist in the first place. Man must eat before he can do anything else – before he can worship, pursue culture or become an economist. When an individual achieves a level of economic well-being such that he can take the basic economic necessities, particularly his daily food, for granted, the urgency of economic need loses its edge. Nevertheless, the primacy remains. The fact that one is not constantly preoccupied with, and motivated by, economic needs, shows that the needs are being met; it does not show they are not of primary importance.

Just as economic need is the primary need, so economic activity is man's primary activity. The primacy of work, that is economic productivity, is the corollary of the primacy of economic need. Man is first and foremost a worker or a producer. It is by man's productive activity that he is able to obtain the economic means which he needs to sustain life. In short, man must eat to live but he must work in order to eat. Thus productive activity is the condition for all other activities. This fact is amply reflected in the popular consciousness, for people invariably identify themselves in terms of their economic role: 'I am a farmer', 'John is an engineer'. It is true that man does not live by bread alone. But it is a more fundamental truth that man cannot live without bread.

The methodological implication of this for the student of society is that he must pay particular attention to the economic structure of society and indeed use it as the point of departure for studying other aspects of society. Once we understand what the material assets and constraints of a society are, how the society produces goods to meet its material needs, how the goods are distributed, and what types of social relations arise from the organisation of production, we have come a long way to understanding the culture of that society, its laws, its religious system, its political system and even its modes of thought. Thus anyone who makes an empirical study of historical societies, including our contemporary societies, will find the following.

1 Those from the economically privileged groups tend to be better educated, 'more cultured', to have higher social status, to be more 'successful' professionally and politically. This means that economic inequality is extremely important, tending to reproduce itself endlessly in a series of other inequalities.

2 Those who are economically privileged tend to be interested in preserving the existing social order; and those who are disadvantaged by the social order, particularly its distribution of wealth, have a strong interest in changing the social order, particularly its distribution of wealth. In this way the economic structure sets the general trend of political interests and political alignments.

3 In so far as there is economic inequality in a society, that society cannot have political democracy because political power will tend to polarise around economic power. Also a society where a high degree of economic inequality exists must necessarily be repressive. This repression arises from the need to curb the inevitable demand of the have-nots for redistribution. We see here economic conditions not only setting the tone of politics but also defining the role of coercion in society.

4 The morality and values of a society tend to support the preservation of the existing division of labour and distribution of wealth in that society. The autonomy of morality and social values is more apparent than real. Contemporary Western morality condemns theft. And we forget that theft as a moral value is something created and dependent on a particular economic condition. Where there is no scarcity and no private property, the idea of theft would not arise.

These propositions show the importance of economic conditions in understanding society. In looking at Africa, this study has given due attention to economic conditions. As we shall see, economic conditions help us to understand why the colonising powers came to Africa, why they established the particular types of political systems that they did, how the nationalist movement arose, etc. By taking cognizance of the economic factors we are able to improve on the traditional treatment of problems such as tribalism and nation-building. In the case of tribalism traditional treatments have failed to grasp it fully because they have regarded it merely as consciousness and failed to situate the consciousness in material conditions. Thus they fail to take advantage of the obvious and important fact that tribalism flourishes mainly because it is useful, especially in the economic sense. It provides access to 'important' people for villagers and the unemployed seeking jobs in the cities; it fills to a considerable extent the gap left by the lack of a social security system in most of Africa; and it serves the economic and political interests of the African bourgeoisie by promoting solidaristic ties across class lines. Our failure to take full account of the economic underpinnings of tribalism has also been detrimental to the effort to solve the 'problem of tribalism'. Attempts to reduce tribalism have suffered from not confronting the issue of making tribal identity less useful economically.

2   The dynamic character of reality

The second major characteristic of the method used here is its particular emphasis on the dynamic character of reality. This is a method which refuses to look at aspects of the world as simple identities, or discrete elements, or as being static. The method encourages us to think of the world in terms of continuity and relatedness and with a keen awareness that this continuity is essentially very complex and also problematic. Above all it treats the world as something which is full of movement and dynamism, the movement and dynamism being provided by the contradictions which pervade existence. The method assumes that the world cannot be understood by thinking in terms of simple harmonies and irreconcilable contrasts. It encourages us to recognise that the seemingly united and harmonious is prone to contradiction, that there is a striving for unity or at least synthesis among the diverse. In short the method looks at the world dialectically.

One of the main weaknesses of mainstream Western social science is its discouragement of dialectical thinking, a weakness that has also spilled over into African Studies. This discouragement of dialectical thinking is related to the ideological commitment of Western social science to the justification and preservation of the existing social order. With this kind of commitment mainstream Western social science has an inbuilt bias in favour of categories such as mechanical and organic solidarity (Emile Durkheim), traditional and bureaucratic authority (Max Weber), universalism and particularism (Parsons), Gemeinschaft and Gesellschaft (Toennies), democratic and totalitarian political systems which are discrete and in sharp contrast and suggestive of good and bad. The categories connoting good are associated with the prevailing Western society being justified; the need to justify by designating as good traps social science into drawing a very sharp distinction between the preferred category and others. Furthermore the penchant for justification traps Western social science into fixing the categories rigidly and minimising the possibilities of change, for if the possibility of the preferred category changing for the better is allowed, it is admitted that the preferred category was imperfect in the first place. So we have come to have a social science of discrete, sharply contrasting and rigidly fixed categories and entities, a science which is inadequate for understanding a complex social world of subtle shades in which change is ubiquitous.

The deficiences of this social science came out very clearly in the study of non-Western societies, especially the less economically advanced ones now designated 'underdeveloped countries'. Confronted with the study of these societies it became quite impossible to conceal the fact that the bulk of Western social science is tendentially geared to the study of order rather than change. The attempt to deal with this is instructive. The methodology and theories of change which were devised to meet this challenge amounted essentially to introducing intermediary categories between the old categories, connoting the preferred state of being, and the others. Examples are Rostow's, *Stages of Economic Growth*, Organski's *Stages of Political Development*, the theories of modernisation which were so influential in African Studies. This attempt to introduce

3

theories of change and make analysis more dynamic only underlined the inadequacies of Western social science. Stringing together a series of categories called stages of development and stating what form of social engineering might be needed to realise a particular stage does not constitute a theory of change. This device did not teach us anything about social change but merely revealed further the ideological bias of Western social science, for what the procedure in question was really drawing attention to was that the Western societies were the peak of social evolution and that in so far as other societies needed to change, the real question was how far they could be like the West. As if to stress this ideological bias and the fundamental lack of interest in change, the new developmental approaches hardly raised the question as to how the preferred categories (Western societies) might change. These types of problem have hampered students of Africa who are studying societies where change is particularly ubiquitious.

3   The relatedness of different elements of society

The third distinctive feature of the method used in this work is that it encourages the student to take account systemmatically of the interactions of the different elements of social life, especially economic structure, social structure, political structure and the belief system. Our method assumes the relationship between all these social structures. Indeed it has an implicit theory of the relationship of these structures and of all aspects of social life. According to this theory, it is the economic factor which is the most decisive of all these elements of society and which largely determines the character of the others. Thus if knowledge of the economic is available the general character of the social system, the political system, the belief system, etc. of the relevant society can be reasonably conjectured. That is not to say that the economic structure is autonomous and strictly determines the others. All the social structures are interdependent and interact in complex ways. Each one of them affects the character of every other one and is in turn affected by it. But our method assumes that it is the economic factor which provides the axis around which all the movement takes place, and imparts a certain orderliness to the interaction.

The points are illustrated in the course of the development of this work. For instance, in the early chapters we concentrate on the material conditions, describing the capitalist penetration of Africa and delineating the economic systems established in Africa by the colonising powers. Once we grasp the structure and the dynamics of the colonial economy we immediately begin to move away from economic factors – merely by following the dynamics of the economic system. Thus by following the dynamics of the economic system we see how it leads to the transformation of existing social structures, and how it leads to the emergence of new social structures, particularly an African petit-bourgeoisie whose interests soon put it in opposition to the colonial system. From then on we move into the politics of the nationalist movement and the overthrow of the colonial political system – but the economic system which generated the changes is itself not overthrown. So we have indigenous leaders who are in political office but with little economic base. This contradiction between economic power and political power becomes a source of further interesting development as the new rulers try to use the only tool they have, political power, to create an economic base in order to consolidate their economic power. At this point we see how the political is influencing and even transforming the economic structures and social structures. In the latter part of this work we examine the structure of the postcolonial economies of Africa as well as the efforts that have been made to achieve economic development. We show how the failure of economic development creates political conditions which seem poised to transform the economic system fundamentally. The dialectic method and our attention to material conditions allows us to move in an orderly manner between the elements of the social system, to delineate the relations between them and the logic of their metamorphosis.

It remains to add that the connectedness of the economic structure, social structure, belief system and political system demands an interdisciplinary approach to the study of society. If society is so connected it cannot be studied in any depth without drawing on each of the specialised social science disciplines used for studying the various aspects of man and society. But it will not do to draw on them in a haphazard and eclectic manner, or to assume that the type of interdisciplinary approach required here is the simultaneous application of the specialised disciplines. What is really required is the forging of a new synthetic discipline, on materialistic foundations, a social science to replace the social sciences.

Some advantages of this method

In the course of outlining the characteristics of our method, some of its advantages have become apparent. However, it is desirable to treat them more explicitly.

1 Insight into the dynamics of the social world

As has been shown, the approach of this book compels attention to the dynamic rather than the static, as the bulk of the conventional methods of Western social sciences are apt to do. For instance in Western political science, the most prominent problem is the problem of political stability and much of the discipline is preoccupied with an attempt to characterise the state of political stability and to define its conditions. It is much the same thing in sociology where so much effort goes into the problem of how interaction evolves roles and eventually cultures and social structures, how social order arises and is maintained. On balance, Western social science is conservative in the sense that it is heavily oriented towards the problem of how to maintain the social, economic or political order. It is unfortunate, though not perhaps so surprising, that social science in Africa is so much in the grip of the methodology of Western social science – unfortunate, because to all appearances the concerns of Western social science, particularly the maintenance of the social order, is quite different from the concerns of a continent in a hurry to develop, and so, interested less in how to maintain the existing order than how to change it. The method used here is surely more suitable for the study of transitional societies such as Africa. It frees the mind from certain attitudes and tendencies which Western social science has tended to inculcate, and which those who are interested in understanding change and bringing it about, as many people in Africa are, can ill-afford to harbour. Among these unfortunate attitudes is the disposition to see consensus everywhere and to prefer it to conflict, a prejudice against disequilibrium and a negative attitude towards contradiction. Those who want to understand the process of change, or who have a vested interest in change, cannot afford to harbour these attitudes of mind, for conflict and contradiction are the very vehicles of change and progress. In this work we will see how contradictions (of capitalism) gave impulse to the colonisation of Africa, how the contradictions of the colonial economy led to political independence, and how contradictions are shaping the general course of development of African societies.

2   The development perspective

The method of this book allows us to see social phenomena in the context of their development. All too often the methods of traditional social science encourage a view of social phenomena as things which happen to be there, fully formed and with set characteristics – as something without a 'natural history'. But the method used here encourages the perception of social phenomena as elements of a continuum, or as moments of an unfolding process. It encourages their perception as things which begin, become, and pass away.

By putting social phenomena in the context of their development we are able to gain greater understanding of them. For one thing we are able to understand not only how they come to be what they are, but also to make reasonable conjecture as to what they might become. The treatment of the problem of underdevelopment by economists sheds some light on this point. The general tendency among western economists who have concerned themselves with the problem of underdevelopment is to reduce the problem to an aggregation of factors such as lack of capital, insufficient saving, lack of technical know-how, lack of entrepreneural skills, lack of diversification of the economy. If it is the presence of these specific effects that causes underdevelopment, then the way to overcome underdevelopment is to remove them. It is easy to see that this conventional way of dealing with this problem is not in the least promising. To begin with the explanation of underdevelopment implicit in this treatment is really a tautology. On analysis, it is soon clear that the things offered by the approach under review as causes of underdevelopment are in fact symptoms of underdevelopment. That is partly why the influence of this approach on development strategy in Africa has been so disastrous. If one looks at underdevelopment from the developmental perspective suggested here, one recognises that it is not reducible to discrete elements, but rather that it is a complex phenomenon whose constituent parts have an organic unity. One will also see that this phenomenon is deeply rooted in the social, economic and political structures of Africa, and that underdevelopment cannot be overcome without a profound transformation of economic, social and political structures.

3 A comprehensive view of society

The fact that this method emphasises the relatedness of social phenomena, particularly the economic structure, the social structure, the political structure and belief system, gives it great advantages as a tool for the study of society. In studying aspects of social life, or in explaining social problems, consciousness of this relatedness compels the student to take a more comprehensive view. The result is that his explanations are likely to have more depth. The fact that conventional Western social sciences have specialised disciplines for studying different aspects of social life – political science for the political system, sociology for the social system and economics for the economic system – unfortunately encourages a fragmentary and incomplete view of society, all the more so as the autonomous disciplines quickly create the illusion of the autonomy of the aspect of social life which each is trying to illuminate.

Worse, the systematic relation of the findings of research in each of the major disciplines of Western social science is at best obscure and at worst confusing and contradictory, so that these disciplines cannot be said to provide particular perspectives which together add up to a coherent body of knowledge, or at any rate a useful tool for the study of social life. In these circumstances it has been very difficult for Western social sciences to resist the temptation of artificially regarding those areas in which there is some fit between social science knowledge and the real world as autonomous, and ignoring the general confusion. The method of this study hopefully offers a better chance of a genuinely comprehensive view of society as well as coherent, cumulative knowledge about society.

4 Treating problems concretely rather than abstractly

One of the most important advantages of the method used here is that it encourages us to treat problems concretely rather than abstractly. In much of the Western social science that prevails in African institutions of higher learning, there is an unfortunate tendency towards abstraction in the explanation of social phenomena. For instance, one explanation of economic backwardness of developing countries which used to be very popular with development economists was something to the effect that the people in the underdeveloped countries lacked achievement motivation. But the concept of achievement motivation was very abstract, and imprecise as well. An attempt was made to quantify it by devising sets of questions by which an attitude survey could be conducted and scored to determine the extent to which achievement motivation existed. But, despite the quantification, the concept of achievement motivation remained abstract because the questions devised to test its existence were themselves abstract and full of ambiguities.

Nevertheless the fact of quantification gave the illusion of a thoroughly scientific and empirically testable explanation. But of course it led nowhere. And it could have led nowhere even if the problems of quantification had not arisen. For there was a more fundamental failing, namely, the fact that the problem of underdevelopment was being explained in terms of attitudes and left at that. The attitudes were treated as if they could be dissociated from actual historical circumstances and left floating in the air. Is it entirely accidental that one set of attitudes prevails in a particular society? If we say yes, we have no explanation. If we say no, then the question arises, what accounts for the prevalence of particular attitudes? Apart from revealing the inadequacy of the explanation of underdevelopment in attitudinal terms, this question also suggests the necessity of going beyond attitudes to the material conditions which underlie them. Attitudes, beliefs, motivation and other forms of consciousness do not exist in a vacuum, nor are they mere accidents. They reflect the history of a people. They are formed by concrete historical conditions. They cannot be understood or meaningfully discussed if they are dissociated from these historical conditions. They evolve over a long period in the course of man's interaction with his human and physical environment. That is why an explanation of underdevelopment in terms of lack of achievement motivation says very little.

Finally, one other advantage of relating the abstract to the concrete is that it helps to expose false assumptions and biases in explanations. The explanation under review illustrates the point. When the achievement motivation is placed in historical context it is found to be the acquisitive drive of capitalist societies.

If that is so, the explanation is highly biased in that it suggests that development presupposes capitalism. And in so far as the acquisitive drive is particularly strong in the industrialised capitalist societies, then the explanation is also a tautology, because it amounts to suggesting that a society is not developed because it does not have the characteristics of a developed society.

This is by no means an exhaustive treatment of the advantages of the method of this work. It is merely an illustration of some of its analytic possibilities. Further treatment of the advantages of the methodology of this work will be done implicitly in the course of the development of the work. For in the final analysis the claims of this methodology cannot rest on a mere theoretical elaboration of its advantages. In the meantime it is necessary to discuss certain basic concepts which shed light on the assumptions and the methodology of this work.

Basic concepts for the study of the economy and socio-economic formations

We have been arguing for the primacy of material conditions, especially the economic, in the study of societies. However, it is not enough to suggest that economic conditions should be given special attention and used as the point of departure for analysis. We have to go beyond this and specify how to look at economic conditions and how to relate them systematically to a conceptual framework. In this section we shall introduce and clarify some major concepts for looking at economic conditions in an orderly manner, and with the aid of these concepts show in outline what the economic system is, and then attempt to place it in the broader context of the social system so that we can begin to see the linkages between the economic structure and other social structures. As much as possible we shall avoid making arbitrary assumptions or choosing concepts haphazardly. In this connection it is useful to note that all the concepts used for this exercise derive from, or are closely associated with, the concept of labour and the labour process. It is necessary to explain why this is so.

Man is above all else a worker or a labourer. Work is the primary condition of his existence. If man does not work, he cannot live. It is true of course that what man needs to support his life exists in nature. However, it rarely exists in a form directly suitable to his needs. It is human labour which ultimately makes nature suitable for human needs. By man's labour the fish in the ocean becomes nourishment, grass and wool become clothing, trees become shelter, the waterfall generates electricity to heat and light homes and cook food. If man did not labour he would soon die, despite the prodigality of nature.

Labour or work is much more than a means of providing the economic means of human existence. It is by labour that man creates and recreates his entire material life. By work he builds dams, irrigates deserts and fashions tools, which give him new capabilities and new opportunities for acquiring knowledge. By creating and recreating his economic and other material conditions man also creates his culture, history and civilisation. Most importantly he also creates his consciousness, for even consciousness is essentially an effect of the 'environment'. In a sense man is as he works. We will now develop some concepts from the idea of labour and use them to conceptualise both an economic system and the broader social system.

Necessary labour and surplus labour

We have seen that man must labour; he must produce in order to live. Now, when a person is producing just enough for his subsistence he is said to be engaged in *necessary labour,* and what he produces for his subsistence is said to be a *necessary product,* necessary because he could not exist without it. It would be very difficult today to find a society in which everyone, or even most people, engage in necessary labour and produce a necessary product. But if we go back in the history of civilisation, including that of Africa, we readily find examples of primitive groups engaged in necessary labour. Before proceeding further, it is interesting to note some implications of this type of society. A society in which everyone produces just what he needs must also be one in which there is no division of labour, or one which has a rudimentary division of labour at best. It will also be a society in which everyone is poor – in the limited perhaps trivial sense – that they have only the necessities they manage to produce for themselves.

Finally, it will also be a society of equality, an equality underpinned by everybody's limited means – everybody has only the bare necessities. Since there is equality there is very limited scope for the oppression of one person by another, and limited scope for the development of those institutions associated with repression. It is interesting how one economic assumption of necessary labour defines the character of this simple society.

Surplus labour and surplus product

When a person produces more than he needs for his subsistence, the product (in excess of what is needed for subsistence) is called *surplus product* or *social surplus product*. The labour expended in this excess production is called *surplus labour*.

The change from a simple society, in which people are engaged in necessary labour and producing necessary products, to the more complex one, in which people engage in surplus labour and produce surplus product, goes hand in hand with the development of the division of labour. The division of labour implies the concentration of each person in what they can do well and, by extension, implies more efficiency and more wealth for the society at large. With more wealth to dispose of, a struggle for the surplus product ensues, and the possibilities of economic inequality arise. Along with economic inequality come political relations of domination and subordination, and the development of institutionalised repression, which is necessary to contain the demand of the economically disadvantaged for redistribution. What emerges is a society which is in many ways the diametrical opposite of the one associated with necessary labour.

We have looked at the distinction between two types of labour, necessary labour and surplus labour and its implications. Now let us look carefully at the labour process itself, because it is through the description of the labour process that the economic system is defined.

The labour process

The labour process consists of three elements.

1 Labour power

This comprises the physical, psychological and intellectual capabilities of man, the worker.

2 The objects of labour

These are the things to which labour power is applied. The examples which readily come to mind are the objects of nature such as coal, oil and the iron-ore in the ground, waiting to be extracted and harnessed to serve human needs, the uncultivated land. Objects of labour may also include things which some human labour has already touched, such as wood which is not yet made into furniture.

3 The means of labour

These are the instruments with which man labours. Means of labour include all tools and other aids for production, such as the access road to the farm, the vehicle which takes the worker to the factory, and the buildings in which the factory is located. The means of labour is a very important aspect of the labour process, for it is what mediates between man and nature. Without it, man's labour power is virtually useless. Without it, nature cannot be harnessed to meet man's needs.

The objects of labour plus the means of labour constitute the *means of production*. The means of production are very important both theoretically and existentially. Without the means of production man cannot produce the material conditions of his existence. A person deprived of means of production becomes helpless and in danger of perishing, for even his labour power (his individual mental and physical assets) cannot help him, since he has no tools to produce with and resources on which to apply his labour. Not surprisingly the distribution of means of production among members of a society is a matter of the utmost importance; it is the foundation of the most fundamental inequalities, conflicts and contradictions of society. As we shall see later, the distribution of the means of production among members of society is also the basis for their classification into classes. More of this later.

The productive forces

The concept of means of production which we have been discussing refers to the combination of two of the three elements of the labour process. Now all three components of the labour process (ie. labour power, objects of labour and means of labour) taken together constitute the *productive forces*. The productive forces express the overall productive capabilities of the society. They tend to develop all the time. When one talks of the development of the productive forces one may be thinking of the quantitative and qualitative improvements in labour power, for instance when people acquire more scientific education and technical skills. One could be thinking of the improvement of natural assets, such as the irrigation of arid land to make it arable. One could be thinking of the development of the technology with which man produces. The importance of the development of productive forces to a society cannot be overemphasised. The state of the development of productive forces decisively influences social organisation, culture, the level of welfare, and even consciousness. The history of Africa itself bears testimony to the importance of productive forces. It was mainly because the development of productive forces stagnated at a certain stage in African history that the colonisers were able to subordinate the continent. Africa's economic backwardness and abject dependence today reflects the state of the development of productive forces. One major reason why we have failed to make sense of politics and other events in Africa is because we have not paid enough attention to the state of the development of productive forces and its powerful influence on everything else. For instance, a lot has been written about the failure of the liberal constitutions with which many African countries came to independence, but liberal democracy could not possibly have been relevant in a situation in which the state of the development of productive forces maintains the existence of feudal relations and patron-client relations, and where the bulk of the population, ill-fed and illiterate, is isolated in villages with very poor, if any, communication linkages. It is much the same situation with the failure of socialism. The attempt to build socialism has tended to degenerate into the redistribution of poverty with immense coercion. Like liberal democracy, socialism cannot be built on good intentions. The state of the development of productive forces greatly affects its possibilities. The political and social-organisational styles being adopted in Africa prematurely (ie. ahead of the development of productive forces), invariably come out as caricatures. So much for the concept of productive forces. Let us now turn to another concept which is closely related to it, namely social relations of production.

Social relations of production

Labour or production is usually social, that is, done in cooperation or at any rate in association with others. Even in the very primitive stages of man's existence, which preceded the formation of fully-fledged societies, there was cooperative labour among members of the same family. In modern times, when a complex division of labour has emerged, labour has become highly social. The production of a single object such as a clock may involve scores of workers each contributing a specialised labour input. Indeed the socialisation of labour has become international, components of machines such as automobiles may be manufactured in several countries and then assembled.

The relations which people enter into with each other in the course of production are called the *social relations of production* or *relations of production* for short. The relations between the peasant and the feudal lord under feudalism is an example of social relations of production. In a modern factory people tend to be organised in a hierachy with a clear line of authority from the assembly line to the manager; this organisation is also an example of the social relations of production. The most famous and most important example of social relations of production is the relation between the ruling classes and subordinate class, which will be discussed soon.

It is useful to note the affinity between the social relations of production and the productive forces. They may be said to be aspects of the same thing. A particular relation of production comes into being because the productive forces are at a particular stage of development. Thus under feudalism productive forces were in a very rudimentary stage of development and land was the major means of production. The social relations of production, notably that between feudal lords and the peasants, devolved around land; obligation and rights were defined in terms of land and the feudal lord was dominant in the social relations of production (over the peasant) because he owned the land. With the development of technology and industrialisation, land became less important as the means of production; the locus of production shifted from land to the factory, and in this way capital becomes 'the means of production'.

These changes in productive forces have given rise to new relations of production, especially that between capitalists and workers. The productive forces are clearly the more dynamic element and largely determine the relations of production.

Nevertheless, the relations of production are not simply passive and dependent. They also shape, or at least influence, the productive forces. In particular they can aid or hinder their development.

The economic system

We have talked of the productive forces and the social relations of production as being really two aspects of the same thing, and we have tried to illustrate their affinity. The organic unity of productive forces and the social relations of production constitute the *economic system*, alternatively referred to as the *mode of production*.

The economic system or the mode of production is the material foundation of social life. It largely determines other aspects of social life, particularly the legal system, the political system, the belief system and the morality. Once the mode of production or the economic system is understood we have a fairly good idea of what the general character of the other aspects of the social system will be like. We have already given some indication of the dominant influence of the economic forces in our discussion of productive forces. In the course of the development of this work we will see more illustrations of the dominance of the economic system; but we will also see that the economic system is not entirely independent, but also subject to the influence of non-economic factors.

The socio-economic formation

The tendency of the mode of production or the economic system to shape the other aspects of social life – the political system, the legal system, the ideological system, etc. – has already been noted. These non-economic aspects of social life that are dependent on the economic system are collectively called the *superstructure*. This is in contrast to the economic system which is called the *substructure*. The substructure and the superstructure – or what is the same thing, the economic system and the superstructure corresponding to it – together constitute the *socio-economic formation*. What we have been referring to rather crudely here as society, or the 'broader society', is more accurately the socio-economic formation.

That completes our exposition of key concepts and our definition of the economic system. We now turn to a more detailed look at a particular type of economic system, or mode of production.

The capitalist mode of production

Two modes of production dominate the contemporary world. These are the capitalist and the socialist mode of production. We will concentrate our discussion here on the capitalist mode of production for two reasons.

First, it is the mode of production which has had the most decisive impact on Africa's history. The integration of Africa into the world capitalist system by Western colonialism and imperialism is the event which has had the most influence in shaping the economic and political development of contemporary Africa. Second, once capitalism is understood, the task of understanding the socialist mode of production is accomplished also, for socialism is a mode of production under which the contradictions of the capitalist mode of production have been resolved.

The capitalist mode of production has two main features. The first is that the means of production are very unevenly distributed to the point that we have, for all practical purposes, a society divided essentially into a small group of people who monopolise the means of production and the rest of the population who have no means of production. The second major characteristic of capitalism is commodity production, which gives capitalist society some of the characteristics of a market. Let us explore each of these features.

Monopolisation of the means of production

The capitalist mode of production polarises into a very small group of people who monopolise the available means of production, and the vast majority who essentially have no means of production. We will not go into how the distribution of means of production gets to be so unevenly distributed, except to say that it is the effect of the struggle for the social surplus product. Instead we shall look at the major implication of this uneven distribution of the means of production. Now, those who have no means of production only have their labour power to fall back on. However, there is not much that they can do with their labour power. As we have seen, labour power is useless for production without objects of labour and means of labour. And yet those with only labour power and no means of production must produce to survive. How do they do it? By hiring their labour power (themselves) to those who have the means of production. The buyer uses the labour for his purposes and in return pays wages to the owner or the labour power. But the exchange is a very unequal one. The buyer of labour power buys it only because it is to his advantage to do so. That means in effect that he buys it only in so far as he pays the wage earner (the seller of labour power) less than what his labour produces. In short he buys it only in so far as he can exploit the wage earner. The basic relation of production in capitalist society is the relation between the few who have means of production and the many who have no means of production and only their labour power. As we have seen, this is a relation of gross inequality, of subordination and domination, of exploitation and antagonism.

This relation to the means of production as owners and non-owners is called a *class relation*. Those who own the means of production constitute a class, and those who have no means of production constitute another class. Under the capitalist mode of production, the class of people who own and control the means of production are the *bourgeoisie*, and the class of people who do not have means of production are called the *proletariat*.

Exploitation under the capitalist mode of production

It is clear from what has been said so far about capitalism that the relation between these two classes has to be a relationship of domination, subjection, exploitation and antagonism. The proletariat class which has nothing but labour power lives only by the permission of the bourgoisie, for if the bourgoisie refuses to buy its labour power, it will soon starve. When the worker sells his labour power he submits to exploitation. The member of the bourgoisie who hires him (ie. buys his labour power) does so only on the expectation that the value of the product of the employee's labour power will be higher than what he pays for the labour power, that is the wage he pays to the employee. The difference between the exchange value of the proletariat's labour power and the value of its products goes into the pocket of the member of the bourgoisie who employs him as unearned income or, more accurately, *surplus value*. In this way the bourgoisie lives off the sweat of the proletariat. The proletariat are allowed to work to produce only if they accept to be paid less than what they produce; that is, they are allowed to produce, and hence to live, only if they submit to exploitation.

The relation of exploitation between capitalist and worker comes out more clearly when we reduce capital to its two components. One is constant capital. This is that part of the investment of the capitalist in non-personal factors such as raw materials, machinery and transportation. This part of capital is said to be *constant capital* because the value of these factors of production remain the same through the production process and are merely transformed. For instance, when a ton of palm-oil goes into the manufacture of soap, its value is not changed, the palm-oil is merely transformed to another state and the value of this particular input at the end of the transformation remains the same. The second component of capital is *variable capital*. This is the personal factor of production, that is the part which consists of human labour. This is the part which brings about the increase in value of capital. All the capitalist's profit or surplus value is created solely by the labour of the worker. The ratio of constant to variable capital is called *the organic composition of capital*. The extent to which the capitalist exploits the worker can be expressed with mathematical precision, as the *rate of surplus value*. The rate of surplus value is the ratio of surplus-value to variable capital. This ratio shows just how much of the worker's product goes to his own upkeep and how much of it goes into producing surplus value for the owners of capital.

Inequality in the production relation of bourgeoisie and proleteriat replicates itself endlessly in a wide variety of spheres – in the distribution of income, the allocation of status, the distribution of political power, the distribution of agreeable and disagreeable jobs, the distribution of the capacity to pursue culture and leisure, etc.

Commodity production

The second major characteristic of the capitalist mode of production is commodity production. To understand clearly what commodity production means it is useful to go back to the word *capital*. Capital is any value or economic asset which is used to generate more wealth or more accurately surplus value. In short capital is self-augmenting value. But how does this self-augmentation take place? How, for instance, does one use an economic asset such as money to augment itself? Essentially by transforming it into goods and/or services which are then sold 'profitably'. Thus the money left under the mattrass is not capital. But when it is loaned at interest it becomes capital; when it is used to build a house in order to generate more money it is capital. In either case it is undergoing self-augmentation.

The capitalist mode of production is one in which capital has penetrated and taken over production. That means that production is geared to sale, and thus becomes commodity production. A commodity is a product made expressly for sale.

Because under capitalism production is so geared to exchange (ie. buying and selling), classical capitalist society is in effect a market. Like a market, it is ruled by the laws of supply and demand. Like a market it is characterised by competition. Producers strive for minimum input for maximum output, to buy cheap and sell dear, and generally to 'corner the market'. The competition among capitalists contributes immensely to the development of productive forces as capitalists seek more efficient ways of production in the quest for profit, fabricate new tools for greater productive efficiency, etc. But the competition also leads to waste, to the divorce of production from need, and to anarchy and gross inequality.

Accumulation and the contradiction of capitalism

The driving force of the capitalist system – we may also call it the major law of the capitalist system – is the production of the maximum surplus value possible which is usually done by the intensification of exploitation and by the expansion of production. This law governs capitalist society to the extent that we may legitimately talk of a capitalist rationality, that is a tendency to behave in a manner compatible with the logic of this law. For instance, in a capitalist country such as Nigeria, capital tends to flow into those investments which yield more surplus value and out of those which yield less, and production in the economy at large is oriented to the augmentation of capital. To realise as much surplus value as possible, the workers are paid low wages, the power of the state is used to prevent them from effectively increasing their wages, attempts are made to increase the productivity of labour so there is less outlay on wages, working hours are extended. The drive for maximising surplus value, which is necessarily a drive for the intensification of exploitation, increases the wretchedness of the workers, their earning power lags behind this general standard of living, and their unsatisified wants increase.

As the wretchedness of the worker increases, his antagonism, real and potential, to the capitalist system, particularly to the bourgeois class, tends to increase. He increasingly recognises the implications of capitalist relations of production and becomes more prone to want to destroy it. So we can already see how in acting out its own internal logic, namely the maximisation of surplus value, the capitalist system tends to generate its own dialectical negation. When two such trends exist – that is, when a tendency inherent in the character of a system or phenomenon produces a tendency which actually or potentially negates the system or another tendency of the system – the system is said to have a *contradiction*.

It is time to turn to the other aspect of the fundamental law of the capitalist system, namely the expansion of production. The surplus value which the capitalist gets by investing his capital is itself a potential source of additional surplus value, that is, if he uses it as capital. And he is prone to do so since he wants to maximise his surplus value. Thus the tendency is for surplus value to be added to capital in order to generate even more surplus value. This *capitalisation* of surplus value is called the *accumulation of capital*. Once it is seen that accumulation of capital generally presupposes the expansion of production, it becomes clear how the drive for maximum surplus value leads to the expansion of production.

The contradictions of capitalism

The drive for maximum surplus value also leads to the expansion of production because it is done in a context in which capitalists are competing among themselves for the market. To compete effectively capitalists try to increase production, because up to a point expansion of production tends to reduce the unit price of the product. If the capitalist can reduce his unit price he is in a position to capture the market.

There are also contradictions inherent in the expansion of capitalist production. To begin with, expansion of production goes hand in hand with the concentration of a large work force in an intricate division of labour and also an absolute increase in the labour force, the victims of exploitation. So expansion creates and concentrates the proletariat, the potential army against capitalism. There is another type of contradiction. As production expands, the organic composition of capital increases, that is that share of capital which goes into material input such as machinery (as opposed to labour power) increases. But to say that the organic composition of capital is increasing means that the share of variable capital decreases. Not surprisingly, this change has consequences for the production of surplus value since, as we have seen, surplus value always comes from variable capital. Decrease of the share of variable capital ultimately reduces the chances of transforming surplus value into capital and hence the expansion of production. To put it more simply, as the organic composition of capital increases, the rate of accumulation of surplus value tends to be reduced.

The decline of the rate of profit due to the increase in the organic composition of capital can be neutralised up to a point by intensifying the exploitation of the worker, that is by increasing the rate of exploitation. But in the long run, the rate of profit will tend to fall. This is so because, from the theoretical point of view, there is no limit to the increase of the organic composition of capital, the side of the equation which is reducing the rate of profit. On the other hand, there is a limit to the intensification of the exploitation of the worker – the side of the equation which counteracts the declining rate of profit. The exploitation of the worker must be limited because part of the product of his labour must go into his own maintenance if he is to live and continue to produce. Having said this, it should be added that this is a simplification of a highly complex point. There is considerable controversy about the validity of the assertion that extended accumulation must ultimately lead to a declining rate of profits, although it would appear that those who dispute this thesis have not succeeded in disproving it.

There is another type of contradiction inherent in the capitalists' natural tendency to maximise surplus value (by increasing production) which also affects the rate of profit. The expansion of production tends to go hand in hand with a rising organic composition of capital. Increase in the organic composition of capital in turn goes hand in hand with the concentration of capital, that is with monopolisation in production. This is so partly because a rising organic composition means, among other things, that machinery is increasingly replacing human labour in production. As a branch of production becomes more mechanised it becomes more difficult for new entrepreneurs to enter that branch of production because of the cost of investing in machines to remain competitive with those who are already in that line of production. When investment requires only human labour, it is obviously much easier for new entrepreneurs to enter that branch of production and remain competitive. It is because of such factors that a rising organic composition of capital leads to *monopolistic capitalism*, a form of capitalism in which the economy is dominated by a few large enterprises who control the market and make it extremely difficult for new entrepreneurs to break into their line of production.

It should be clear that while the monopolisation of capital may be said to be an effect of rising organic composition of capital, it may also be said to be caused by the competition among capitalists. For the increase in the organic composition of capital is largely an effect of the struggle among capitalists for profit. Looked at from this point of view, we see that competition leads to monopoly which is a negation of competition. This contradiction entails another one. When competition reduces the number of enterprises to a few large ones, these few large enterprises will tend to cooperate to reduce competition among themselves by fixing prices and dividing the market. Such an arrangement will offer a better prospect of maximising surplus value than the continuation of unrestricted competition. However, such an arrangement on the reduction of competition will invariably entail limiting production in order to keep prices high. Limitation of production ultimately entails limitation of the accumulation of capital, that is the conversion of surplus value into capital to produce even more surplus value. So the expansion of capital production tends to negate itself in the long run.

Finally, the basic contradiction which has already been touched on in an earlier context should be mentioned again. The competition among capitalists leads to enormous development of the forces of production, and with that a complex division of labour and economic interdependence among people – even among those who may be separated by vast distances. The tendency for production to become a collective effort involving more and more people is called the progressive *socialisation* of production. But the socialisation of production goes hand in hand with the growth of large-scale enterprises, and the monopolisation of capital. If capital is being monopolised it must mean that fewer and fewer people are exploiting more and more people and taking more and more of the wealth of the society; it must mean, in other words, increasing *private appropriation*. So there is a singular contradiction here, more and more people cooperate to produce, but the product is appropriated by an increasingly small number of people. This is the fundamental contradiction of capitalism.

It can be reformulated in terms of another vocabulary which is already familiar: there is a contradiction between the forces of production and the relations of production. The forces of production under capitalism develop in the direction of the socialisation of production. However, the social relations of production develop in the direction of greater private appropriation, that is in the direction of fewer people taking an ever larger share of the social product. These two conflicting tendencies of the forces of production and the relations of production cannot continue indefinitely. Society cannot develop indefinitely in the direction in which an ever increasing number of people is cooperatively producing for the appropriation of an ever diminishing number of people. Sooner or later the development of the forces of production burst asunder the fetters which the social relations of production impose. This bursting asunder of the constraint is the 'revolution' which puts an end to capitalism. The point of the 'revolution' will be to bring into being a new relation of production, one in which the social product belongs to all and not just to a few. When this happens the relations of production are restored into harmony with the development of the forces of production in the direction of the socialisation of production. This is supposedly the aim of socialism; it seeks to usher in an epoch in which all cooperate to produce, and in which the product belongs to all.

Capitalism and colonialism

The contradictions of capitalism not only transform it, they also transplant it. The transplanting of capitalism arises from those contradictions which reduce the rate of profit and arrest the capitalisation of surplus value. Confronted with these effects, it was inevitable that the capitalist, forever bent on profit maximisation, would look for a new environment in which the process of accumulation could proceed apace. Capitalists turned to foreign lands attacked and subjugated them and integrated their economies to those of Western Europe. To date, the experience of Western imperialism, particularly colonisation, remains the most decisive event in the history of Africa. It is to this phenomenon that we now turn.

Imperialism and Africa

In the preceding section we examined the nature of the capitalist mode of production and saw how its internal contradictions tend to hamper the accumulation of capital. As these contradictions developed, Western capitalists tried to counteract their effects on accumulation, first by making internal adjustments but eventually and inevitably by transporting capitalism to new lands. This transplanting of capitalism from Western Europe to Africa was accomplished through colonising imperialism. As is well-known, the imperialist incursion into Africa by Western capitalism had the most profound influence on the economic and political history of Africa. Western imperialism in Africa took many forms at different stages – the pillage of Africa's natural resources, trade, and colonisation. But it is the manifestation of imperialism as colonisation that is of the most interest for the purposes of this book. For it was colonisation that acted as the major vehicle of capitalist penetration in Africa.

Imperialism

Since the phenomenon of imperialism is so important for Africa's economic history, it is necessary to begin by understanding it.

What is imperialism? It has already been defined implicitly in the preceding comments. It is the economic control and exploitation of foreign lands arising from the necessity for counteracting the impediments to the accumulation of capital engendered by the internal contradictions of the domestic capitalist economy. Following Michael Barratt Brown's *The Economics of Imperialism* (p. 22), the concept may be more broadly defined as follows: 'the outward drive of certain peoples . . . to build empires – both formal colonies and privileged positions in markets, protected sources of materials and extended opportunities for profitable employment of labour. The concept has thus been associated with an unequal economic relationship between states, not simply the inequality of large and small, rich and poor trading partners, but the inequality of political and economic dependence of the latter on the former'.

This is a useful definition from the point of view of the fact that it builds on some familiar and common sense notions of imperialism. But it might have done well to mention explicitly the relation between capitalism and imperialism. This link is in fact the critical factor in imperialism; it is the essence of the technical definition of imperialism which made the concept of powerful analytic tool ever since Lenin wrote his famous book, *Imperialism: The Highest Stage of Capitalism*. So much for the concept. Let us now turn to the phenomenon.

Theories of imperialism

The major classical writers on imperialism, namely Hobson, Lenin and Schumpeter, appear to agree that the impetus for imperialism comes from economic interests, that imperialism is related to the process of capitalist accumulation. But they differ in their accounts of the precise nature of the character and manifestations of these interests, and the precise nature of the relationship between capitalist accumulation and imperialism.

Hobson

To begin with, let us consider the account of imperialism in Hobson's

Imperialism: A Study (1902). Hobson considers some of the psychological motives which have been put forward as an explanation of imperialism such as national pride, quest for glory, and bellicosity. While admitting that these factors might be relevant to the explanation of imperialism, he dismisses them as not constituting a major cause. He asserts that the dominant motive for imperialism was the quest for markets as well as opportunities for higher returns on investments. According to Hobson, the need for this quest arises partly because as a result of the development of capitalism in the West industry was more productive and needed greater imports of raw materials, more food for the urban population growing in response to industrialisation, and products to meet the rising demand for luxury goods created by a rising standard of living. Hobson maintains that a more important cause of imperialism was the tendency for production to outgrow consumption, a tendency towards oversaving and over-investment and under-consumption. Associated with the tendency for investment to outstrip consumption is the distribution of income which gives too much money to employers and too little to employees.

Hobson posits that the attempts to deal with this dilemma of oversaving and under-consumption fall into three categories. First is an attempt by organised labour and the state to ensure that workers obtain a larger share of the surplus. This would increase the purchasing power of the workers and also increase effective demand. The second is the restriction of output. Such restriction can be achieved by financial control of enterprises by sharing the market, or otherwise regulating it, and by imposing production quotas and tariff barriers.

The third option is for those who own capital to persuade the state to aid them in securing new markets by the establishment of protectorates, colonies and spheres of influence. This was the option which led to imperialism. One interesting thing about Hobson's explanation of imperialism is that it does not rest on the benefits of imperialism to the British economy. He argues that British imperialism with all its militant aggression did not bring economic benefits to a broad spectrum of the British people. It meant heavy taxes for the taxpayer and was only marginally beneficial to the British manufacturer and trader. He considers that when account is taken of all the expenditure on arms, wars, etc. imperialism was too costly on investment for 'a small, bad, unsafe increase of markets'. However, although it might have been bad business for the nation, it was very good business for the British investor who needed more profitable foreign outlets for his capital. In the final analysis, Hobson concludes, imperialism is really the vehicle of the growing cosmopolitanism of capital.

Another interesting aspect of Hobson's account of imperialism needs to be noted. He rejects the explanation of imperialism as an inevitable and integral aspect of industrial progress. To do this, he raised the question as to why there should be under-consumption or why there should be more saving than could be profitably and usefully employed? He answers that if the economy was such that consumption power or incomes were distributed according to needs there would be no under-consumption, that since human needs are not finite, consumption would rise with productivity and there would be no excess saving. He then goes on to point out that it is quite otherwise in an economy where income distribution bears no relation to need and some people have far more income than they could possibly consume. In that kind of economy, according to Hobson, there is bound to be under-consumption. In so far as this type of distribution and under-consumption are necessary attributes of capitalism, Hobson is saying in effect that imperialism is a logical outcome of capitalism.

Schumpeter

It is not clear whether Schumpeter can properly be considered a major writer on imperialism. But since his views are well-known, unique and interesting, it is useful to consider them. Schumpeter's views on imperialism are to be found in his essay, 'Zur Soziologie der Imperialismus' which was published in 1919. This essay was subsequently translated into English by Heinz Nordon and issued under the editorship of Paul Sweezy as *Imperialism and Social Classes* in 1951 by Harvard University Press.

In this essay Schumpeter explains imperialism mainly as an atavism. Imperialism is characterised as an aggressive expansionism which has no objective beyond itself. In other words imperialism cannot be explained in terms of concrete interests, economic or otherwise. Besides, says Schumpeter, it is never satisfied by any interest. The further implication of this is that imperialism is non-rational.

What is the explanation of this non-rational impulse? It comes from the habits and instincts that moulded peoples and classes into warriors under pressure of the struggle for survival and supremacy. The psychological characteristics and social structures which are developed in the course of such situations of threat survive even when the danger is gone and manifest themselves as imperialism. Situations of threat in the historical past created these warlike instincts, but later when the aggressive instincts create the threat they need to nurture them.

The main thrust of Schumpeter's essay is to establish that, far from being the cause of imperialism, capitalism is in fact antithetical to it. He develops this argument by drawing attention to the modes of thought and action associated with the capitalist mode of production. According to Schumpeter, capitalism is associated with the emergence of a specialised and a mechanised world, the growth of individualism and democratisation. Most importantly capitalism is associated with rationalism. This is so because in the conditions of capitalist competition, survival demands a highly calculating and rationalist bent. In so far as people become so rationalist they are less disposed to imperialism – which is, as already indicated, a manifestation of the instinctual. In a purely capitalist world people will direct their energies towards pursuing their economic interest as well as other activities which are similarly rational. They will be less inclined to direct their energy to wasteful and risky adventurism.

On a closer look it is clear that Schumpeter's treatment of imperialism has little merit. Much of the difficulty of this treatment comes from his definition. To begin with, he defines imperialism as expansionism pursued specifically with military force. This is too narrow. Other writers on imperialism fully recognise that the subjugation of foreign lands can be accomplished and is often accomplished by means other than military, for instance by economic power.

Of course there is a sense in which definitions are 'arbitrary' and Schumpeter is entitled to his narrow definition. Indeed a definition may be all the more analytically useful for being narrow. Unfortunately it is not true in this case. Schumpeter's definition causes confusion by its narrowness. His definition is so narrow that he and the other major writers on imperialism are really talking about different things. If Schumpeter is indeed talking of something such as the familiar idea of the subordination of other lands by military force, then it should be called just that and not confused with the more complex phenomenon which other people are calling imperialism.

The other objectionable aspect of Schumpeter's definition is his notion that imperialism is not resorted to in order to promote or realise concrete interests. On this score Schumpeter's definition is also a source of confusion. The objective of interests and expansion are so integral and so fundamental to the other writers' definitions of imperialism that their exclusion from Schumpeter's definition really makes his notion of imperialism so different from those of other writers that they are really talking of different things. Among the writings on imperialism, it is an oddity which is really a source of confusion.

The main case against Schumpeter's definition is that it is not useful analytically. This is amply shown by his attempt to explain imperialism, an attempt which fails. He begins by saying that imperialist aggression is something that occurs for no purpose and without reference to the realisation of any concrete interests. When he goes on to examine how this non-rational behaviour occurs, he merely says that it is because in the past some people had acquired the disposition to be irrational. As an explanation this begs the question. People act irrationally because they have historically acquired some disposition to be irrational. Why these historically-acquired dispositions to be irrational should manifest themselves as imperialism is not clear.

Schumpeter's attempt to dissociate capitalism from imperialism fails dismally. He argues that capitalism could not lead to imperialism because it is rationalistic, whereas imperialism represents the non-rational. It is conceivable that one country can attack another militarily from pure aggression. But it is also possible that such an attack could be made on a rational calculation of some concrete interest which it might realise, in other words capitalism can also lead to aggressive expansionism. Schumpeter can of course insist that his dissociation of capitalism from imperialism still stands since only aggressive expansionism which is 'objectless' is really imperialism. In that case he would have been arbitrarily emphasising one aspect of his definition and the relationship or the lack of it which he attests between capitalism and imperialism will be true by definition only. Any attempt to carry it beyond this formality will lead to insurmountable problems and absurdities. For instance, one would have to be able to determine for all historically-given instances of aggressive expansionism those instances which were motivated by concrete instance and those in which aggressive expansionism was an end in itself. The difficulty and absurdity of trying to do so will soon be obvious to anyone who attempts it.

It must be said that Schumpeter's thesis on the rationalist character of capitalism is rather surprisingly crude. To be sure, capitalism is associated with some of the characteristics that he mentions, particularly rationalism. But it all depends on the perspective from which one looks at capitalism and on the level of analysis with which one is concerned. The individual capitalist needs to behave rationally to survive. He must be alert to the opportunities of the market-place and strive to take advantage of them, and he must strive to be as efficient as possible. One of the interesting things about capitalism is that it looks so rational from the perspective of the individual competitor but quite irrational from the point of view of the whole system. The multiplicity of centres of economic decision-making, necessarily a feature of capitalism, leads to a waste of resources, competition and anarchy; and the gearing of production to effective demand means that production is often dissociated from want. And so on. The notion that capitalism is too rational to lead to imperialism is too crude to be useful. In the final analysis, the value of Schumpeter's *Imperialism and Social Classes* may be its failure to dissociate imperialism from capitalism.

Marx

Marx's treatment of capitalism contains an implicit theory of imperialism which is very important. This theory says essentially that imperialism is a necessary outcome of capitalism. Marx throws light on imperialism in his analysis of the process by which surplus value is converted into capital, a process called accumulation. It is well to begin by recalling what surplus value is. Roughly, surplus value is value of the product of the workers less what the capitalist pays him. In pursuit of profit this part of the gross product, surplus value has to be converted into a means of creating more wealth. It is rather like using profit to make more profit. The process of using surplus value to engineer more surplus value is the capitalisation of surplus value. If surplus value is to be used to generate more wealth, it has to be converted into means of production as well as means of subsistence for workers. But it is easier if cruder to think of capitalisation of surplus value as their ultimate use in commodity production. The progressive use of surplus value to produce more and more commodities entails the more intensive use of existing labour, or the employment of more labour, usually the latter unless one makes highly limiting assumptions. Thus one inescapable consequence of capitalist accumulation is the production of more or bigger capitalists and more workers. In other words it reproduces and expands capitalist relations of production. Capitalism is inherently expansionary. The capitalist cannot survive and remain competitive without progressive accumulation or the continuous reproduction of his capital on a continuously expanding scale. This in itself suggests a relationship between capitalism and imperialism.

However, the relationship emerges in sharper relief when the contradictions inherent in the process of accumulation are considered. One is related to the gross inequality between the capitalist and the worker, reproduced and invariably deepened by the process of accumulation. Because of the poverty of the worker his demand for commodities is 'weak'. But more importantly the wealth of the capitalist leads to too much saving over investment, idle capacity and lower rate of profit. This is one way in which accumulation falls into contradiction.

A related contradiction inheres in the tendency of capitalist competition to develop the productive forces. The development of capitalism has gone hand in hand with the increasing use of machinery in production. This application of machinery enhances productivity and allows the capitalist to stay ahead of his competition, or at any rate keep pace with it. But it also entails the increase in the organic composition of capital, that is increase in the ratio of constant to variable capital. As the organic composition of capital rises the rate of profit tends to decline. There is very little that the capitalist can do about this dilemma that is at all satisfactory in the long run. He can opt for oligopolistic competition, but this restricts an increase in productivity. He can increase the rate of exploitation. But this is limited because the worker must earn enough to reproduce himself. One of the most promising things he can do is to redeploy capital to other lands where the organic composition is still relatively low. In places where the organic composition of capital is low, the surplus value per unit of labour will be comparatively high. Without being very explicit about the phenomenon, Marx sheds a lot of light on imperialism, and its relation to capitalism. He shows that capitalism is inherently expansionary and that the contradictions of capitalist accumulation will tend to transport capitalism to economically backward countries.

Lenin

Like Marx, Lenin holds that imperialism grows out of the logic of the capitalist system. But Lenin goes somewhat beyond Marx in asserting that imperialism symbolises a particular stage in the development of capitalism. It reflects a transitional stage of capitalism to a higher economic order, a transitional stage characterised by the 'displacement of capitalist free competition by capitalist monopoly'. According to Lenin 'Imperialism is capital in that stage of development in which the dominance of monopolies and finance capital has established itself; in which the export of capital has acquired pronounced importance; in which the division of the world among the international trusts has begun, in which the division of all territories of the globe among the biggest capitalist powers has been completed'.

Although the economic foundation of imperialism is monopoly, this monopoly which has grown out of capitalism 'exists in the general environment of capitalism, commodity production and competition, in permanent and insoluble contradiction to this general environment'. The monopoly stage of capitalism is, not surprisingly, also a stage in which the 'accumulation of capital has reached gigantic proportions'. The super-abundance of capital exists side by side with the poverty and starvation of the masses. Indeed the super-abundance of capital and mass impoverishment are two sides of the same coin. According to Lenin, this is so because 'uneven development and a semi-starvation level of existence of the masses are fundamental and inevitable conditions and premises of this mode of production. As long as capitalism remains what it is, surplus capital will be utilised not for the purpose of raising the standard of living of the masses in a given country, for this would mean a decline in profits for the capitalists, but for the purpose of increasing profits by exporting capital abroad to the backward countries.' That is one aspect of the relation between capitalism and imperialism.

Another aspect emerges from the tendency of monopoly to engender stagnation and decay or loss of dynamism. Because the monopolist can, up to a point, fix prices at least temporarily, his incentive continuously to revolutionise his means of production is greatly reduced. Indeed he may well stand in the way of technical progress. Lenin cites the example of a machine invented by a certain Owens which revolutionised the manufacture of bottles. A cartel of German bottle manufacturers bought the patent in order to ensure that the machine would not be put to use. Lenin sees all this as being indicative of the fact that capital has become 'overripe' and cannot find avenues of profitable investment, a situation which compels the export of capital.

More contemporary writings have elaborated, criticised and expanded aspects of these classical writings on the nature of imperialism. In *Accumulation of Capital* (1913) Rosa Luxemburg shows the tendency of capitalist accumulation to lead to overproduction and hence to create demand for new markets. In *Unequal Exchange* Emmanuel has drawn attention to the imperialism of trade, the exploitation of one nation by another based not on colonial subordination but on gross inequalities inherent in their trade relations. In a more recent work, *The Geometry of Imperialism* (1978), Giovanni Arrighi has pointed to the limitations of Lenin's theory of imperialism to the understanding of the contemporary world, and urged the necessity of going beyond Lenin. Other useful discussions of imperialism include Michael Barratt Brown, *The Economics of Imperialism*, Samir Amin, *Accumulation on a World Scale*, Nabudare, *The Political Economy of Imperialism*, and Harry Magdoff, *Imperialism*.

Imperialism in Africa

We have seen that imperialism is a necessary outcome of capitalism. It is important to bear this in mind not only because it helps to cut through the confusion over the motives of Western colonisation in Africa but also to shed light on the colonial experience in Africa and its effects on Africa's development. The colonisation of Africa occurred mainly in the last three decades of the nineteenth century. There is considerable disagreement among historians and social scientists about the causes of the colonisation of Africa and other lands in this period. It would be crude to reduce colonialism to a single motive because several factors contributed to it, but economic factors played the central role.

To understand the colonising imperialism of the late-nineteenth century, it is useful to begin by noting the relation of the industrial revolution to international trade. In his *Industry and Empire*, Hobsbawm tackles the problem of explaining the industrial revolution; why did the phenomenon occur in Britain and not in another country? Why did it happen at the end of the eighteenth century and not later or even before? He finds the answer in the changing character of the relation of Western

Europe, and Britain in particular, to the wider world economy. The significant change was the growing scope and greater intensity of commerce. 'The powerful, growing and accelerating current of overseas trade which swept the infant industries of Europe with it – which, in fact, sometimes actually created them – was hardly conceivable without this change. It rested on three things: in Europe, the rise of a market for overseas products for everyday use whose market could be expanded as they became available in larger quantities and more cheaply; and overseas the creation of economic systems for producing such goods . . . and the conquest of colonies designed to serve the economic advantage of their European owners' (p. 52). Britain benefited greatly from this development. According to Hobsbawm, colonial trade, which amounted to about 15% of British commerce by around 1700, had risen to about 33% by 1775. The growth in colonial trade 'provided a limitless horizon of sales and profit for merchants and manufacturer', an opportunity on which Britain greatly capitalised. Hobsbawm concludes that the industrial revolution was generated in these decades, 'after the 1740s when this massive but slow growth in the domestic economy combined with the rapid – after 1750, extremely rapid – expansion of the international economy; and it occurred in the country which seized its international opportunities to corner a major share of the overseas market'.

The relation between the industrial revolution and international trade comes out even more clearly in Phyllis Deane's *The First Industrial Revolution*. Phyllis Deane discusses several ways in which foreign trade helped to make the industrial revolution possible. It greatly enhanced the demand for manufactured goods and so encouraged expansion of production and specialisation. Foreign trade made the requisite raw materials available, at low prices. Trade enhanced the purchasing power of foreign and less economically developed trading partners of Britain to the benefit of British industry. Trade generated the economic surplus which helped to finance the industrial revolution. The institutional base of the industrial revolution was in part created under the stimulus of foreign trade. 'The system of orderly marketing, insurance, quality-control and standardisation of product which grows up out of the needs of foreign trade were important aids to improving productivity at home'. Finally, foreign trade was a major cause of the growth of large towns such as Liverpool, Manchester, Glasgow and Birmingham. The growth of large towns expressed as well as encouraged the shift of the balance of the economy from an agricultural base to an industrial base, and it stimulated the massive investments in transportation, a major aid to industrial expansion. The details on foreign trade underline these points. Working from official trade statistics, Phyllis Deane concludes that 'the volume of domestic exports multiplied by between 2 and 2½ times in the second half of the eighteenth century. . . . Undoubtedly domestic exports grew faster than population in the second half of the eighteenth century. Measured at 1796/8 prices the value of English domestic exports rose from barely £2 per head in 1752/3 to about £2 15s per head of the population in 1797/8. This must have represented a substantial addition to average incomes, more especially for the sectors which were producing for the export trade.' Even more interesting than the volume of trade was the change in its composition. Domestic export was shifting increasingly to manufactured goods, particularly the goods being produced by the new industries. For instance, in 1750 the export share of cotton yarn and fabric was negligible, but by 1800 it had risen to 24%.

This relationship between industrial revolution and colonialism sheds some light on what happened in the period 1875–1914 in which a new and virulent wave of colonialism engulfed Africa. The vigour and fury of the new wave of imperialism was remarkable. 'This new vigour in the pursuit of colonies is reflected in the fact that the rate of new territorial acquisitions of the new imperialism was almost three times that of the earlier period. Thus, the increase in new territories claimed in the first seventy-five years of the nineteenth century averaged about 83,000 square miles – a year. As against this, the colonial powers added an average of about 240,000 square miles a year between the late 1870s and World War I (1914–1918). Hence, 'in 1914 as a consequence of this new expansion and conquest on top of that of preceding centuries the colonial powers, their colonies, and their former colonies, extended over approximately 85% of the earth's surface'. (H. Magdoff, *Imperialism*, 1978, pp. 34–5.)

This upsurge of colonising imperialism was fuelled by competition among the European powers for colonies; the competition was fuelled by a heightened consciousness of the economic advantages of colonies, and the declining competitive superiority of Britain relative to other European countries.

The industrial revolution had inevitably spread to other European countries. The countries which entered the industrial revolution narrowed the technological gap between them and Britain very quickly, and they were often better able to further develop and apply the new advances in science and technology to the benefit of industrial development. For instance, Britain pioneered critical advances in the electro-technics field such as the electric telegraph and the carbon – filament incandescent lamp, yet Germany quickly overtook Britain in the volume of their output, and according to Hobsbawm by 1913 the output of the British electrical industry was little more than a third of the German, its exports barely half. In the area of automatic machine tools the story was the same except that it was America which quickly overtook Britain, where the pioneering work in this area was done. In the all-important iron and steel industry, Britain pioneered critical advances such as the Gilchrist-Thomas base process, the Siemons-Martin open-hearth furnace and the Bessemer Converter. But Britain was quickly outstripped by France, America and Germany, who capitalised on these developments and advanced them further.

The European countries which entered the industrial revolution after Britain were anxious to reduce the negative effect of the competitive superiority of Britain on their economies. They limited the influx of British goods and tried to nurture their infant industries behind protective tariff barriers. In the face of this protectionism, Britain doggedly propagated the idea of laissez-faire, but to no avail; discrimination against British goods by America, France, Germany, Russia and Austro-Hungary increased, and Britain's export market contracted. Economic depression ensued. This was hardly surprising.

Despite the increasing and lucrative ties with the empire the bulk of Britain's exports and foreign investment went to the industrialising European countries. According to John Hatch in *The History of Britain in Africa*, 'during the 1860s, for instance, only 32 per cent of exports and 36 per cent of investments found their way to the Empire' (p. 174).

Against such threats Britain became very anxious to promote free trade, to find new markets and new outlets for investment, but most importantly she became very anxious to defend her empire and the commercial privileges she enjoyed by her connection with them. At the same time Britain's competitors were also in an aggressive and expansionist mood. As Hatch points out, they were convinced 'that British commercial and industrial power was a consequence of the existence of a British Empire'.

Thus Germany jumped into the race for colonies. Bismarck, who had rejected the idea of colonies, reversed policy, arguing that colonies were necessary for 'winning new markets for German industries, the expansion of trade and a new field for German activity, civilisation and capital'. In 1867 Lother Bucher, who was a colleague of Bismarck, had argued that 'Colonies are the best means of developing manufactured export and import trade, and finally a respectable navy'. By the 1880s this was clearly an idea whose time had come. In France the mood was the similar, where propagandists such as Jules Ferry and Leroy-Beaulien supported by commercial interest groups argued the necessity of colonies for the development of French industry and French power. Italy too caught the expansionist fever and proceeded to seize Ethiopia. Belgium jumped into the fray too, and soon claimed the Congo. In Britain the case for colonies was well orchestrated by writers such as John Seeley (*Expansion of England*) and Charles Dilke (*Greater Britain*), and by organisations such as the Liberal Imperial Federation League and the Tory Primrose League, and by politicians such as Disraeli.

When propaganda gave way to action, Africa found itself the focal point for the action; the scramble for Africa began. In 1876 King Leopold II of Belgium formed his African International Association, to found commercial and scientific stations across Africa between Zanzibar and the Atlantic, and soon annexed the Congo basin, designating it the Congo Free State. In 1882 Britain took Egypt. The French, infuriated by this, consolidated and expanded their holdings in West Africa. Between 1883 and 1885 Germany took Cameroons, Togoland and South West Africa, fearful of the consequences of the colonial gains of Germany and France. Britain became singularly aggressive. She moved to consolidate her hold on Gambia, Sierra Leone, Nigeria and the Gold Coast and turned to Eastern, Southern and Central Africa, where she soon established her rule over Bechuanaland, Northern Rhodesia, Nyasaland, Zanzibar, Kenya and Uganda. Within a few years after King Leopold had triggered off the scramble for Africa in 1876, Africa was divided among the European powers and colonised.

Bibliography

AFANASYEV, L. ET AL., *The Political Economy of Capitalism*, Moscow, 1974.

AKE, C., 'The Scientific State of Political Science', *British Journal of Political Science*, 2, 1972.

AKE, C., *Social Science as Imperialism: The Theory of Political Development*, Ibadan, 1979.

ALAVI, H., UNESCO, Paris, SS-79/Conf. 602/1/8, 1979.

ALAVI, H., 'Imperialism Old and New', in K. A. Miliband and J. Savile eds., *Socialist Register*, Merlin Press, 1964.

AMIN, SAMIR, *Accumulation on a World Scale: A critique of the Theory of Underdevelopment*, 2 vols., New York, 1974.

ARRIGHI, G., *The Geometry of Imperialism*, London, 1978.

ARRIGHI, G. AND SAUL J., EDS., *Essays on the Political Economy of Africa*, New York, 1973.

BARAN, P., *The Political Economy of Growth*, New York, 1957.

BARRATT BROWN, M., *The Economics of Imperialism*, Harmondsworth, 1974.

BUKHARIN, N., *Imperialism and the World Economy*, Merlin Press, 1970 (first published 1927).

COPANS, JEAN, 'Pour une Histoire et un Sociologie des études Africaines', *Cahier d'Etudes Africaines*, 11, 43, 1971.

DOBB, M., *Political Economy and Capitalism*, London, 1945.

DOBB, M., *Studies in the Development of Capitalism*, revised edition, New York, 1964.

EATON, J., *Political Economy*, New York, 1966.

EMMANUEL, A., *Unequal Exchange: A Study of the Imperialism of Trade*, London, 1972.

GLYN, A., 'Capitalist Crisis and Organic Composition', *Conference of Socialist Economists' Bulletin*, Winter, 1972.

GUTKIND, P., AND WATERMAN, P., *African Social Studies: A Radical Reader*, New York, 1977.

HAVENS, A. E., 'Methodological issues in the Study of Development'. *Sociological Ruralis*, 12, 1972.

HILFERDING, R., *Finance Capital*, Vienna, 1923.

HOBSON, J. A., *Imperialism: A Study*, London, 1938 (first published 1902).

HODGKIN, T., 'Africa and Third World Theories of Imperialism' in R. J. Owen and R. B. Sutcliffe eds., *Studies in the Theory of Imperialism*, London, 1972.

JAKUBOWSKI, FRANZ, *Ideology and Superstructure in Historical Materialism*, trans. Anne Booth, London, 1976.

KEMP, T., *Theories of Imperialism*, London, 1967.

LAZARSFELD, P., AND ROSENBERG, M., EDS., *The Language of Social Research*, Glencoe, 1955.

LENIN, V. I., *The Development of Capitalism in Russia*, Moscow, 1967 reissue.

LENIN, V. I., *Imperialism: The Highest Stage of Capitalism*, Little Library, 1933 (first published in Petrograd 1919).

LEONTYEV, L., *Political Economy*, Moscow, 1972.

LUXEMBURG, R., *The Accumulation of Capital*, London, 1951.

MAGDOFF, H., *The Age of Imperialism*, New York, 1969.

MAGDOFF, H., 'Imperialism without colonies', in R. J. Owen and R. B. Sutcliffe eds., *Studies in the Theory of Imperialism*, London, 1972.

MARX, KARL, *Capital Vol. 1*, Allen and Unwin (first published 1867).

MARX, KARL, *A Contribution to the Critique of Political Economy*, Moscow, 1970 (first published 1859).

MARX KARL, *The Communist Manifesto*, first published 1848.

MURRAY, R., 'Productivity, Organic Composition and the falling rate of Profit', *Conference of Socialist Economists' Bulletin*, Summer, 1973.

NEWLYN, W. AND ROWAN, D. *Money and Banking in British Colonial Africa*, Oxford, 1954.

NKRUMAH, KWAME, *Neo-Colonialism: The last Stage of Imperialism*, London, 1965.

PALLOIX, C., *The World Capitalist Economy*, Paris, 1971.

RHODES, R. I. ED., *Imperialism and Underdevelopment: A Reader*, New York, 1970.

ROWTHORN, 'Imperialism in the Seventies – Unity of Rivalry? *New Left Review*, 69, 1971.

RYNDING, M. AND CHERNIKOW, G., EDS., *The Political Economy of Capitalism*, Moscow, 1974.

SCHUMPETER, J. A., *The Theory of Economic Development*, 1934.

SCHUMPETER, J. A., *Capitalism, Socialism and Democracy*, London, 1943.

SCHUMPETER, J. A. *Sociology of Imperialism*, Meridian Books, 1955 (first published 1919).

SMITH, A., *The Wealth of Nations*, first published in 1776.

SWEEZY, P., *Theory of Capitalist Development*, New York, 1942.

TAYLOR, J., *From Modernisation to Modes of Production: A Critique of the Sociologies of Development and Underdevelopment*, London, 1979.

WARREN, B., 'Imperialism and Capitalist Industrialisation', *New Left Review*, 81, 1973.

WATERMAN, P., 'On Radicalism in African Studies', *Politics and Society*, 3, 3, 1973.

2 Colonialism and the capitalist penetration of Africa

This chapter will deal with the question of the penetration of Western capitalism into Africa and the subsequent integration of African economies into the world capitalist system. The treatment of the topic here will be limited to broad principles and tendencies in order to avoid repetition, for the details required for its treatment are also pertinent to the discussion of the character of the colonial economy which is the subject of the next chapter.

It is very important to understand the process of capitalist penetration of African economies. The process is easily confused with its effects. For instance, it can be confused with economic domination. African economies were and are dominated, but the domination is the effect of the particular manner in which they have been integrated into the Western capitalist system. Much the same thing might be said of dependence. The dependence of African economies is the effect of the integration of African economies into the world capitalist system and not the essence of this process of integration. The salient feature of the process under review is that it 'joined' African economies to the Western capitalist economies in what was essentially an organic relationship. This process was brought about by colonialism, but that is not to say that it is a necessary effect of colonialism, it was just the effect of the particular mode of articulation of colonialism in Africa. What was this particular mode of articulation of colonialism and how did it bring about the process of integration? This question will be considered under three headings: the monetisation of African economies, the imperialism of colonial trade, and metropolitan investment and infrastructure development.

Monetisation

A non-monetised economy cannot really be integrated into a capitalist economy. The monetisation of a precapitalist economy is necessary for its integration into a capitalist one. As has been shown earlier, the essence of the capitalist mode of production is that it penetrates and takes over the production process. To say that capital has taken over production means that production is geared to the output of commodities or, what is the same thing, that production occurs for the purpose of exchange. This process, which may be called pervasive commodification, requires a universal medium of exchange – money.

The rudimentary elements of a market economy, particularly money, existed for centuries before the colonisation of Africa. Among the currencies which had been in use in precolonial Africa were gold dinars or mithqals, gold dust, cloth money, copper rods, iron, cowries and manillas. There is some uncertainly about the precise character and role of these earlier currencies. Some have seen them as being currencies in a very limited sense in that they were often used for particular forms of exchange in a particular locality. Some have argued that these earlier currencies were little more than a thin disguise for what was still essentially trade by barter. What is clear is that these earlier currencies had some notable deficiencies as means of exchange. The physical character of some of them made them very inconvenient to handle, for instance cloth money was unwieldy. They were not convertible into international currencies. In some cases they were supplied by the big European firms trading in Africa. This encouraged monopoly, inhibited the expansion of commerce and rendered the currencies unstable, as the firms who produced them sometimes deliberately overproduced and depreciated the currency.

The inadequacies of these precolonial currencies had become very serious by the nineteenth century and they began to decline rapidly, not only because of their inherent weaknesses but also because of other developments. It was now much cheaper, because of technical advances and the availability of new sources of supply, to produce and deliver them. The tendency to over-issue was reinforced by competition among European firms for the African trade. The result was a serious depreciation of the value of these currencies, and inevitably confidence in them was lost. At the same time European currencies, particularly British and French, were coming increasingly into use. This greatly accelerated the decline of the precolonial African currencies. That the European currencies accelerated the decline was not in the least surprising because they were much more convenient. They were easy to handle, they offered the flexibility of a system of standard multiples, they were freely convertible, they were no longer under the control of particular firms, and they could not be easily depreciated by the whim of particular firms. By the third quarter of the nineteenth century the precolonial currencies had fully declined and European currencies had assumed dominance in trade. In a sense the monetisation of African economies had begun before colonialism.

Nevertheless it is still correct to say that it was colonialism which monetised African economies. Monetisation of an economy does not simply mean the presence of money as a means of exchange. To conceive the term this way is to trivialise it to the extent of rendering it analytically useless. More fundamentally, monetisation implies the pervasiveness of money as a medium of exchange in the economy at large, the development of the attributes of what we now call the modern monetary system, including the credit system. In this sense, the precolonial economies were only marginally monetised. The monetary sector was very small, limited to those who traded with Europeans. Large sectors of the economy still depended on barter in some form or another, and there was hardly any wage labour.

How then did colonialism monetise African economies? First economies were monetised by annihilating the precolonial currencies which had represented a rudimentary monetisation, but which were so limited as currencies that they would have been a serious obstacle to fundamental monetisation. They were annihilated by depreciation and displacement so that the way was paved for the development of a modern monetary system. With precolonial currencies displaced, and the European currencies firmly installed in their place, the real task of monetisation began, and this was mainly the task of making the new medium of exchange thoroughly pervasive in the economy. First they encouraged wage labour often by force – for instance, by appropriating arable land from Africans and thus reducing them first to squatters and eventually to wage labourers on their land. The expansion of wage labour not only had the advantage of monetising the economy but also of facilitating the control of the economy and a more reliable supply of labour. Second, African economies were monetised by imposing taxes and insisting on payment of taxes with the European currency. The experience of paying taxes was not new to Africa. What was new was the requirement that the taxes be paid in European currency. Compulsory payment of taxes in European currency was a critical measure in the monetisation of African economies as well as the spread of wage labour. For instance, colonisation brought European traders and farmers in direct competition with their African counterparts. Because of the power of the colonial state and the technical progress behind them, the Europeans were able to ruin many of their African competitors, some of whom had no choice but to become wage earners.

Along with the ascendancy of European currencies came the introduction of the modern credit system as attempts were made to set up modern banking systems. Among the first to be successfully established was the Banque Du Senegal, established in 1854. The geographical and economic scope of the bank was widened and it was changed into the Banque de l'Afrique Occidentale in 1901. Another famous bank, the Bank of British West Africa, was established in 1894. Associated with these developments were new arrangements for monetary control, in particular the issue of currency, control of money supply, reserves, etc. When the Banque de l'Occidentale was established in 1901, it was again given the privilege of being the only bank allowed to issue currency in the whole of French West Africa. It was also given the responsibility of maintaining appropriate reserves, ensuring convertibility into the metropolitan currency. The Bank of British West Africa played a similar role in British West Africa by becoming the bank of issue. But the British government felt dissatisfied with the role of the British Bank of West Africa. It was especially dissatisfied with the effects of concentrating so many roles in regard to the colonial monetary system on the bank. Consequently it created in 1912 the West African Currency Board, which was to issue a separate currency for the colonies in West Africa and to manage it.

It is easy to see that the monetisation of African economies under colonialism was also the process of tying these economies to those of the metropole. For all practical purposes the colonial monetary system was an extension of the monetary system of the colonising power.

The currency was tied to that of the metropole and both were freely convertible. It was the colonial authorities who directly or indirectly through institutions such as the West African Currency Board determined the monetary practices of the colony, including the ratio of reserves to money in circulation and the issue of currency. By means of such control the colonial monetary policy became an integral part of the mechanism by which the goals of the monetary policies of the metropole were achieved. This control structured the colonial economy to serve the interests of the metropole, at the expense of the colony.

In both the British and French colonies the regulation of money supply was determined primarily by the balance of payments. If the demand for the colony's exports was strong and the terms of trade favourable, the money supply was increased. But if there was a recession in the colonial export trade and a balance of payments deficit, the money supply was reduced appropriately so that incomes fell, and demand for imports weakened until a new lower equilibrium between imports and exports was reached. This was a highly unfavourable arrangement for the colony. For one thing it reduced its monetary policy into being merely an instrument of exchange with very little, or no, potential for stimulating economic development. The insistence on a balanced budget made money extremely tight to the detriment of development. On the other hand, this particular form of monetary control was designed to ensure that no burdens were placed on the metropolitan country, for instance it dispensed with the necessity of the metropolitan country having to shore up the reserves of the colony in case of a heavy deficit in its balance of payments. In the meantime the colony financed the economic expansion of the metropolitan country with its reserves held by the metropole and freely used for its own purposes.

But the important point of immediate relevance here is not the exploitative character of the colonial monetary system and monetary policies. What needs to be noted is the nature of the colonial monetary system as a cause, as well as an effect, of the integration of African economies into Western capitalism. The process of monetisation went hand in hand with the spread of capitalist relations of production, particularly because it led to the proleterianisation of the African peasant as well as some African entrepreneurs. It also went hand in hand with the development of capitalist institutions such as the money market. The monetary system not only helped to create a capitalist economy, but also a capitalist economy structurally dependent on foreign economies. Thus the colonial currency was tied to that of the colonising power, and the money supply was determined mainly by the social and economic forces in the metropole, particularly the demand for the colony's exports. The dependence of the colony's prosperity on the export demand of the metropole reinforced not only the export orientation of the colony, so that it became complementary to the metropolitan economy, but it also compelled its specialisation on primary products, a specialisation which further reinforced its organic unity with the metropolitan economy.

The imperialism of trade

Trade between the colony and the colonising power was a critical mechanism for the integration of African economies into the European capitalist system. How trade played this role is quite easy to understand.

To begin with, trade was, in the early years of colonisation, the vehicle for extending capitalism into the colony. It helped to create consummerist orientations, it stimulated the growth of a money market and capitalist financial institutions, extending the scope of the money economy. Most importantly trade stimulated primary production. To appreciate this point one has to distinguish between the impact of trade on the colonies before and after colonisation. There was trade before colonisation but its impact on the transformation of the economy of the overseas territory was rather limited. Trading activity centred mainly in the entrepots. The Europeans were relatively indifferent to what went on in the interior. They were content to leave the production and the delivery of whatever products they wanted to local entrepreneurs and middlemen. But with colonisation the situation changed. It has to be remembered that colonisation, as opposed to the previous commercial contact, was to a large extent the effect of the rivalry between European countries and the struggle to secure markets for manufactured goods as well as the supply of raw materials. This aim could not be accomplished without control of the economy, particularly the control of what to produce, how, when and in what quantities. It also meant control of the structure of demand in the colony as well as the growth of the economy. So with colonisation the Europeans took an interest in the development of an infrastructure, at least to the extent that it would serve their interest; they invested in primary production, exercised control over production and effected changes in the social structure which necessarily correlated to the type of economic development they wanted. All these changes were coextensive with the penetration of the capitalist mode of production, for they were brought about by the invasion of a capitalism struggling to defeat its internal contradictions. Extending primary production and developing new sources of raw materials meant extending the capitalist mode of production. It also meant the extension of capitalist social relations, the extension of agrarian capitalism, the proletarianisation of some peasants, and the rudimentary development of a local bourgeoisie. In these ways trade promoted the integration of African economies into the world capitalist system.

The capitalist penetration of African economies created some fundamental affinities between the African economy and that of the colonising power. The controlled development of the African economy in the interest of the metropole, which went along with the expansion of colonial trade, meant structural links and structural interdependence, for instance in the division of labour between primary production and manufacture, and in the dependence of economic growth in the colony on the metropole's demand for colonial imports. At the same time the emerging class division of the colony which trade stimulated and nourished was soon to create a critical link between the colony and the metropole. This critical link was the common interests of the colonising bourgeoisie and the African bourgeoisie.

The essence of the role of trade in the integration of African economies into the world capitalist system was that it promoted complementarity, or interdependence, albeit an 'unequal interdependence' between the African economies and the metropolitan economies. Trade created interdependence through complementarity by encouraging specialisation in the primary production of raw materials needed by the metropole, while the metropole specialised in manufacture. This specialisation was not simply one of 'commodities' produced; it was also reflected in the division of labour.

How this particular aspect of the complementarity and interdependence of colonial and metropolitan economies started is obvious enough. Even before the period of effective colonisation, raw materials were needed by Western countries and overseas territories had them to offer. At the same time European countries wanted to sell manufactured goods. So in the exchange of manufactured goods and raw materials trade was following the line of least resistance, so to speak. As trade grew between the colony and the metropole the complementarity and interdependence along the lines of manufacture and primary production were reinforced.

First, the money income accruing to the colony from colonial trade went largely to the consumption of imported manufactured goods from the metropole. The colony's ability to purchase manufactured goods depended on its export earnings from primary products. So the growth of incomes arising from trade merely encouraged ever-rising demand for metropolitan imports and encouraged its specialisation in the production of manufactures. Now, since the colony's ability to purchase manufactured goods depended on its export earnings from primary products, the expansion of incomes in the colony and the growth of demand for manufactured goods also meant the increasing specialisation of the colony in primary production. This trend was all the more so because generally, as incomes rise, a higher proportion of the rise in income tends to be spent on luxury goods (which is what the metropole's cheap manufactured goods were in the colonies) as opposed to basic necessities. This trend would reinforce the export orientation of the colony. This is so because of the monopolistic character of early colonial trade, which was a carry-over from the precolonial era. Early colonial trade was to a considerable extent dominated by powerful African middlemen who made it difficult for competitors to break in. The colonisers could of course break the monopoly of these middlemen and sometimes did. But on the whole, the colonisers found the system of middlemen quite efficient for purposes of distribution, and while they attacked particular middlemen, they were favourably disposed to the middlemen as an economic group. The implication of the monopolistic character of colonial trade was that a rather limited number of Africans had a lion's share of the new wealth coming from the expansion of trade. Since the wealthier people are, the greater the proportion of additional income they spend on luxury goods, the distribution of income among the African population was highly biased in favour of consumption of metropolitan exports.

The European demand for African primary products, and the brutally self-interested way in which it was satisfied, led to a form of development which made the African economies heavily dependent on the metropolitan economies. Like good capitalists, the colonisers went for minimum input for maximum output. The expansion of trade required some amount of development, especially in regard to infrastructures. A minimum of infrastructure development was allowed to take place in just those places where they were necessary for tapping particular primary products of interest to the metropole. Roads and railways and other modes of communication were developed to link the sources of raw materials to the points of exit to Europe. Thus in so far as colonialism brought about development it was a very haphazard development, the development of enclaves which bore little relation to the other areas of the economy. The African economies became incoherent, incapable of autocentric growth, and dependent. The net effect of all this was that the escape route of the African economy from primary production was blocked.

Third, colonial trade tended to destroy the traditional crafts and craftmanship in Africa. This is because it flooded the market with substitutes which were cheaply produced but considered exotic, more desirable or more functional by the African population than the traditional substitutes. Colonial trade merely encouraged primary production with its emphasis on unskilled labour. Thus colonial trade was in effect bringing about a regress in the development of production forces. In doing this it was also reinforcing the division of labour between the metropole and the colony as well as their interdependence.

In addition to these there were other factors which reinforced the complementarity and the interdependence of the colonial economy with that of the metropole. They cannot all be mentioned here, but two more deserve brief mention. One is that the colonising power ensured the specialisation of the colony in primary production by adopting a system of quotas and tariffs which heavily favoured unprocessed primary commodities from the colonies. The other is that in so far as metropolitan capital came into colonial commerce, it tended to go into primary production. One reason for this was that this was a fool-proof way of ensuring that the capital and profits could be easily repatriated. The capital could be retransferred automatically in the form of primary commodities. Also primary production was on balance relatively more efficient in the colony than manufacture, at least in the earlier colonial period.

The impact of foreign investment

The pattern of foreign investment in the colonial African economies reinforced the complementarity between these economies and the Western economies, and the structural dependence of the former on the latter.

But before going into the question of complementarity and dependence, it is useful to mention that foreign investment increased the integration of the African economies into the Western capitalist system by promoting the spread of the capitalist mode of production. As Western capital flowed into the colony, capitalism spread. And as capitalism and capitalist-related institutions took root, the economies of the colony became more compatible with Western economies and this aided integration. Foreign investment created linkages between the metropolitan and colonial economies. For instance, while stimulating primary production in the colonies it directed its forward linkages outwards to the metropole. The spread of capitalism in the colony was integrative in more subtle but nevertheless effective ways. It encouraged the growth of a small class of indigenous capitalists who had common interests with foreign capital.

Now to return to the question of integration by the promotion of complementarity and dependence. As already noted it was necessary for Western capital to encourage investment in some infrastructure development and the development of an administrative system. Much of this infrastructure development was achieved by public investment. The foreign component of this public investment in infrastructure development was not usually written off as necessary costs or a reasonable contribution to the welfare of the colonies. Rather, the emphasis was on recovering this investment with a good return in the shortest possible time. That meant a lot of emphasis on the improvement of the balance of payments. And that in turn placed pressure on primary production. This was all the more so because primary commodities requiring relatively unskilled labour could be efficiently produced in the colonial economies. Despite the low wages in the colony the real costs associated with the production of manufactured goods were so high that the production of manufactured goods was rarely efficient. Also, as already noted, there was far less uncertainty about the repatriation of capital invested in primary production.

The pressure in favour of primary production in the colonial economy only reinforced the existing division of labour between the colony and the metropole, as well as reinforcing the structural dependence of the colony. The possibilities of changing this division of labour and of making the African economies less dependent were greatly limited. To begin with, as Raul Prebish has shown, market forces in the global economy tend to work towards the transfer of income from poor countries to rich ones. Incomes in the African economies rose too slowly to be very significant in producing internally-generated industrialisation or even growth. And the pattern of the distribution of this income with its associated low propensity to save did not help much. Also the investment in primary production did very little to generate external economies. Since there was very little processing, the stimulation of production brought by foreign investment did not contribute much to the improvement of knowledge or the improvement of techniques, in short, the development of productive forces. The expansion in the production of primary commodities did not involve radically new techniques, but largely the methods already in use, with perhaps a little more efficiency. In sum, because foreign investment increased primary production without significantly raising incomes, improving the development of productive forces or even capital accumulation, it did not hold much hope of the colony breaking away from its role in the division of labour established in the early periods of colonialism between the colony and the metropole.

It would appear that this discussion has concentrated on foreign investment in primary production and neglected the relatively heavy investment of foreign capital in the mining sector. The point is that a special and lengthy consideration of the investment in the extractive sector would hardly make any difference to the argument here. To be sure there was some development of the extractive sector. According to a United Nation economic survey (*UN Economic Survey of Africa since 1950*, New York, 1959) in 1938 Africa produced 97% of the world's diamond output, 95% of the cobalt, 46% of the gold, 40% of the chrome, 35% of the manganese and 21% of the copper. This must have entailed considerable investment as well as development effort. The influence of foreign capital in mining and the development of this sector did not do much to change the role of Africa as a primary producer complementing the manufacturing activity in Europe. For the purposes of elaborating this point, it is useful to divide mining activity into two types. First is the type of mining activity that requires very limited capital investment such as diamond mining. In such cases the expansion of mining needed a very limited level of skilled labour. And the few highly skilled operations were performed by Europeans. So there was little here that was conducive to the development of the forces of production. Also the spread effect of such mining activity was limited. It paid low wages to a labour force which could not have been a highly significant proportion of the population. The linkages from mining were externally oriented to the metropole, since the colonisers realised economies by processing in the metropole. The second type of mining activity is that requiring very heavy capital investment. These were also the type of mining activity which involved very sophisticated technology and mechanisation. Here again this type of mining was much like the first one as far as the effect on maintaining Africa's role in the international division of labour was concerned, as well as the underdevelopment of the productive forces in Africa. The number of people employed was limited by mechanisation, the highly skilled operations required were done by European labour; Africans were largely relegated to the role of supplying unskilled labour. As usual all the forward linkages were in Europe, the development of the sector drew on few domestic inputs, the carry-over from the mining export sector to the rest of the economy was limited by fragmentation of the economy and the relative isolation of the 'modern' sectors as well as market imperfections, caused by colonial industrial regulations. And heavy foreign investment meant heavy repatriation of capital. The colonial economy had a negligible share of capital formation from the mining sector, and on balance gained little more than a hole in the ground.

Conclusion

To sum up, in this chapter we have tried to shed some light on the capitalist penetration of Africa under colonialism. To this end, we have examined some of the salient features of the process and we have seen how it promoted the structural integration of African economies into the Western capitalist system. The process of penetration and integration had a decisive influence on the nature of Africa's colonial economies. The next chapter, in which we examine the character of Africa's colonial economies, will thow further light on the process of penetration and integration.

Bibliography

ADERIBIGBE, A., 'Trade and British Expansion in the Lagos Area in the Second Half of the Nineteenth Century,' *Nigerian Journal of Economic and Social Studies*, 4, 1962.

AMIN, S., 'Underdevelopment and Dependence in Black Africa – Their Historical Origins and Contemporary Forms', *Journal of Modern African Studies*, 10, 1972.

ANJORIN, A., 'European Attempts to Develop Cotton Cultivation in West Africa, 1850–1910', *Odu*, 3, 1966.

BARBER, W. J., 'The Movement into the World Economy' in M. J. Herskovits and M. Harwitz eds., *Economic Transition in Africa*, Evanston, 1964.

BOHANNAN, P., 'The impact of Money on an African subsistence Economy', *Journal of Economic History*, 19, 1959.

BRETT, E. A., *Colonialism and Underdevelopment in East Africa*, London, 1973.

CHARLE, E., 'English Colonial Policy and the Economy of Nigeria', *American Journal of Economics and Sociology*, 26, 1967.

CLANSEN, G., 'The British Colonial Currency System', *Economic Journal*, April, 1944.

DIKE, K., *Trade and Politics in the Niger Delta 1830–1885*, Oxford, 1956.

DOMAR, E., 'The Effect of Foreign Investment on Underdeveloped Countries', *Journal of Political Economy*, Feb. 1953.

FIELDHOUSE, D., *Economics and Empire 1830–1914*, London, 1973.

FLINT, J. E., 'The Wider Background to Partition and Colonial Occupation' in R. Oliver and G. Mathew eds., *History of East Africa*, Oxford, 1963.

GALLAGHER, J. AND ROBINSON, R., 'The Imperialism of Free Trade', in A. G. Shaw ed., *Great Britain and the Colonies*, London, 1970.

GANN, L. H., AND DUIGNAN, P., EDS., *Colonialism in Africa, 1876–1960*, Cambridge, 1969.

GIFFORD, P., AND LEWIS, W. EDS., *France and Britain in Africa*, New Haven, 1971.

GOULD, P., *The Development of the Transportation Pattern in Ghana*, Evanston, 1960.

HAWKINS, E., 'The Growth of a Money Economy in Nigeria and China', *Oxford Economic Papers*, 10, 1958.

HIGGINS, B., 'The Dualistic Theory of Under-Developed Areas', *Economic Development and Cultural Change*, January, 1956.

HOPKINS, A. G., 'Economic Imperialism in West Africa, Lagos 1880–92', *Economic History Review*, 21, 1968.

HOPKINS, A. G., 'The Creation of a Colonial Monetary System: The Origins of the West African Currency Board', *African Historical Studies*, 3, 1970.

HOPKINS, A. G., 'The Currency Revolution in South-West Nigeria in the Late Nineteenth Century', *Journal of the Historical Society of Nigeria*, 3, 1966.

HOPKINS, A. G., *An Economic History of West Africa*, London, 1973.

HOWARD, R., *Colonialism and Underdevelopment in Ghana*, London, 1978.

JOHNSON, M., 'Cotton Imperialism in West Africa', *African Affairs*, 73, 1974.

LATHAM, A., 'Currency, Credit and Capitalism on the Cross River in the Pre-Colonial Era', *Journal of African History*, 12, 1971.

MARX, K., *Pre-Capitalist Economic Formations*, translated by J. Cohen, ed., by E. Hobsbawm, New York, 1964.

MARX, K. AND ENGELS, F., *On Colonialism*, 4th ed., Moscow, 1968.

DOBB, MAURICE, *Studies in the Development of Capitalism*, London, 1964.

MENSAH, A., 'Monetary Relations Among African Countries', *Africa Development*, 4, 1, 1979.

MOSELEY, K. P., 'The Political Economy of Dahomey', *Research in Economic Anthropology*, 2, 1979.

MUNRO, J., *Africa and the International Economy 1800–1960*, London, 1976.

PEARSON, R., *The Economic Imperialism of the Royal Niger Company*, Food Research Institute Studies, 10, 1, 1971.

PERHAM, M., *Colonial Sequence, 1930–1942*, London, 1967.

POULANTZAS, N., 'Internationalisation of Capitalist Relations and the Nation State', *Economy and Society*, 3, 2, 1974.

PHIMISTER, I., 'Peasant Production and Underdevelopment in Southern Rhodesia, 1890–1914', *African Affairs*, 73, 1974.

REYNOLDS, E., *Trade and Economic Change in the Gold Coast 1807–74*, London 1974.

REYNOLDS, E., 'Economic Imperialism: The Case of the Gold Coast', *Journal of Economic History*, 35, 1, 1975.

SZERESZEWSKI, R., *Structural Changes in the Economy of Ghana 1891–1911*, London, 1965.

TARABRIN, E. A., *The New Scramble for Africa*, Moscow, 1974.

VIGNES, K., 'Etude sur la rivalité d'influence entre les puissances Européennes en Afrique equatoriale et occidentale depuis l'acte général de Berlin jusqu'au seuil du xxe siècle', *Revue Française D'Histoire d'Outre-Mer*, 48, 1961.

WOLFF, R. D., *The Economics of Colonialism: Britain and Kenya, 1870–1930*, New Haven, 1974.

3 The colonial economy

We have seen how the contradictions of Western capitalism impeded the accumulation of capital and how it became necessary to resort to imperialism, particularly the colonisation of foreign lands, in order to counteract the obstacles to capitalist accumulation arising from the internal contradictions of the capitalist mode of production. We have also seen that in Africa colonisation went hand in hand with capitalist penetration. This chapter is an outline of the main features of the economic system which colonialism and the capitalist penetration of Africa created. Up to a point the chapter might also be said to be a highly abbreviated account of the underdevelopment of Africa, for, to understand the main features of the structure of the colonial economy is also to understand why Africa is so underdeveloped today.

Disarticulation

The colonial economy was characterised by *disarticulation* or *incoherence*. But what does it mean in more specific terms to say that an economy is disarticulated or incoherent? To begin with, a disarticulated economy is one whose parts or sectors are not complementary. In a coherent economy there is regional and/or sectoral complementarity and reciprocity. One region specialises in agriculture while another supplies the agricultural sector with manufactured goods. Along with this general type of regional or sectoral reciprocity of exchanges will be a system of what economists call forward and backward linkages in production. For instance, when the demand of an industrial centre for coal makes the exploitation of known reserves of coal economic, we have a backward linkage. Linkages can also go forward, for instance when the establishment of an iron and steel industry stimulates the local manufacture of bicycles. A coherent economy is ideally a system of such linkages, its regions and sectors will be complementary, and there will be reciprocity of exchanges between them. The colonial economy generally lacked these linkages, complementarity and reciprocity.

It is necessary to go into the specifics of this disarticulation and the elements of colonial policy associated with it. To begin with, let us consider the coloniser's effort at development. As mentioned earlier, the colonisers could not exploit the colony's wealth at no cost at all. In some cases the extraction of the colony's resources entailed some investment in infrastructure development – roads, water resources, railways, electrical power, and administrative structures. Following the capitalist rationality of minimum input for maximum output, they invested only in what they had to, and where they had to. Not surprisingly the places in which colonialism fostered some development were in places which were convenient collecting centres for commodities, such as Kano; places from where the commodities could be shipped abroad, such as Lagos, Mombasa, and Dar es Salaam; places where the climate was to the taste of Europeans and which could be used as administrative headquarters, such as Nairobi. These centres gradually assumed a character quite different from that of the surrounding country. Some of them had factories for processing raw materials such as palm-kernels, amenities such as tap-borne water, electricity, railway stations, a scattering of buses, cinemas, hotels, tarred roads, and excellent recreational facilities in the European sections. These centres were a piece of Europe in Africa. They represented in a concrete and poignant form the fact of colonialism and the contradictions between the coloniser and the colonised. The contrast between the amenities in these centres and lack of amenities in the villages, between the commodious living of the European districts and the intolerable wretchedness of the peasant's lifestyle, brought the meaning of colonialism home. These centres or enclaves, as some people prefer to call them, made the colonial economy even more incoherent. There they stood, alienated, hostile and incomprehensible to their environment.

Disarticulation of the transport system

This haphazard development is amply illustrated by the story of the transport system, especially railways. It would appear that the building of railways was dictated by the collection of export commodities. In what is now known as Zaire, there is the Chemin de Fer de Bas-Congo au Katanga, built to connect the mineral rich Katanga to the sea. In Congo there is the Congo-Ocean Railway, built expressly to facilitate the transportation of manganese ore from Gabon, as well as forest products. In Nigeria the Kano-Apapa railway line was built to facilitate the collection of cotton, groundnuts and cocoa for export. And the Enugu-Port Harcourt line was built to serve the oil-palm trade. Among other railway lines built specifically for export commodities were the Marampa-Pepel line in Sierra Leone, the Fria-Conakry line in Guinea, the entire railway system of Liberia, the Dakar-Niger railway line in Mali and Senegal, and the Port Etienne-Fort Gouraud line in Mauritania. As if to emphasise the fact that the railway was purely functional for gathering and exporting the commodities of the colonies, the Germans in Togo actually named their railway lines after the particular primary commodities and minerals which they were supposed to transport. Thus there were the cotton line, the cocoa line, the coconut line, the iron line and the palm-oil line.

The railway systems of colonial Africa are an excellent example of the disarticulation of the colonial economy. They did not constitute in any country a coherent system of communications. Neither did they contribute to the building of a coherent economy. They were built *ad hoc* according to the metropolitan interests of the moment and the availability of funds. The incoherence of the railway system rendered related ancillary communication facilities chaotic as well. For instance, the ports tended to be built at the terminals of the railways; since the location of the railway was invariably determined by the location of the desired commodity rather than by the location of the prospective port of exit, it meant that the ports were not necessarily located where they would yield the maximum benefit to the development of the country. The same was true of the road system. According to Michael Crowder in *West Africa under Colonial Rule*, the road system was usually seen as 'adjuncts not competitors of the railways'. Crowder sums up the chaos of railway development succinctly: 'the railways were all directed to the coast, with no links between them, of different gauges, so that a rationalisation of the railway system of West Africa today is impossible'.

Disarticulation and the development of export commodities

Something similar to the development of railways happened in the development of primary commodities under colonialism. Colonial capitalism was naturally interested only in the most profitable primary commodities. To obtain an adequate supply of the preferred commodities it was sometimes necessary to discourage the production of some other commodities. When this necessity arose it was accepted without too much thought being wasted on the implications of encouraging or discouraging the production of particular commodities. It was assumed that what was good for international capital was good for the colony. More often than not colonial capitalism used persuasion or force to compel a concentration of effort on the production of particular export crops. This upset the balance of the traditional economy, as was the case in Ghana. It was after the colonisation of Ghana that cocoa was successfully grown in the colony. But the production of cocoa grew so rapidly that it soon began to dominate the Ghanaian economy. Ghana had not started exporting cocoa until about 1885. By 1901 the country was already the biggest producer of cocoa in the world. By 1939 cocoa accounted for about 80% of the value of Ghana's exports. This sort of change led to disequilibrium, for instance shortages in the supply of traditional food crops, changes in land use creating changes in land tenure, the ending of some old farming methods, unsatisfied demand for new farming skills, displacement of people and shifts in population, the uneven development of different regions, the dependence of the economy on a few export crops, and associated with all these, profoundly unbalanced economic growth.

Disarticulation of the agricultural economy caused by colonial policy was compounded by some of the 'natural tendencies of subsistence agriculture towards disarticulation'. When agricultural producers are producing mainly to feed themselves, that is producing primarily use-values, as opposed to exchange-values, there is necessarily some degree of disarticulation. In that kind of situation the market mechanism is weak, because exchange is so limited. And it is the market mechanism which acts as an integrative force, not only among small producers but also between small producers and the wider economy. Also, subsistence agriculture implies that there is highly limited functional specialisation, a critical factor producing the organic unity of economies.

The manufacturing sector

It remains to touch on the manufacturing sector, the development of which was most neglected in colonial Africa. The colonial government did not do very much to encourage the development of manufacturing. Their interest in a colony lay primarily in the fact that it was a source of raw materials as well as a market for selling metropolitan manufactured goods. The companies such as the Royal Niger Company, which were given wide powers and privileges in the colonies as well as the obligation to develop them, did not consider that industrialisation of the colony merited serious attention. The agencies which were charged specifically with promoting the industrialisation of the colonies such as the Colonial Development Advisory Committee and the Empire Marketing Board, appear to have had little or no enthusiasm for the task. According to Brett in *Colonialism and Underdevelopment in East Africa* (1973), the Annual Reports of the Colonial Development Advisory Committees indicate that by March 1939 it had allocated just under £8 million, out of which only £151,000 was for industrialisation-related projects, and of this sum only £23,000 had actually been spent. Manufacturing was further discouraged by the rudimentary development of infrastructures in the colony as well as the limited possibilities of economies of scale. However, some degree of development in manufacturing did take place. The type of manufacturing or industrial activity was of a most rudimentary nature: food and beverages, tobacco, base metal, non-durable consumer goods, textiles, basic chemical products, building materials, furniture, leather and leather products.

The causes and manifestations of disarticulation in the manufacturing sector are readily discernible. To begin with, it should be noted that those who were making the investment decisions were making their decisions according to the necessities of the process of accumulation, particularly the quest for maximum return on investment in the minimum amount of time. In the circumstances the incoherence of this sector was inevitable. The factors associated with the incoherence of the manufacturing sector may be summed up as follows: the multiplicity of decision centres, the *ad hoc* and particularist interest-oriented character of investment decisions, the reliance of the industrial sector on imported inputs, the chaotic development of infrastructures which inevitably influence the development of manufacturing, especially the type of investment and its location. To this should be added the less obvious factors, especially the small number of industrial establishments as well as the smallness of the scale of operations, the simplicity of much of the technology involved, the thrust towards non-durable consumer goods, the concentration of the industrial establishments in the isolated modern enclaves. All these factors are not favourable to the spread of manufacturing activity. So much for disarticulation. Let us now turn to another salient feature of the colonial economy.

Market imperfections and monopolistic tendencies

The colonial economy was characterised by market imperfections and monopolies. This characteristic of colonial capitalism is an important element in the link between colonisation and underdevelopment. From the very beginning the European economic presence in Africa has been associated with monopolisation. This might have had something to do with the conditions of the period of more intensive contact between Europe and Africa. For instance, given the state of communications in the fifteenth century, only large-scale enterprises could afford the risks of the long, sometimes hazardous expeditions across the seas to Africa for slaves or primary commodities. Apart from the risks involved, such expeditions involved immense expenditure on sailors, provisions, ships, navigation research and equipment – not to mention the fortification of trading posts. Not surprisingly, in the precolonial days, European trade with Africa was done mainly by large-scale state-owned or state-supported companies, such as the Royal African Company (1672), The Royal Adventurers into Africa (1621), the Compagnie du Senegal (1673), The Dutch West India Company (1621), and the Compagnie du Guinea (1684). This tendency continued in the period of effective colonisation in the 19th century. At this time, it was reinforced by several factors, especially the rivalry between European imperialisms of which the scramble for Africa itself was only one manifestation. This rivalry between Great Britain, Belgium, Germany and France made it mandatory to establish an effective and forceful presence in order to better protect sources of raw materials and to secure markets for manufactured goods. This created a strong prejudice in favour of monopolies. Indeed in the general enthusiasm for protecting economic interests through effective monopolies, commercial enterprises were given some of the functions of the state.

The story of the Royal Niger Company illustrates this phenomenon very clearly. The creation of the company was achieved under the inspiration of Sir George Goldie, a former officer in the British army. Goldie had an interest in one of the British companies trading on the Niger. In 1877 he came to the conclusion that the British companies in the Niger were too weak, that it was necessary to amalgamate them in order to compete effectively with the German and French companies. The amalgamation which Sir George Goldie advocated was achieved in 1879. The new company was called the United Africa Company, but the name was changed two years afterwards to the National African Company.

Sir George Goldie soon began to exert pressure for a charter from the British government; a charter would make the company effectively the government over its sphere of influence. In 1886 the charter was granted and the name of the company was changed to the Royal Niger Company. By the charter the company was empowered to maintain law and order, to levy and collect duties, to maintain free trade, to administer justice, and to secure the abolition of slavery. It is difficult to imagine a commercial enterprise having these governmental functions in contemporary society. But as Fage shows in *A History of West Africa*, the power of the Royal Niger Company was even greater than its governmental role suggests. The company not only administered part of the British empire but it helped to extend British imperialism by trade and by force of arms. It was the Company which compelled the Sultans of Sokoto and Gwandu to accept its monopoly of the exploitation of their territories. It conquered and subordinated the emirates of Ilorin and Nupe, and it had great success in thwarting French and German imperialist ambitions. It was the success of the Company's violent imperialism which provided the British government with the grounds for its protectorate status over the Fulani emirates during the Berlin Conference.

Despite the extraordinary power of the Company it was not in fact unique in colonial Africa. There were other very powerful companies, for instance Compagnie du Senegal, and the Compagnie Française de l'Afrique Equatoriale. In East Africa the British East Africa Company played a role very similar to that of the Royal Niger Company in West Africa. In the wake of the Anglo-German agreement of November 1886, which demarcated the spheres of influence of Germany and Britain in East Africa, the administration of the British African territories was given to the company. It was originally called the British East African Association. In 1888, when it obtained a royal charter from the British government, its name was changed to the British East Africa Company.

The discussion has drawn attention to the enormous political power of the big trading companies in Africa under colonialism. But this should not lead us to forget that the mission of these enterprises was the economic exploitation of Africa and not political power as such. At best their political power, as great as it was, was merely a means to economic power. That is why it is important to emphasise their monopolisation of economic power. Indeed it is in this that their greatest significance to African history lies, for it was their economic power and economic activities which appear to have had the more decisive impact on African history. It was their economic power which was the more durable. It continued to endure long after their political power had dwindled. In some cases they continue to endure even to the present day as the activities of companies such as the United Africa Company.

The monopoly of economic power in the colonies which the metropolitan companies enjoyed arose from their political power as well as the specific economic functions which the home government gave them, such as the power to levy duties. One of the functions which contributed most to the creation and consolidation of their monopoly status in the economy was the power to take overall charge of the economic development of the colony. Among the companies given this charge were the Imperial British East Africa Company in Kenya and Uganda, the British South Africa Company of Rhodesia (Zimbabwe), the Royal Niger Company in Nigeria, the Portuguese Mozambique Company, the Compagnie du Congo pour le Commerce et l'industrie, the Comité Spécial du Katanga, Compagnie des Chemins de Fer du Congo Supérieur aux Grands Lacs Africains, Comité National du Kivu, Société du Haut-Ogooué, and the Deutsche Ostafrikanische Gesellschaft. The power to oversee the economic development of the colony gave these companies the right to intervene and to regulate and manipulate the economy to further capitalist accumulation.

Another aspect of the monopoly character of colonial economies was the granting of concessions to favoured companies by the home government and the colonial government. For instance, in Angola the Angola Diamond Company was given exclusive rights to prospect for and mine diamonds in a large area of about 1 million square kilometers. Petrangol enjoyed a similar concession in regard to petroleum in Cabinda. Belgian and Portuguese interests had concessions covering 400 million tons of coal deposits in Mozambique. In East Africa an investment syndicate called the East African Syndicate and based in London and Johannesburg was given lease of 300,000 acres of land east of the rift valley, an area in which there was a large settlement of Masai. The action led to the resignation of Sir Charles Eliot, the Protectorate Commissioner from 1903 to 1904.

These monopolistic characteristics of the colonial economy were unavoidably associated with a series of market imperfections, discontinuities and contradictions. The very distribution of economic and political power between these enormous monopoly enterprises and the indigenous enterprises and the indigenous population was a source of serious contradiction, made all the sharper by the divergent interest of the companies and the indigenous population. The uneven distribution of power invited abuse, and a brutally intense form of capitalist exploitation. It is useful to mention a few examples of these contradictions and of the impediments on the free play of market forces. The voracious demand of European farmers and companies for land meant landlessness for millions of peasants; the flooding of the African market with cheap European manufactures ruined the African artisan; the demand for export crops in Europe meant an inadequate supply of staple foods for the African population; the demands of white settlers and foreign enterprises for labour meant a massive assault on the liberty and the dignity of the African peasant.

It remains to raise the question of the significance of this particular characterisation of the colonial economy in Africa. What makes the features so salient? First, an understanding of the characteristics in question helps us to gain a more sophisticated understanding of the nature of African economies. We very commonly talk about the capitalist penetration of Africa, about periphery capitalism, and about the prevalence of the capitalist mode of production in colonial and postcolonial Africa. The capitalist character of the economies is agreed. However, it is necessary to go beyond that to specify the uniqueness of this capitalism. One important characteristic we have described is its monopolistic tendency and associated market imperfections. The capitalism of colonial Africa displays a pathological maturity, like a highly accelerated ageing process. It has, so to speak, attained the weaknesses of old age without having had time to take advantage of the benefits of youthfulness, it suffered the disadvantages of monopoly without having enjoyed the advantages of competition. What is this advantage that is lost and why is it so important? The capitalist thrives by the continuous capitalisation of surplus value. But this presupposes that he is able to create and sustain a demand for the goods and services which he offers. And if he is able to beat his competitors and corner the market, all the better for him. To improve his competitive position, the capitalist tries to expand production to take advantage of economies of scale and reduce his unit cost. He may also try to increase the productivity of labour by introducing mechanisation and thereby increasing the organic composition of capital. Here lies the positive role of capitalism. The competition among capitalists leads to the development of productive forces – as capitalists expand production to reduce costs, develop new tools, introduce new machines that make things better or cheaper, gain new sources for the supply of raw materials, and develop new processes of production. Capitalism has contributed more to the development of productive forces than all the modes of production which preceded it and it has been able to do so because of the dynamics of competition inherent in it. In colonial Africa capitalism short-circuited history, so to speak, and moved directly to a monopoly stage. Just to give an idea of the uncompetitive nature of this capitalism, commerce in colonial Africa was dominated by a small number of powerful firms, especially the Compagnie Française de l'Afrique Occidentale, the United Africa Company, and the Société Commerciale de l'Ouest Africain. These three companies handled as much as 70% of West Africa's foreign trade. The United Africa Company alone controlled about 50% of West Africa's foreign trade in the 1930s. The same monopoly tendencies occurred in other spheres of economic life such as shipping and banking. In shipping the monopoly power of Elder Dempster and Company was roughly analogous to that of the United Africa Company in commerce. In British West Africa, banking was monopolised by the Bank of West Africa until 1926 when Barclays Bank was founded. The French established one vast banking monopoly in their overseas territories. This was the Banque de l'Afrique Occidentale. These monopoly tendencies hampered the development of productive forces by discouraging competition. This point bears importantly on our understanding of the persistence of underdevelopment.

There are other implications of the monopoly tendencies which are subtler but just as important. These will only be mentioned here because this is not the proper place to go into the complex questions which they raise. One of these is that the monopoly tendencies under review contributed greatly to the rise and persistence of statism, that is, the large and all-important role of the state in society, particularly in economic life. As will be clear later, statism has had an important influence on the accumulation of capital in Africa and the prospects of overcoming underdevelopment. Second, is the fact that the monopoly tendencies in question helped to create the contradictions between economic and political power which became a very important contradiction in the post colonial era. Third, is that these tendencies are so strong that they are apt to obscure the boundary between capitalist accumulation proper and primitive accumulation. To appreciate this it is helpful to remember that the capitalist is dominated by two passions, greed and fear, greed for more and fear of losing in the quest for more. How these passions find equilibrium depends on several factors, one of the most important being the power behind opposing interests. The monopolies in Africa could discount the power of opposing interests to a considerable extent, and this affected their behaviour in the accumulation of capital. Encouraged by their power they began to act crudely, to take short-cuts and sometimes to prefer naked coercion backed by state power. The result was that the accumulation of capital often began to look like primitive accumulation. As we shall see, this tendency to recede into primitive accumulation has important consequencies not only for the nature of capitalist development in Africa but also for the persistence of underdevelopment.

Reliance on a few export commodities

The colonial economy in Africa was characterised by reliance on a few export commodities for foreign exchange earnings and development funds. The tables assembled here are indicative of this, and characteristic of African colonial economies as a whole.

TABLE 3.1 Uganda, domestic exports: principal commodities by value, 1959–61 (£000)

Commodity	1958	1959	1960	1961
Coffee, not roasted	20,827	18,688	16,987	13,979
Tea	979	1,186	1,453	1,472
Animal feeding stuffs	1,104	1,654	1,677	1,425
Hinds and skins	764	941	1,146	816
Raw cotton	18,141	15,428	14,930	16,716
Copper and alloys (unwrought)	2,065	2,781	3,689	2,961
All others	1,528	1,413	1,676	1,826
Total	45,408	24,091	41,658	39,195

Source
Work for Progress: Uganda's Second Five-Year Plan, 1966–1971, Entebbe, p. 1

TABLE 3.2 Nigeria, domestic exports: main commodities by tonnage and value, 1956–58

The table represents the seven most important agricultural exports, with the average annual f.o.b. value and tonnage exported over the 3 years, 1956, 1957, 1958. These items make up 96% of Nigeria's agricultural exports, or 82% of Nigeria's domestic exports.

Commodity	Tonnage	Value (£)
Palm kernels	433,000	19,616,000
Palm-oil	174,000	13,777,000
Groundnuts (including oil and cake)	507,000	30,267,000
Cocoa	113,000	25,605,000
Cotton lint	29,000	7,098,000
Cotton seed	42,000	925,000
Rubber	40,000	7,024,000
Bananas	78,000	2,822,000

Source
Adapted from *Economic Survey of Nigeria 1959*, Lagos Government Printer, 1959, p. 27

It might be tempting to attribute this narrow base for foreign exchange earnings to the natural endowments of the colony – its mineral endowments, its climatic conditions and the types of crops that will flourish in particular localities. But this would be quite mistaken because the colonial experience had much to do with it. The problem of a narrow resource base is related to the basic fact that the colonisation of Africa was done in the interest of capitalist accumulation and not in the interests of African development. In the main the colonisers tried to market what

TABLE 3.3 African export economies wholly or mainly dependent on a single commodity, 1938–54 (table shows millions of national currency and percentage of total exports)

Country and item	1938	1950	1951	1952	1953	1954
Egypt (UAR)						
Total exports	28.6	173.0	200.6	142.8	135.9	136.7
Exports of raw cotton	21.2	149.8	164.1	126.4	116.4	113.1
Exports of raw cotton as percentage of total exports	74.1	86.6	81.8	88.5	85.6	82.7
Ethiopia						
Total exports	–	–	109.7	112.1	147.8	172.2
Exports of coffee	–	–	56.6	58.8	83.1	112.4
Exports of coffee as percentage of total exports	–	–	51.5	52.4	56.2	65.2
Gambia						
Total exports	–	2.2	3.0	3.7	2.6	2.9
Exports of groundnuts	–	2.1	2.7	3.6	2.5	2.2
Exports of groundnuts as percentage of total exports	–	97.2	88.7	96.2	95.0	76.5
Ghana						
Total exports	11.2	76.2	90.0	84.3	88.0	113.3
Exports of cocoa	4.5	54.6	60.3	52.5	56.1	84.6
Exports of cocoa as percentage of total exports	40.2	71.7	67.0	62.3	63.8	74.7
Sudan						
Total exports	5.4	32.1	61.0	41.2	43.0	38.9
Exports of raw cotton	3.4	22.9	46.5	29.0	26.8	21.7
Exports of raw cotton as percentage of total exports	63.7	71.3	76.2	70.4	62.3	55.7

Source

United Nations, *Economic Survey of Africa since 1950*, New York, 1959, p. 167

manufactured goods they could, they encouraged the development of export commodities when and where it was profitable to do so, and did not really bother themselves much with the question as to how their economic activities fitted in with the overall development of the colony – at any rate this question was secondary. The mining of gold by the British in Chunya in Uganda was typical of the essentially exploitative character of the economic activity of colonial capitalism. The British simply took away the gold as quickly as possible, and with considerable damage to the environment. When the gold vanished they simply moved on. The people of Chunya remained just as poor as they were, and the only difference was that their physical environment had become badly scarred.

Colonial capitalism encouraged export crops *ad hoc* in response to the demands of capitalist accumulation. In some cases this meant introducing entirely new cash crops. For instance, the first experiments with cocoa growing in Ghana were conducted by members of the Basel

TABLE 3.4 Semi-diversified export economies of Africa: selected principal exports 1938/1950–57 (table shows millions of national currency and percentage of total exports)

Country and item	Value 1938[ad]	Value Average 1950–1957[bc]	Percentage 1938[a]	Percentage Average 1950–1957[bc]
Algeria				
Total exports	5,639	129,102	100.0	100.0
Citrus fruits	140	8,310	2.5	5.6
Wine	2,756	57,687	48.9	39.7
Iron ore	317	9,987	5.6	6.8
Phosphates and chemical fertilizers	53	2,129	0.9	1.5
Total for items listed	3,266	78,112	57.9	53.6
Liberia				
Total exports	2.0	39.0	100.0	100.0
Rubber	1.0	30.2	50.8	76.3
Iron-ore		4.8		13.2
Palm-kernels	0.5	1.7	23.3	4.3
Total for items listed	1.5	36.7	41.1	93.9
French Equatorial Africa				
Total exports	228	11,653	100.0	100.0
Coffee	10	628	4.6	5.4
Cotton, raw	49	4,297	21.4	36.9
Wood and wood products	95	3,831	41.5	32.9
Diamonds	2	398	0.8	3.4
Total for items listed	156	9,154	68.3	78.6
Rhodesia and Nyasaland, Federation of[f]				
Total exports		145.8	100.0	100.0
Copper[e]		80.1		54.1
Tobacco		104.2		16.9
Total for items listed		104.2		71.0
Sierra Leone				
Total exports	2.1	10.2	100.0	100.0
Palm-kernels	0.6	3.5	21.4	34.5
Iron-ore	0.6	2.8	30.2	27.8
Diamonds, uncut and unworked	0.9	1.5	40.2	14.4
Total for items listed	2.0	7.8	91.8	16.7

a For Liberia, 1937
b For Liberia, average for 1951–1956
c For Federation of Rhodesia and Nyasaland, averages for 1950–1958
d For 1938, value in French metropolitan francs
e Including other precious stones
f Figures prior to 1954 are totals for the three countries that were subsequently federated

Source
United Nations *Economic Survey of Africa since 1950*, p. 168

Mission in the 1860s. But by 1911 Ghana was the world's largest producer of cocoa and by 1939 cocoa accounted for about 80% of the value of Ghana's export commodities.

The case of Ghana was not uncommon. As a general rule, if a country was particularly suitable for producing a cash crop for which overseas demand was good, the country was made to put in a lot of effort in the production of that commodity by a combination of incentives and sanctions. Very soon the country began to specialise in the production of the new commodity. This was what happened in Ghana. Before the introduction of cocoa in Ghana her export had been dominated by palm-oil and palm-kernels, commodities that had accounted for more than half of Ghana's export crops. But already by 1910 the introduction of cocoa had reduced their share to under 10%. In Northern Nigeria the amount of groundnuts produced was quite insignificant until the first world war. But after that the British made a major effort to expand production. Groundnut production in the area expanded so rapidly that it soon became the major export commodity. Up to the middle of the nineteenth century Senegal hardly exported groundnuts, but under the impact of European trade and colonisation it rapidly became predominantly a groundnut economy. Gambia had a similar experience. Before she was effectively colonised almost all of her exports consisted of hides and beeswax. These commodities probably accounted for as much as 90% of the value of Gambia's exports. Under the impact of American and British trade, and especially after its colonisation, the production of groundnuts in Gambia was vigorously promoted, so that by the middle of the nineteenth century groundnuts accounted for just over 60% of Gambia's exports. This attitude of latching on to opportunities for profit and pressing it to the very limit did not aid the diversification of the colonial economy. One would have expected that diversification would have been aided by these situations (and they were many) in which foreign capital found entirely new opportunities for profitable investment. But not so. Instead of adding to the old sources of foreign exchange the new commodities tended to replace some of the old ones, so that the composition of export commodities changed without achieving diversification. Thus in Ghana cocoa tended to replace palm-kernels and palm-oil instead of supplementing them. The same thing happened in Gambia with the successful promotion of the production of groundnuts. One of the most dramatic examples of this phenomenon is the replacement of palm-kernels, palm-oil, groundnuts and cocoa – indeed almost every other export crop – by petroleum in postcolonial Nigeria.

The tendency for economic expansion to lead to replacement of one export commodity by another instead of diversification was not due merely to the capitalist quest for profit. It was helped by the nature of primary products. Primary products are subject to price fluctuations, and their supply tends to be relatively inelastic in the short run. A fairly protracted period of slack in the overseas demand for an export crop could easily lead to a loss of interest in the production of that crop, and to the allocation of the land and other inputs to alternative uses.

Dependence

There are some serious problems connected with the concept of dependence. But we will not dwell on them here. For present purposes a crude definition of the concept will suffice. An economy is dependent to the extent that its position and relations to other economies in the international system and the articulation of its internal structure make it incapable of autocentric development. All the colonial economies of Africa were heavily dependent by the criteria of this definition. Let us look at some concrete manifestations of the dependence of Africa's colonial economies.

Dependence of the monetary system

To begin with there is the dependence of the monetary system of a colony. The monetary system of a colony was invariably an extension of that of the metropole. Control of a colony's reserves and of the issue of currency rested in the metropole. Such control was justified by arguing that it gave the colony monetary stability and international status and helped its trade. However, monetary dependence was essentially a means of exploitation. For instance, the colonial banks mobilised capital from African savings and loaned it to European businessmen. These banks avoided giving loans to Africans. Sometimes this discrimination against Africans was even given legal sanction. For instance, a notorious ordinance of colonial Kenya held that debts owed by Africans over Sh.200 (about £12) were not enforceable by law. This law naturally became an excuse for denying loans to Africans.

The exploitation of the colony's monetary dependence appears to have been done mainly through the manipulation of the colony's reserves and currency. In British colonies the system worked like this. The local currency of the colony issued by the West African Currency Board (established in 1912) or The East African Currency Board (established in 1919) was to be backed by sterling reserves held in Britain. Now, the foreign exchange which the colony earned by the sale of its exports was held in Britain. The British authorities then authorised the issue of local African currency equivalent to the foreign exchange earning. This amounted to forcing the colony to put its foreign exchange completely at the disposal of the metropolitan country. By 1955 Africa's sterling reserves in Britain were £1,446 million, which was more than 50% of the total reserves of Britain and the Commonwealth.

Financial dependence

In the early days of Africa's colonisation there was very little indigenous capital to mobilise for investment and development. The level of domestic savings was small for reasons which need not detain us here. A high proportion of the wealth accruing to the indigenous people from colonial trade was spent on imports. Colonial capitalism, with its tendency to lapse into primitive accumulation, left the indigenous population little scope to accumulate wealth. All these factors led to

TABLE 3.5 Tanzanian development budgets, 1948–61 (£000)

Year	Capital expenditure	Financed from:		
		Reserves and other domestic sources	External grants	Loan funds
1948	996	354	340	311
1952	4,989	1,985	1,080	1,924
1954/5	3,337	792	530	2,015
1955/6	4,084	1,136	677	2,271
1956/7	5,282	1,160	922	3,200
1957/8	5,454	1,668	899	2,887
1958/9	5,159	1,529	1,283	2,347
1959/60	3,939	852	1,361	1,726
1960/1	5,672	866	1,974	2,832

Source
Republic of Tanzania, *Statistical Abstract 1963*, Dar es Salaam, 1964, p. 110

TABLE 3.6 Financing of capital formation in French tropical Africa and Madagascar, 1952–57 (billions of metropolitan francs)

Item	1952	1953	1954	1955	1956	1957
Estimated gross fixed capital formation	223	231	211	227	264	329
Financing:						
Public Resources	107	87	101	107	110	139
Local, Public and semi-public	20	18	32	34	27	37
Metropolitan public funds	87	69	69	72	82	101
Direct expenditures	45	41	11	7	12	21
Subsidies			35	40	50	53
Loans	42	28	22	25	19	28
Foreign (IBRD loans, ECA)	–	–	–	1	2	–
Public resources as percentage of gross capital formation	48	38	47	46	42	38
Private resources:						
French	116	114	110	118	151	191
Foreign	–	–	–	2	3	–

Source
United Nations, *Economic Survey of Africa since 1950*, p. 216

dependence on foreign capital. While capital resources were so drastically limited, the need for them was very great. In particular, infrastructures, especially railways, roads and energy resources, had to be developed to some extent, if not to ensure the colony's development then at least to maximise its exploitation. The lack of domestic capital resources on the one hand, and the pressure for investment capital on the other, made the African colonial economy highly dependent. The tables shown on p. 56 both illustrate Africa's financial dependence.

Trade dependence

The colonial economies of Africa depended primarily on the metropolitan countries which colonised them for their external trade. This dependence reflected the exploitative structural integration of the colonial economy to the capitalist system of the metropole. The structural integration was also a function of the coercive measures which the colonising powers used to gear the colonial economy to their interests. The following tables on the directions of trade in colonial Africa give an idea of the extent of the dependence of a colony on trade with the metropole. The Nigerian situation revealed in Tables 3.7 and 3.8 is shown to be typical of the rest of Africa in Tables 3.9 and 3.10.

TABLE 3.7 Nigeria, directions of trade: exports and re-exports to principal customers, 1948–50/1957–58

| | 1948–50 | | 1957–58 | |
	Average annual value (£ million)	Percentage of total exports	Average annual value (£ million)	Percentage of total exports
United Kingdom	62.3	80	76.8	58.5
Netherlands	2.0	2.5	15.4	11.5
West Germany	0.4	0.5	8.5	6.5
USA	9.8	12.5	7.8	6.0
Italy	0.16	–	7.4	5.5

Source
Economic Survey of Nigeria 1959, Lagos Government Printer, p. 94

TABLE 3.8 Nigeria, directions of trade: Principal suppliers of imports, 1948–50/1957–58

| | 1948–50 | | 1957–58 | |
	Average annual value (£ million)	Percentage of total imports	Average annual value (£ million)	Percentage of total imports
United Kingdom	29.2	54	69.4	43.5
Japan	5.0	9	18.5	11.5
West Germany	2.7	5	13.0	8
USA	3.2	6	8.9	5.5
Netherlands	1.2	2	8.4	5.5

Source
Economic Survey of Nigeria 1959, p. 94

TABLE 3.9 Francophone countries of Africa, including Madagascar: distribution of trade, 1950–55 (millions of dollars)

Country or area	1950	1951	1952	1953	1954	1955
Imports						
France	317.8	488.9	467.5	409.3	475.6	467.3
Other French franc countries	34.0	51.9	52.1	48.4	57.5	64.4
Total, French franc countries	351.8	540.8	519.6	457.7	533.1	531.7
United Kingdom	7.3	11.4	21.6	17.1	19.2	18.7
Other sterling area countries	16.5	17.2	26.4	21.1	18.3	20.5
Total, sterling area	23.8	28.6	48.0	38.2	37.5	39.2
United States	43.6	38.9	43.4	27.9	28.8	38.5
Other dollar area countries	–	3.2	5.1	6.0	4.4	3.6
Total, dollar area	43.6	42.1	48.5	33.9	33.2	42.1
Non-sterling, non-French franc OEEC countries	21.1	55.4	67.0	63.6	82.6	81.8
Other	24.9	12.6	21.3	16.4	18.9	20.2
Total	465.2	679.5	704.4	609.8	705.3	715.0
Exports						
France	234.3	294.5	302.7	318.6	380.4	333.0
Other French franc countries	24.5	42.7	43.2	52.5	52.4	49.1
Total, French franc countries	258.8	337.2	345.9	371.1	432.8	382.1
United Kingdom	9.7	9.0	5.6	9.7	13.9	14.1
Other sterling area countries	6.9	15.0	16.8	13.1	10.9	9.7
Total, sterling area	16.6	24.0	22.4	22.8	24.8	23.8
United States	8.9	11.1	12.8	18.3	45.5	51.1
Other dollar areas countries	–	0.2	1.3	2.8	3.0	2.6
Total, dollar area	8.9	11.3	14.1	21.1	48.5	53.7
Non-sterling, non-French franc OEEC countries	26.7	47.1	52.9	58.1	68.1	85.0
Other	23.4	5.3	9.2	11.5	10.5	9.2
Total	334.4	424.9	444.5	484.6	584.7	553.8

Source
United Nations, *Economic Survey of Africa since 1950*, p. 177

Technological dependence

This is one of the most critical forms of dependence of the colonial economy. When we go back to the analysis of the labour process in the first chapter, its special importance is soon understood. We saw that the instruments of labour are the critical factor in the labour process. Without instruments of labour man's physical, intellectual and psychological assets cannot do him much good in meeting his needs. Without the instruments of labour man cannot survive in spite of all that nature has to

TABLE 3.10 Anglophone countries of Africa: distribution of trade, 1950–55 (millions of dollars)

Country or area	1950	1951	1952	1953	1954	1955
Imports						
United Kingdom	436.8	520.6	633.1	640.8	578.4	693.4
Other sterling area countries	160.2	229.3	250.8	255.3	284.9	312.5
Total, Sterling area	596.9	749.9	883.9	896.1	863.3	1,005.9
United States	41.8	48.4	66.5	57.9	49.9	58.6
Other dollar area countries	6.1	8.7	9.9	7.8	11.6	10.6
Total, dollar area	47.8	57.1	76.4	65.7	61.5	69.2
Non-sterling OEEC countries	99.6	194.1	208.4	199.5	247.1	269.9
Other	69.2	106.6	118.5	80.0	108.8	187.9
Total	813.6	1,107.7	1,287.2	1,241.3	1,280.7	1,532.9
Exports						
United Kingdom	513.6	674.0	767.2	749.2	804.5	770.4
Other stering area countries	129.1	178.3	180.6	145.4	164.8	168.4
Total, sterling area	642.7	852.3	947.8	894.6	969.3	938.8
United States	160.2	183.8	172.8	198.1	171.6	182.5
Other dollar area countries	17.6	15.9	12.1	20.5	17.8	15.7
Total, dollar area	177.8	199.7	184.9	218.6	189.4	198.2
Non-sterling OEEC countries	119.0	192.4	208.1	192.9	315.6	327.0
Other	30.5	38.6	51.9	39.1	49.2	43.1
Total	970.0	1,283.0	1,392.8	1,345.3	1,523.5	1,507.1

Source
United Nations, *Economic Survey of Africa since 1950*, p. 178

offer. Instruments of labour are the vital link between labour power and the objects of labour. It is instruments of labour which make it possible for man to apply his labour power to the objects of labour, and thus to harness nature to meet his needs. It we realise that instruments of labour are crudely equivalent to technology, we can then understand why technological dependence is so critical. Colonial Africa depended on the capitalist West for virtually all her technology. This put the colonial economy in a position analogous to that of a producer who has no instruments of labour. Such a producer is helpless and totally at the mercy of those who are in a position to give him the use of instruments of labour. It is precisely this helplessness that underlies the worker's exploitation by capital. Similarly, technological dependence underlies the exploitation of the colonial economies by the metropolitan economies. Like the disparity in the distribution of means of production between capital and labour, the disparity in the distribution of technology reproduces itself endlessly in a series of inequalities.

Complexities and discontinuities in the social relations of production

The contradictions and discontinuities of the social relations of production in colonial Africa arise mainly from the impact of Western imperialism, particularly the penetration of the capitalist mode of production, its most critical aspect. But there would have been enough complexities of discontinuities even if Western imperialism had not been associated with the penetration of capitalism, but merely restricted itself to primitive accumulation.

The colonial territory in Africa was typically an aggregation of disparate modes of production and social formations. A colonial territory could contain, all at once, a simple commodity mode of production, primitive community mode of production, and vestiges of feudal and slave modes of production. What really happens as the colonial state tries to forge an economy and social formation out of this constellation? More importantly, what happens as the capitalist mode of production is juxtaposed to, penetrates, and dominates these precapitalist modes of production? Do the precapitalist modes of production disappear, become distorted or transformed? Or do they form a new complex totality? If so, what is the nature of this complex totality? What is the mode of articulation of colonial capitalism? Is this colonial capitalism unique or does it obey the familiar laws of motion of capitalism? These are very difficult questions which students of Africa and students of underdevelopment have been grappling with for a long time, with only limited success. While these questions are pertinent and interesting we will not pretend to solve them here. The point of raising them is to indicate the difficulties of a related problem, the problem immediately before us here, namely that of outlining the social relations of production in the colonial economy. The questions raised above have to be solved before the social relations of production in the colonial economy can be adequately delineated. If the characterisation of the very process of capitalist penetration is problematic, and if the characterisation of the dominant capitalism is also problematic, then the characterisation of the social relations of production of the colonial economy will be necessarily problematic. In what follows an attempt will be made to outline the salient features of the social relations of production under colonial capitalism. This will be a crude outline, but hopefully adequate for our limited purposes here.

The capitalist sphere

We may think of the colonial economy as consisting of two related spheres, a capitalist sphere and a precapitalist one. The capitalist sphere comprises those enclaves in which the capitalist mode of production has successfully penetrated and become dominant and indeed virtually exclusive. If one limited oneself to this sphere then the characterisation of the social relations of production is not very difficult. In these enclaves the essential means of production comprise capital, commodification is pervasive, producers are separated from the means of production,

production is social, capital and labour confront each other in contradiction, the former exploiting the latter through the mechanism of exchange. In short, despite imperfections and distortions caused by the environment of the capitalist enclaves, the social relations of production are essentially those associated with extended reproduction – the socialisation of production, the social concentration of producers, the incremental consciousness of their solidarity, the antagonism between labour and capital, and relations of domination and subordination between labour and capital.

But it ought to be added that these relationships of production are mediated and distorted, and transformed by the environment of these capitalist enclaves and the peculiar features of colonial capitalism. It is useful to take note of one effect of this mediation. This is the tendency for race to be coextensive with class, the capitalist class being mainly Europeans while the working class is African. This was more true particularly in the early years of colonisation, but less so of the later years when colonisation was increasingly creating an African petit-bourgeoisie, some of whom became co-opted into the white ruling class. This overlap of class with race became a source of contradictions within the capitalist class as the ruling class became indigenised. Among other things the contradictions influence the particular forms of the capitalisation of surplus value, but this will not detain us here. The overlap of class and race also encourages false consciousness and makes possible some solidaristic identification across class lines, thereby helping to maintain a political atmosphere favourable to capitalist accumulation. Let us now turn to the precapitalist sphere.

The precapitalist sphere

Some of the effects of the impact of colonial rule and the penetration of the capitalist mode of production are reasonably clear. Some of the precapitalist modes of production were rapidly displaced under the impact of colonialism. The conditions for their reproduction could not survive. I am referring specially to the tributary, feudal and slave modes of production. The exclusive claim of the colonial regime to political power quickly undermined the power stratification system, which was essential for the reproduction of these modes of production. Only the odd vestige of these modes of production were able to survive and it should be said that their survival does not constitute a competitive mode of production but merely a source of distortion of the dominant capitalist mode of production.

The precapitalist modes of production which have tended to persist, albeit in a modified form in the face of the impact of capitalism, are the primitive commodity mode of production and the simple commodity mode of production. To all appearances the predominant mode of production in the precapitalist sphere is a new totality which is a mix of the primitive community mode of production and simple commodity mode of production, along with features which reflect the influence of capitalism. For expositional convenience we shall refer to all those who live in the context of this mode of production as peasants. The main features of this new totality are as follows:

1   The family, immediate or extended is the basic unit for the organisation of production.
2   Land is the essential means of production.
3   Land tends to be communally owned but usually privately 'exploited' subject to certain obligations.
4   Commodity exchange among relatively equal petty producers who produce predominantly use-values.
5   Limited production of exchange-values and intermittent contact of some petty producers with wage labour.

Now comes the critical question. What is the relationship between the capitalist in the capitalist sphere and these peasants?

It would seem that the relation between the capitalist and the peasant is radically different from that between the capitalist and the worker in the capitalist enclaves. Indeed it would seem that there is hardly any relationship at all between the capitalist and the peasant, much less the relationship of exploitation, subordination and domination, antagonism and struggle, which exists between the capitalist and labour. The peasant does not appear to be separated from his means of production, and so is not obliged to submit to exploitation. But this is more apparent than real. The relationship between the capitalist and the peasant is very much like that between the capitalist and the worker in the sense that it is a relationship of exploitation and antagonism, domination and subordination. But how can this be when the peasant is an independent producer? The answer to the question is that the colonial state on behalf of its capitalist clients engages in exploitative manipulation of the conditions of production and exchange in the precapitalist sphere.

The manipulation of peasant production

Capital uses state power to regulate the conditions of peasant production by (a) making laws about who might produce what, as was the case in colonial Uganda; (b) imposing agricultural development programmes which put the peasant in the position of using inputs such as fertilizers, and different techniques and tools; the process of compelling the use of these inputs and techniques was ostensibly to help the peasant, but in fact they aid the integration of the peasant into exploitative commodity relations; (c) imposing laws which standardise products and production processes.

It is easy to see how these measures facilitate the expropriation of the peasant by the capitalist, even though the capitalist does not directly control production, and even though the peasant technically still remains independent by virtue of the fact that he is not separated from the means of production. First these measures change the distribution of productive effort into those commodities which are to the benefit of the capitalist clients of the colonial state, and which may be to the disadvantage of the peasants. Second, and following from the first point, the measures increase the supply of the commodities which are more profitable to the capitalist. The increase in the supply of such commodities may pose threats of starvation to simple commodity producers (eg. in the event of a shift from food crop to cash crop production) and reinforce his marginalisation (eg. as the new techniques he is forced to adopt lead him into dependence and debt). Third, these measures often entail an increase in the rate of exploitation, in the sense that they compel the peasant producer to put in more labour-time and more costly inputs, which increase the profit of the capitalist while yielding to the peasant producer a return possibly much less than his increased input. Fourth, they effectively devalue the peasants labour-time by channelling his productive effort into areas, techniques and commodities which render him less competitive with the capitalist.

Let us look at some examples of how the regulations emanating from the state (and enforced through agencies such as Marketing Boards) controlled the product of the peasant producer and even his choice of techniques and made him more dependent. In the Southern Cameroons, cocoa beans was usually dried on smokey fires. Cocoa dried by his process was likely to have some smokey beans. Because of this the cocoa dried by the process was sold at a discount of £5 to £12 a ton. The colonial government forbade drying over smoky fires and at the same time introduced special cocoa drying ovens. Soon all the peasant producers were obliged to adopt the new technique. In Nigeria, price incentives were used by the colonial government to encourage a good quality palm-oil with no more than $4\frac{1}{2}\%$ free fatty acid. This particular grade of oil was needed for making products such as margarine and was considered more profitable to the capitalist class than the inferior oils. The price incentive for the production of the quality palm-oil was supported by the introduction of hand presses for extracting the oil. The higher prices induced peasant producers to produce the better quality palm-oil. But to do this they needed the hand presses. The capitalist class succeeded admirably, for the supply of the special grade oil rose from 0.02% of marketed palm-oil in 1950 to 77% in 1958. Much the same thing happened in the case of groundnuts. In 1955 a premium price was paid for a 'special grade' of groundnuts containing no less than 70% by weight of whole nuts. The point was to reduce the free fatty acid content on delivery to Europe. Farmers were persuaded to purchase a special decorting machine which was less prone to breaking the nuts than the old method of decorting by pestle and morter. The peasant producer had to buy the new machine and adjust to the new technique, especially when the North Regional Marketing Board insisted on buying only the special grade. The capitalists got their supply of the preferred quality groundnut, the proportion of this special grade supplied in the Northern region rising rapidly from 22% in the 1955/6 season to 97.7% in the 1957/8 season.

Exchange

The capitalist class also subordinates and expropriates the peasant through mechanisms of exchange, which it is able to set up by the use of state power. These include crop grading. The grading of the crop determines the price, and those who control the grading system are able to use it as a means of appropriation of surplus value. They can easily ensure that the peasant producer gets much less than the value of his product.

But the more common and more effective form of subordination and expropriation of the peasant producer in the sphere of exchange is the compulsory marketing of products through monopolistic agencies such as Marketing Boards. To illustrate this, all of colonial Nigeria's four main export crops were collected and marketed through Marketing Boards, namely the Nigerian Cocoa Marketing Board (1947), the Nigerian Palm Produce Marketing Board (1949), the Nigerian Groundnut Marketing Board (1949), and the Nigerian Cotton Marketing Board (1949). The arrangement proved so profitable to local and international capital that more and more commodities were brought into the scheme. By 1954 the four Marketing Boards were replaced by four regional Marketing Boards (one in each of the four regions of Nigeria). These new Marketing Boards were all-purpose Boards, that is, each one controlled all the commodities which were placed in the Marketing Board scheme. By 1954 the list of the commodities controlled by the Marketing Boards had grown to include palm-oil, sesame, soya beans, cocoa, palm-kernels, benni seed, cotton and groundnuts. The collection of the commodities from the producers was left to the licensed agents of the Marketing Boards. The Marketing Boards took over the commodities at the port and then handed them over to the Nigerian Produce Marketing Company, which was a wholly-owned subsidiary of the four Marketing Boards. It was this company which arranged for the shipping and the sale of the commodities overseas.

The official justification of the Marketing Boards is interesting. It was claimed that the arrangement avoided price fluctuations during the buying season because the minimum price payable was announced ahead of the buying season and adhered to. This supposedly helped to stabilise the income of the peasant producer and helped him to rationalise his activities. It was claimed that regulation of the quality of commodities by the Marketing Boards, and the payment of higher prices for better quality products, gave the producer incentive to produce better quality products and to increase his earning power. Finally it was claimed that the arrangement helped to protect the peasant producer against the fluctuations in the world price of their commodities. This was possible because the Marketing Boards could pay less in seasons in which the world demand was strong by putting some of the surplus in a buffer fund to be used to pay more in seasons when the world demand might be particularly weak. So the argument goes.

There is some truth in these arguments. That can be admitted without prejudice to the fact that the thrust of the Marketing Board arrangement was overwhelmingly exploitative. They paid the peasant producer a small fraction of the value of their product in the world market. Groundnuts bought from producers for £15 per ton by the West African Produce Board sold for £110 per ton in Europe. A ton of palm-oil bought from producers for £17 sold for £95 in Europe. The scale of this exploitation can be deduced from the following. In Nigeria in the mid 1950s the commodities under the control of the Marketing Boards amounted to 85% of the total value of Nigeria's agricultural exports, as well as 72% of her total domestic exports. This means that the lion's share of the internal contribution to the development budget came from the surplus extracted from the peasants by the Marketing Boards. The extent of the expropriation becomes more impressive yet when it is realised that the bulk of development expenditure in the postwar period in Nigeria came from internal sources. According to the *Economic Survey of Nigeria, 1959*, of a total development expenditure of £339.1 million, required for the period 1955 to 1962, £264 million or 78% was to come from internal sources. Theoretically the large surplus appropriated through the Marketing Boards was public revenue and not profit for the capitalist class. However, much of it was appropriated by the capitalist class through forms of investment which serviced capitalist enterprises such as infrastructures. Also, appropriation took place by using the surplus for projects from which the capitalists benefited as contractors, etc.

We have now seen that the capitalist class is able (largely through the use of state power) to manipulate the conditions of production and exchange is such a way as to appropriate surplus value from the peasant producers. The relationship between the capitalist and the peasant producer is not unlike the relationship between the capitalist and the worker in the capitalist enclaves. The difference is that the control of production is indirect and the appropriation of the surplus is mediated and disguised through a series of mechanisms devised by the state. So it is not contradictory to say that while the peasants are not separated from the means of production and remain independent producers, they are nonetheless in a relationship of exploitation, domination and subordination to the capitalist class. By extension they are also in a relationship of antagonism and even of struggle, as evidenced by illegal product marketing, reduction of output, opting out of commodity relations, migration, subversion of quality regulations and the occasional uprising. So much for the salient features of the colonial economy.

Our main interest in the features of the colonial economy lies in their significance for understanding what happened in Africa, what is happening and what might happen. It would then seem pertinent to go into a discussion of their implications. However, this will not be done here in order to avoid repetition. Much of what remains of this study will deal directly or indirectly with the implications of the structure of the colonial economy. There is the additional consideration that treating the implications here is bound to be abstract and unsatisfactory. It will be more useful to treat them concretely in a context in which we try to understand specific phenomona, such as the contradictions and the dynamics of the colonial economy and the problem of underdevelopment.

Bibliography

AMIN, S., 'Underdevelopment and Dependence in Black Africa', *Journal of Modern African Studies*, 10, 4, 1972.
AMIN, S., *Unequal Development: An Essay on the Social Formations of Peripheral Capitalism*, New York, 1976.
BAUER, P., *West African Trade*, Cambridge, 1954.

CHARLE, E., 'An Appraisal of British Imperial Policy with Respect to the Extraction of Mineral Resources in Nigeria', *Nigerian Journal of Economic and Social Studies*, 6, 1964.

CHINWEIZU, *The West and the Rest of Us. White Predators, Black Slavers and the African Elite*, New York, 1975.

CROWDER, M., *West Africa Under Colonial Rule*, London, 1968.

CROWDER, M., *Colonial West Africa*, London, 1978.

DOS SANTOS, T., 'The Structure of Dependence', *Economic Review*, 60, 2, 1970.

FAGE, J., *A History of West Africa*, Cambridge, 1969.

FRANK, A. G., *Capitalism and Underdevelopment in Latin American*, New York, 1976.

FURTADO, C., 'Development and Stagnation in Latin America: A Structuralist Approach', *Studies in Comparative International Development*, 1, 11, 1965.

HANCE, W., *African Economic Developmant*, New York, 1967.

HVEEM, H., 'The Extent and Type of Direct Foreign Investment in Africa', in C. Widstrand ed., *Multinational Firms in Africa*, Uppsala, 1975.

JALEE, P., *The Pillage of the Third World*, New York, 1968.

JALEE, P., *The Third World in the World Economy*, New York, 1967.

JEWSIEWICKI, B., 'The Great Depression and the Making of the Colonial Economic System in the Beligan Congo', *African Economic History*, 4, 1977.

KAMARCK, A., *The Economics of African Development*, New York, 1967.

KAY, G., *The Political Economy of Colonialism in Ghana*, Cambridge, 1972.

LEUBUSCHER, C., *The Processing of Colonial Raw Materials: A Study in Location*, Colonial Office, London, 1951.

LEYS, C., *Underdevelopment in Kenya: The Political Economy of Neo-Colonialism*, London, 1974.

LIEDHOLM, C., 'The Influence of Colonial Policy on the Growth and Development of Nigeria's Industrial Sector' in C. Eicher and C. Liedholm eds., *Growth and Development of the Nigerian Economy*, East Lansing, 1970.

LUGARD, F., *The Dual Mandate in British Tropical Africa* Edinburgh, 1922.

McPHEE, A., *Kenya*, New York, 1968.

McPHEE, A., *The Economic Revolution in British West Africa*, London, 1926.

MUNGEAM, G., *British Rule in Kenya 1895–1912*, Oxford, 1966.

MURRAY, R., 'Colonial Congo', *New Left Review*, 17, Winter, 1962.

REY, P., *Colonialisme, neo-colonialisme et transition au capitalisme: Example de la 'camilog', 1971, au Congo-Brazzaville*, Paris, 1971.

RODNEY, W., *How Europe Underdeveloped Africa*, London, 1972.

STAHL, K., *The Metropolitan Organization of British Colonial Trade*, London, 1951.

SURET-CANALE, J., *French Colonialism in Tropical Africa*, London, 1971.

SZERESZEWSKI, R., *Structural Changes in the Economy of Ghana, 1891–1911*, London, 1965.

UNITED NATIONS, Department of Economic and Social Affairs: Economic Commission for Africa, *Economic Survey of Africa since 1950*, New York, 1959, E/CN 14/28.

WAYNE, J., 'Some Notes on the Sociology of Dependence: The Underdevelopment of Kigoma Region Tanzania', East Africa Social Science Conference Paper, Dar es Salaam, 1973.

WILLIAMS, G., *The Political Economy of Colonialism and Neo-colonialism in Nigeria* in P. Gutkind and P. Waterman eds., *African Social Studies: A Radical Reader*, London, 1976.

WOLFF, R., *The Economics of Colonialism: Britain and Kenya, 1870–1930*, New Haven, 1974.

UDO, R., 'British Policy and the Development of Export Crops in Nigeria', *Nigerian Journal of Economic and Social Studies*, 9, 1967.

4 Contradictions of the colonial economy

In the preceding chapter we took an essentially static view of the colonial economy. We merely described its main characteristics and noted their implications. This chapter will look at the colonial economy from a dynamic perspective, namely from the point of view of its contradictions and their consequences for change or continuity of the colonial system.

The colonial economy was ridden with contradictions which had repercussions for its stability. Contradictions are dynamic, and the contradictions of the colonial system subverted and changed it. But what they changed was an aspect of its superstructure – the political system – while the economic structure of the colonial system remained essentially unchanged. Before going into detailed discussion of specific contradictions, it is useful to review briefly the general movement of colonial economic history in Africa. This history may be divided into three phases.

Phase one: before c. 1930

It was in this period that new commodities were introduced to the colonies and aggressively promoted, with the result that exports rose substantially and a few countries such as Senegal might be said to have enjoyed intermittent boom conditions. Nevertheless it was a period of conflict and bitterness. For one thing, the process of military consolidation was still going on. Lugard was still battling with the Fulani emirates of Northern Nigeria and continued doing so until 1906. The French were fully occupied until 1915 with military expeditions, especially to the Ivory Coast and French Guinea. Germany continued to fight for the establishment of its authority in Togo and Cameroon up to the beginning of the first world war. The conflict between coloniser and colonised was intensified by the very policies which the colonial government used to create the export boom, such as forced labour, the alienation of land and the commercialisation of agriculture.

To give just two examples on the question of forced labour, the French rounded up thousands of Africans and sent them to work on the Brazzaville-Point-Noire railway, which was started in 1921. The African labourers slaved under such inhuman conditions that an estimated 25% of them died annually. The British also practised forced labour in this period. The records of the Gold Coast transport department for 1908 give us some idea of the British abuse of African labour. The records talk of African carriers walking constantly for a twelve month period, averaging about 400 miles a month. Naturally many of the men became incapacitated, their soles 'almost completely worn through'. With characteristic insensitivity the British officials dealt with the problem by tarring the carriers feet. The report goes on to boast that the results 'have proved quite good and many carriers are now able to keep to the road who would otherwise have to lie up'. The use of forced labour in British colonial Africa was so widespread and so abused that it became necessary to enact a law in 1923 restricting it. However, the law was not effective and it is not clear whether it was even intended to be.

Discontent with colonial rule in this phase was reinforced by the hardships and constraints of the first world war, 1914–18. Then came the economic hardships in the wake of the brief postwar boom. It was in these circumstances that there developed the urban-based opposition which ultimately led to the collapse of the colonial regime. To illustrate this, in 1923 the workers on the Dakar-Niger railway went on strike. This was an echo of the strike by the dock workers of Conakry in 1919. Riots broke out in Porto Novo in 1923. There was a chain of strikes by railway workers in Sierra Leone and Nigeria between 1919 and 1926. Most ominous of all, for the fate of colonialism, was the general strike of the Gold Coast public service in 1919 and 1921. In short, even in this first phase, when there was considerable economic expansion, the contradictions of the colonial situation asserted themselves decisively.

Phase two: 1930–1945

In this second phase, the period of the great depression, the contradictions inherent in the integration of the African colonies to the world capitalist system are shown in very clear relief. We can sum up the effect of the great depression in Africa by saying that it caused an immense change for the worse in both the *barter terms of trade* and the *income terms of trade*. These are now concepts which need clarification. The barter terms of trade refers to the ratio of export prices to import prices. The income terms of trade refers to what we get when we multiply the barter terms of trade by an index of export volume. The income terms of trade allow us to measure the ability of an economy to purchase imports. Some idea of the effect of the depression on Africa can be glimpsed from the fact that in 1939 a given unit of exports could only purchase about 60% of the imports which it would have purchased between 1870 and 1880.

Why did the depressed state of world commerce during the great depression have a particularly disastrous effect on colonial Africa? First, the revenue of the African colonial governments was derived predominantly (indeed overwhelmingly) from customs earnings. In some parts of colonial Africa, such as French West Africa, customs receipts fell by as much as 47%. But while income was falling off so sharply expenditure on fixed commitments such as salaries was stable or rising: this magnified the depression of the economy. There was another factor peculiar to the colonial government, namely its domination of the economy through its control of the export sector. When government revenues declined sharply with the collapse of the export sector, the reverberations echoed throughout the colonial economy, and all the other sectors which depended on the export sector suffered. For instance, as incomes of the African labour force in the export sector fell, the farmer received less for his food crops, demand for crafts and livestock fell, so traders received less for their goods, and so on.

Second, the logic of the colonial situation dictated responses to the depression which eventually worsened the problem. For instance, one of the colonial government's responses was to increase import duties. This was a natural reaction in the context of an economy dominated by the export sector, and a government which had no other significant source of revenue than customs receipts. While the increase in duties put a little more money into the pockets of the colonial government, its major impact was to make life even more difficult for Africans by raising the prices of imported goods. Africans were earning less and paying more for manufactured goods. Another line of policy which the colonial governments adopted was to reduce government expenditure. Once more, this was a logical response considering the circumstances: the government was not getting the revenue in the way it knew how, and it was contrary to capitalist rationality to transfer capital charitably from the mother country to the colony. This response increased the adverse effects of the depression, for it meant fewer public projects, less earnings, less demand for services and less employment.

The third type of policy which the colonial government used to deal with the depression was the regulation of trade. For instance, Marketing Boards were set up as the monopoly marketers of the colonies' commodities. Quotas were imposed on foreign goods imported into the colonies. A system of preferences was introduced. The preference system was a protectionist measure by which the colony and the mother country gave preferences to each other's exports. These measures were geared to the interest of the colonising powers and became more emphatically so under pressure of the war effort. Because of the structure of the colonial economy and the relation of the colonial economy to that of the mother country, they greatly compounded the problems of the depression in Africa. The quota system prevented Africans from taking advantage of cheaper goods from other parts of the world, such as Japan, at a time when their incomes were falling. The preferential system increased the integration of the colonial economy into the world capitalist system, made it more responsive to the pressures of the western capitalist economies, and more exploitable. As for the Marketing Boards, they turned out to be an instrument of robbery, since they were used to force African producers to accept prices well below the world commodity prices.

It remains to consider the reaction of the European firms in Africa to the great depression. The companies reacted to the depression in the following ways. They cut back on investment and on the scale of operations. Then they reduced competition among themselves by dividing the market. One such agreement was the Merchandise Agreement of 1937. The reduction of investment only served to worsen the depression, while the trade agreements allowed the European companies to save themselves at the expense of the Africans. The events of this period contributed greatly to the radicalisation and politicisation of the contradictions of the colonial social formation. By the end of this period it was already clear that colonialism would have to beat a hasty retreat.

Phase three: 1945–1960s

This was the period of the postwar boom. But the impact of the boom on the amelioration of economic conditions in Africa was limited. First, the effects of the boom were felt mainly in those parts of Africa which produced the commodities most in demand in Europe, and much of this production came from just a few places. Second, the large expatriate companies were able to use the regulations of the war period to monopolise the benefits of the boom. As far as the African population was concerned, the economic amelioration of the postwar period was too small and too late. If anything, it merely raised aspirations which could not be fulfilled, and dramatised the inequalities and the exploitative character of the colonial situation. Discontent with colonialism grew faster than economic expansion. The period of the postwar economic expansion was also the period when anticolonial protest assumed a decisive militancy. There were several serious strikes and disturbances in French West Africa, such as that of the railway workers in Dakar in 1947–48. In Nigeria the militancy and industrial action of coal miners led to their massacre at Enugu in 1949. In the Gold Coast there were riots and an organised boycott of European companies. There were strikes on a national scale, such as the national strike of Nigeria in 1945. By 1945 the contradictions of the colonial situation had fully revealed themselves and Africa was well on the march to independence.

We have surveyed the general trends in the economic history of Africa following the period of effective colonisation, and we have seen how these trends reflect the contradictions of the colonial situation. We will now turn to specific types of contradictions. They will be treated both theoretically and empirically, and an attempt will be made to indicate how they assumed political significance and contributed to the negation of the colonial system, or the political system of colonialism at any rate.

The contradictions of the colonial social formation may be grouped into three broad categories: (a) contradictions between colonial capital and the emerging African petit-bourgeoisie; (b) contradictions between colonial capital and African labour; and (c) contradictions between colonial capital and peasants.

Contradictions between colonial capital and the African petit-bourgeoisie

It was the African petit-bourgeoisie which led the battle against colonialism. This petit-bourgeoisie was itself a creation of the colonial system. Its creation was one of the most interesting contradictions of colonialism. The colonising power would have liked to avoid creating its own grave-diggers but it was unable to do so. How did the colonial system create an African petit-bourgeoisie?

Education was perhaps the single most important factor contributing to the creation of a petit-bourgeoisie in indigenous colonial society. Colonial educational policies reflected the typical contradictions of colonialism. The colonisers' attitudes to education were ambiguous. On the one hand they wanted to avoid investment in education. They had come to Africa to do well and not to do good and investment in education could be justified to only a very limited extent as a way of minimising the expropriation of the colony. Educating the African might leave him less in awe of the European; it might make him more assertive, less inclined to resign himself to the humiliation and exploitation of colonisation.

And yet there were also good reasons for educating Africans. You cannot fully dominate without educating, without penetrating the personality and culture of the person to be dominated. And the penetration has to be accomplished not so much by coercion as by education. The same goes for exploitation. You cannot fully exploit without educating. The untutored and unskilled is a tool of very limited use; more is got out of him when he is tutored and skilled. Indeed one might generalise that the major function of education in all societies is to facilitate domination and exploitation.

In addition to these considerations there were more practical reasons for paying attention to education. One of the most compelling was that the colonisers did not have enough manpower to administer and exploit the colony. The manpower shortage was particularly acute in the British colonies. To illustrate this, in Northern Nigeria there was one British administrator to 100,000 Africans. In Southern Nigeria there was one British administrator to 70,000 Nigerians. In addition to administrators there was the need for a pool of technical and supervisory staff and skilled labour. For instance, foremen were needed to supervise railway workers, low-level technicians were needed for building construction and to maintain machinery. Also needed was a large cadre of junior administrators, accountants, agricultural extension workers, medical auxillaries, etc. It would have been too expensive and too inconvenient to import all these workers from the mother country.

In the circumstances it was inevitable that the colonisers should make some concession to the education of Africans. But it was a very grudging concession. The education budgets of the colonial governments were extremely small. Here are the 1929 budgets for the three largest British colonies in West Africa:

Nigeria	£304,626
Sierra Leone	£ 44,141
Gold Coast	£218,052

Michael Crowder in his book *West Africa under Colonial Rule* estimates that 'there were less than six hundred pupils at government and post-secondary schools in French West Africa in 1934'. By the middle of the nineteenth century, Sierra Leone had only 42 schools with approximately 6,000 pupils. By 1948, only one out of twenty children eligible for primary school in the Ivory Coast was in school. The situation as regards to post-primary education was worse still. For instance, the entire Federation of French West Africa had only one higher institution, the Ecole Normale William Ponty in Senegal.

Colonial education sought to realise two objectives: to increase semi-skilled labour and to create a cultural and political atmosphere favourable to the maintenance of the colonial system. Those two objectives need to be borne in mind because they underlie the contribution of colonial education to the development of the contradictions of the colonial system.

The content of colonial education was attuned to the realisation of these objectives. First, it was designed to inculcate basic literacy in aspects of Western culture. The point here was to inculcate some minimal skills in reading, writing, Western thinking, and accepting the coloniser's ideology. The values in the programmes emphasised the superiority of the coloniser's culture, the virtues of submission and obedience, and the necessity of collaboration with the colonial system. The following passage from a well-known French children's story book published in 1919 for use in African village schools is a good example. 'It is on the one hand, an advantage for the native to work for the white man because the whites are better educated, more advanced in civilisation than the natives and because, thanks to them, the natives will make more rapid progress, learn better and more quickly, know more things, and become one day really useful men. On the other hand, the blacks will render service to the whites by bringing them the help of their arms, by cultivating the land which will permit them to grow crops for Europeans, and also by fighting for France in the ranks of native troops. Thus the two races will associate and work together in common prosperity and happiness of all. You who are intelligent and industrious my children, always help the whites in their task. This a duty.' (L. Sonolet and A. Peres., *Moussa et Gli-gla: Historie de deux petite Noires.*)

Second, colonial education inculcated technical skills – the basic skills needed by auxiliary 'technical' staff such as accountants, workshop-foremen, medical orderlies, fitters, plumbers, electricians, etc. Much of the technical education was acquired as on-the-job-training to people who already had a basic literary education.

How did colonial education contribute to the creation of an African petit-bourgeoisie? The people who were able to take advantage of the limited opportunities of colonial education were immediately in a very special position. They had some opportunities for upward mobility, and they acquired a fresh status by virtue of their new proximity to the coloniser's world. The new status and their new skills placed them in a position of becoming leaders and, by the same token, of accumulating some wealth. This effect of colonial education, which would have occurred as a matter of course, was intentionally reinforced by the colonial governments. They used education consciously to create an African elite. But they wanted to create an elite completely dominated by their own values, and therefore willing to collaborate in their design. For example, a circular issued in 1910 by Ponty, Governor-General of French West Africa stated: 'After we have formed an elite of young people destined to aid our own efforts, we must occupy ourselves with the education of the whole race and attempt to give the greatest number of our subjects if not assimilation, at least, a French imprint'.

The formation of this elite to collaborate with colonisers was promoted in the following ways. First, there was the creation of a few distinctive schools whose students had social and economic advantages over the students that went to the other schools. Example of these special schools were the Bo School founded in Sierra Leone in 1906, Achimota College in Ghana, Kings College, Lagos, Ecole Normale William Ponty for French West Africa, and Kisubi College and Kings College in Uganda. Second, there was the concentration of educational opportunities on the people who already had high socio-economic status in traditional society, particularly the sons of chiefs. Thus the former Governor-General of Nigeria, Lord Lugard, was very preoccupied with the education of the sons of the Fulani rulers of the emirates of Northern Nigeria, in order to give them 'English Public School boys' ideas of honour, loyalty and above all responsibility . . . [to] become really efficient, reliable, and honest cooperators with the British. . . .'. Some of the colonial schools such as Bo School were founded specifically to give educational opportunities to the sons of chiefs and other prominent people. The point was to ensure that (a) the potentially influential were indoctrinated and (b) that the ones who had been exposed to indoctrination were also the ones who had the opportunities for leadership roles and upward mobility. Third, the very limitation of educational opportunities helped the colonisers' aims. Because educational opportunities were so limited, the advantages of the few who were able to get education was all the greater, and so was the ability of the colonial regime to ensure the indoctrinated potential rulers had access to leadership roles. That was how it worked out in practice. For instance, on the eve of independence nearly all the most important leaders of French West Africa were graduates of the only institution of higher education in French West Africa: Modibo Keita, President of Mali; Félix Houphouet-Boigny, President of Ivory Coast; Quezzin Coulibaly, Prime Minister of Upper Volta; Djibo Bakary, Prime Minister of Niger; Mmadu Dia, Prime Minister of Senegal; Hubert Maga, President of Dahomey (Benin). It was along these lines that colonial education started to create class differentiation among the indigenous population. There were other contributory factors to class differentiation. The exploitation of the colonies' resources, the reorientation of the colonial economy outwards and the growth in international trade associated with it, gave opportunities which enabled some of the indigenous people to become marginal capitalists, for instance by acting as lower level middlemen in the export trade. The concentration of the labour force in specific geographical locations, which came with capitalism, created demands for services such as shops, tailoring, food and furniture supplies. Some Africans were able to take advantage of such opportunities, to become marginal capitalists.

The administrative arrangements which the colonial system introduced also provided similar opportunities. Consider the native administration system, for instance. A few powerful chiefs and other nominees of the colonial regime who occupied responsible positions in the system had comparatively good salaries. For instance, the Emir of Kano was being paid a salary of £7,700 in 1960. Even more important than the salaries of these people was the power and patronage which their new status gave them – to punish, to collect taxes, to administer customary law, to supervise public works, and to run some public services such as dispensaries. The power and patronage associated with these duties was very often taken advantage of to accumulate wealth.

Before proceeding with the discussion it should be noted that neither the colonising bourgeoisie nor the African petit-bourgeosie were homogenous social entities. Each of these classes was full of contradictions, but in the case of the African petit-bourgeoisie the internal contradictions did not become very significant until the very eve of their independence. From the very beginning of colonisation, the contradictions within the colonising bourgeoisie were visible and significant. There were three social types in this class: the higher officials of the colonial state who maintained the political conditions of accumulation; European capitalists resident in Europe with substantial investments in the colonies; and European capitalists in the colony itself. Within each of these groups there were contradictions, for instance between those in commerce, those in the service sector and those in agriculture. So when one talks about the interests of the colonial bourgeoisie, or treats it as an undifferentiated whole, this is being rather simplistic. Having said this, it should be added that expositional convenience does not always allow attention to the contradictions in question. But this will not be so misleading if we bear in mind that when an interest is attributed to the bourgeoisie, it does not mean that it applies to all the groups or factions within the bourgeois class.

The contradictions between the bourgeoisie and the African petit-bourgeoisie arise primarily from the monopolistic character of colonial capitalism. As we saw in the preceding chapter, in colonial Africa economic and political power was highly concentrated. Largely because of this concentration, capitalist accumulation was carried on with a singular crudeness and brutality; the arrogance of power was reinforced by contempt for the indigenous people and nurtured by a racist colonial ideology which insisted that Africans had to be subjected to colonial domination in their own interest because they were less than human. Not surprisingly, the colonial bourgeoisie would not easily bring themselves to understand that Africans might have interests, much more conceive that they could assert their interests against those of their colonial masters.

The antagonism and struggle between the colonial bourgeoisie and the emerging African petit-bourgeoisie has to be seen against this background to be understood. The process of class formation which colonialism could not help promoting made it increasingly difficult to maintain the colonial system, for the few indigenous people who were educated became highly skilled, conversant with the coloniser's culture and in some cases imbued with his values, and became assertive. Their education, professional success and penetration of the mystique of the coloniser's culture gave them confidence and raised their expectations. For the most part they shared the capitalist values of their colonial masters and hoped that their education and evident ability would give them the lifestyle and privileges that the European bourgeoisie enjoyed.

However, this expectation was frustrated. Equal treatment for them was against the very logic of colonial ideology. Insurmountable obstacles were placed in their way. Those of them who were professionals found themselves placed below Europeans who possessed far lower qualifications. Amilcar Cabral, the famous leader of Patido Africano da Independencia de Guinea Y Cabo Verde (PAIGC), illustrates the point: 'To take my own case, a member of the petit bourgeoisie group which launched the struggle in Guinea, I was an agronomist working under a European who everybody knew was one of the biggest idiots in Guinea: I could have taught him his job with my eyes shut but he was the boss; this is something which really matters. This is of major importance when considering where the initial idea of the struggle came from'.

Those members of the African petit-bourgeoisie in the private sector were similarly frustrated. African businessmen had to contend with the first few decades of colonial rule. For one thing the banks were averse to giving credit to indigenous entrepreneurs. They insisted on conditions which were extremely difficult for African entrepreneurs to meet; and prospective African borrowers had to contend with traditional property rights which made putting up adequate collateral for a loan difficult. They also had to contend with racist prejudices against African business methods, competence and integrity. These prejudices and other factors, detrimental enough to African entrepreneurs, were in some cases reinforced by discriminatory laws. For instance in Kenya there was the notorious Credit to Africans Ordinance of 1948, which stipulated that debts of over 200 shillings owed by Africans could not be legally enforced in court. It would have taken considerable rashness on the part of credit institutions to grant substantial loans to Africans in the face of such legislation.

The entrepreneural drive of the African petit-bourgeoisie was thwarted by laws designed to protect, or create monopoly status for the European, or to prevent him from engaging in certain forms of economic activity altogether. For instance, in Kenya the Coffee Plantations Registration Ordinance of 1918 prevented African farmers from growing coffee, the most profitable export commodity of the colony. The reasons for this legislation are interesting: permitting Africans to grow coffee would make too many of them independent producers and reduce the supply of labour to European farms; if Africans grew coffee, theft of coffee from European farms would increase for Africans could then legitimately possess coffee. African participation in coffee growing would reduce the quality of the product and the export price – a similar argument was made for barring Africans from growing pyrethreum. Another example of discriminatory laws against African producers was Kenya's Marketing of Native Produce Ordinance of 1935. This law restricted marketing (especially wholesale marketing) to Europeans and Asians. Europeans and Asians could use the law to prevent Africans from growing virtually any cash crop in commercial quantities by simply refusing to buy from the African producer. Measures such as these inevitably turned some members of the African petit-bourgeoisie into implacable opponents of colonialism.

The monopoly tendency of the colonial social formation was not only economic in character but political as well. The severe limitation of the economic participation of the African petit-bourgeoisie was matched by their political marginality. The logic of colonialism compelled the colonisers to make an exclusive claim to political power. Africans would not be allowed any significant political participation, for once this was allowed the assumption that they were less than human, the assumption which sustained the massive assault on their dignity by colonialism, could no longer hold. The exclusive claim of the colonisers to political power was also dictated by economic necessity. Economic power and political power tend to fuse. If the indigenous population was allowed any significant political power, it would soon enhance its ability to acquire economic power, thereby making exploitation, as well as the maintenance of the colonial system, all the more difficult.

This exclusive claim to political power, so necessary for the colonial system, plunged the same system into an acute contradiction. Once the contradiction between the colonial bourgeoisie and the African petit-bourgeoisie became political, the latter had to match this claim with their own exclusive claim to power. If they had opted for incremental political participation they would have been accepting the racist assumption that they were less than human. They had to reject the assumption. But to reject the assumption was tantamount to rejecting the claim of the coloniser to rule – alone or with African participation.

So one exclusive claim to political power was confronted with another. What did this mean for the structure of colonial politics? It meant among other things that in politics the important question was who should rule, not how to rule. It meant that politics became a zero-sum game. Here then was the contradiction: that the coloniser's monopolisation of power created its own dialectical negation, that it created a condition in which the demands of the political outsiders could not be met by reform and accommodation, but only by the complete displacement of those who exercised political power.

To sum up, we have seen how the colonial system produced a petit-bourgeoisie which for reasons of self-interest led the struggle against colonialism. At first this petit-bourgeoisie had very limited ideological clarity, but eventually this changed and a formidable political front gradually emerged. For instance, in Sierra Leone the bourgeoisie fought colonialism in a disorganised way as a set of interest groups, notably the Civil Servants Association (founded in 1907), the African Progress Union (1919), the Aborigines Protection Society (1909) and the Sierra Leone Bar Association (1919). Gradually these interest groups began to federate as the struggle clarified their objective situation and consciousness, and as they progressively recognised their common enemy and common interests. One manifestation of this federation was the Sierra Leone branch of the National Congress of British West Africa, a transterritorial organisation of the rising bourgeoisie, conceived in 1913 and founded in 1920. One more example of the link between the rising bourgeoisie and the nationalist movement will suffice. In the Ivory Coast some of the more successful African farmers had become increasingly frustrated by economic discrimination against them and in favour of the white farmers. In 1944 they banded together to form an interest group called Syndicate Agricole Africain (SAA). The organisation grew rapidly, due to the astute leadership of Houphouet-Boigny, and its membership rose to 20,000. Already by 1945 the SAA had become explicitly political and joined forces with the Communist Study Group which had arisen in Abidjan. The two organisations constituted a political party called the Parti Democratique de la Côte d'Ivoire (PDCI). This bourgeois party quickly gave itself a mass base by championing popular grievances against colonialism, especially the practice of forced labour. It was the PDCI which led the Ivory Coast to independence and still rules the country today.

Contradictions between capital and labour

The emergence of an African proletariat was itself a manifestation of the contradictions of colonialism in much the same sense as the emergence of an African petit bourgeoisie. The penetration of the capitalist mode of production entailed the generation of a proletariat. This proletariat eventually became the base of the political movement of the petit-bourgeoisie against colonialism. In what follows, we shall review the development of the contradictions between labour and capital.

We shall start by considering the contradictions connected with urbanisation and the lack of a social welfare system. The process of capitalist accumulation encourages the socialisation of production and the spatial and social concentration of producers. In Africa the penetration of the capitalist mode of production went hand in hand with urbanisation.

In *West African Urbanisation*, Kenneth Little has provided statistics on Abidjan which are typically suggestive of the rapid rate of urbanisation under colonialism. Abidjan, a small fishing village of 720 people in 1910, rose to a population of 5,371 by 1921. Between 1939 and 1960 the population of Abidjan grew from 18,000 to 180,000. That of Dakar grew from approximately 94,000 to 400,000 in the same period. The population of Lagos was about 99,000 in 1936, but by 1962 it had risen to an estimated 673,000. The increase in urbanisation went hand in hand with the process of proletarianisation. We get a picture of the process of proletarianisation from the following statistics. In Accra 57% of all families had income from wage labour in 1953. In the case of Kumasi, it was roughly 34% in 1955. It was higher in Sekondi-Takoradi – about 69% in 1955.

How this concentration of population and process of proletarianisation helped to negate the colonial system is easy to understand. It brought out the exploitative character of colonialism and expressed with pointed simplicity the contradictions between coloniser and colonised. The urban centres expressed with brutal clarity the class character of the colonial society. On the one hand was the European section of the town with large airy buildings, well-kept gardens, tennis courts, golf courses, well-paved roads, lighted streets, etc. On the other hand, the African quarters consisted of crowded slums served by no amenities. Because of the physical proximity of the two sections of town and their dramatic contrast, it was easier for the African town dwellers to appreciate the exploitative character of colonialism.

Colonial rule was cheap rule. The necessities of profit maximisation did not encourage investment in street lighting, sewage disposal, drainage systems, comfortable housing, good roads, pipe-borne water and other such amenities for the African population. Even more serious than lack of such physical amenities was the lack of social welfare schemes such as unemployment insurance, medical care, medical insurance, a credit system for hard-pressed families, and recreational facilities. Urban Africans tried to cope with this situation as best they could. Rather surprisingly, all over colonial Africa they tended to respond in the same way to the situation, by the formation of urban associations, which were in effect substitutes for a welfare system.

The names of these urban associations give us a hint of their character: the Ibibio Welfare Union, the Calabar Improvement League, the Ibo State Union, and the Igbarra Progressive Union in Nigeria. Those in the Ivory Coast included Union Fraternelle des Originaires des Six Circles de l'Ouest; Odienne Idéal; Association pour la Defense des Interêts des Autochtones de la Côte d'Ivoire. The spread of this phenomenon can be gauged from the following: in 1925 the Freetown-Shebro-Bonthe areas of Sierra Leone had 23 of these associations with a total membership of approximately 13,440 people. It must mean that a very high percentage of the adult population of the area belonged to these associations, since the total population of Freetown around 1921 was only about 44,000.

As Kenneth Little shows, these associations fulfilled a wide variety of functions. Among the most important was the modernisation of the rural society from which their members came. They raised money to build schools, roads, dispensaries and other such facilities. But more relevant for our purpose was the role which these associations played in the urban centres. We can sum up their role by saying that they tried to provide the social welfare services which the colonial government failed to provide. More specifically, they loaned money to their members to do business, gave them money to lighten the financial burdens of marriages, burials, unemployment, sickness, etc. For instance, the aim of the Jubilee Society, a voluntary association founded in Sierra Leone in 1865, was 'relief of members during sickness, death, loss in fire'. In addition they organised recreational activities for their members, pooled their labour to improve their physical surroundings, and awarded scholarships for the education of members' children. The Ibibio Welfare Union of Nigeria awarded several scholarships for study in Britain and America, and educated many of the leading politicians of the Calabar area.

While this phenomenon was a natural outcome of the capitalist logic of colonialism, it stood in contradiction to the colonial regime. To begin with, the associations were fulfilling what is perhaps the most fundamental function of the state, namely the social welfare of its citizens. They supplanted the colonial state, depriving it of the opportunity to mask its nature as a hostile, alien and exploitative force. Thus it became easier to mobilise the indigenous urban population against the colonial system. Apart from this the urban associations provided the organisational basis and leadership training for the nationalist movements of Africa. Most of the early nationalist leaders were people who had benefited from the educational programmes of the urban associations. Many of them had their first experience of politics and organisation through their involvement in these secondary associations.

The contribution of the associations to African nationalist movements went beyond this. They provided ready-made organisational structures for the African petit-bourgeoisie who led the opposition against colonialism. For instance, Nnamdi Azikiwe's nationalist polical party, the National Council of Nigeria and Cameroons, started as a coalition of these urban-based self-help associations. In both East and West Africa most of the nationalist parties built on such associations. This is true of the Convention People's Party, the Kenya African Democratic Union and the Kenya African National Union, to mention just a few. It is thus clear that in giving impetus to urbanisation, and in refusing to attend to the social welfare of its subjects, the colonial regime was creating the conditions for its own negation.

Before leaving this theme it is useful to discuss one more aspect of the conditions negating colonialism because it is also related to the role of the urban associations and the lack of social welfare. It has been indicated that the urban associations were not only interested in the welfare of their members in the cities but also in the rural communities from which their members came. Many of them taxed themselves to bring development to these rural areas. In a sense they regarded themselves as trustees of their rural communities who had a special responsibility for bringing them the benefits of modern life. The developmental activity of the associations in the rural areas helped to maintain very strong ties between city dwellers and rural dwellers. These ties were further reinforced by the intensive exploitation of the urban proletariat, who were often obliged to keep a small farm in the village in order to survive; this peasantisation of the urban proletariat was quite a widespread phenomenon under colonialism. These ties between peasantry and labour made it easy for the petit bourgeoisie to weld them into an irresistible nationalist movement. The trust and legitimacy which the urban associations had won by their remarkable achievement in bringing amenities such as pipe-borne water, schools and clinics to the villages meant that once the urban association embraced the nationalist cause, it was very easy to win over the rural areas from which its members came.

Contradictions between capital and the peasantry

This discussion will be based mainly on the colonial experience of Kenya, because there was a large body of white settlers in colonial Kenya, and because many of the white settlers were farmers. The presence of a settler farming community brings out in sharper relief the effects of colonialism in general, and agrarian capitalism in particular, on the peasantry.

One major source of contradiction between the colonial bourgeoisie (mainly the white farmers in this case) and the peasants was the bourgeoisie's demand for land and labour. Let us consider the demand for land first. In Kenya, African interests in land were originally protected by the Protectorate Regulations of 1897, which forbade the alienation of land which was regularly used by Africans. But this protection was short-lived. The Crown Lands Ordinance of 1902 and the Orders-in-Council of 1901 and 1902 gave the government jurisdiction over all land, but this jurisdiction was limited by the right of occupancy of Africans. That meant of course that the right of ownership by Africans was no longer recognised. Then the Crown Lands Ordinance of 1915 made it quite clear that Africans had no right to land, legal or otherwise. So the way was paved for the appropriation of African lands and the confinement of Africans into reserves. The most striking instance of this was the appropriation of the 16,700 square miles of the best farming land in Kenya for the exclusive use of Kenya's European farmers. In the wake of this massive alienation of African lands came land hunger, civil strife and eventually the Mau Mau rebellion, one of the bloodiest events in African colonial history.

The colonisers needed not only land but labour also. Indeed the need for labour was far more fundamental than the need for land, since wage labour is the very foundation of capitalism. The need for labour was also more widespread among the colonial bourgeoisie. For it was not only those in the agricultural sector who needed it but also those in commerce, the services and manufacturing. An adequate supply of labour was the chronic problem of colonial capitalism in Africa.

Unfortunately for colonial capital, the much-wanted labour was not forthcoming and it was necessary to resort to all sorts of coercive devices to ensure its supply. Taxation was imposed and made payable in the official currency only. By refusing the payment of taxes in kind, the colonial government forced Africans to enter the money economy and to engage in wage labour. The relation of the hut tax introduced in Kenya in 1902 to the supply of labour is clear from the official discussions which preceded its introduction. For instance, it was suggested that the tax could be waived in lieu of a certain amount of labour. Later on a poll tax was also levied. Nevertheless by 1907 the shortage of labour had become so acute in Kenya that many European farmers quickly acted to rectify the situation. In 1910 a Masters and Servants Ordinance was introduced to regulate the conditions of African labour employed by Europeans. The Ordinance defined standards of sanitation, feeding and accommodation. It was hoped that the supply of labour could be increased by improving the deplorable conditions of African wage labour. Characteristically, the colonial government had more faith in coercive measures. A Resident Native Ordinance (also passed in 1910) regulated the conditions under which Africans might leave the reserves and settle as squatters on uncultivated parts of European farms. In 1912 a Native Authority Ordinance was passed, which gave the government power to compel Africans to do communal work for six days in every quarter. Then came the much detested Native Registration Ordinance in 1915, which required Africans leaving their reserve to seek work to carry a certificate containing their fingerprint and their periods of employment. These certificates, called *kipande*, were housed in a small metal container which was usually worn around the neck with a string. The *kipande* was bitterly opposed and came to be a symbol of colonial oppression. In 1937 the Resident Native Labourers' Ordinance was amended. The amendment, which came into effect in 1940, held the squatters on European farms were no longer tenants, that they had rights only in so far as they worked for the European farmer. This is by no means a comprehensive list of the measures taken to ensure the supply of labour to capital. It is difficult to say whether an adequate supply of labour could have been obtained with less coercion and less indignity to Africans. For all the coercion the supply of labour remained problematic. However, the coercion against the independent producers created strong antipathies against the colonial system in rural society and so paved the way for the mobilisation of peasants against colonialism.

Another notable source of contradiction between capital and the peasantry was the attempt by capital to bring the peasants into commodity relations and to extract surplus value from them by manipulating the conditions of production and exchange. We have already encountered some examples of these measures. But to recapitulate, in the sphere of production, agricultural improvement schemes and legislative measures were used to manoeuvre peasants into producing particular commodities to particular specifications, in certain preferred quantities and with specific inputs, tools and techniques. This was done not in the interest of the peasant but in the interest of the people who made the rules and launched the agricultural development schemes. They got the peasant to produce it in a manner most to their advantage. At the same time the peasants became more dependent and more exploitable. In the sphere of exchange the peasant was exploited through control of commodity collection and marketing by monopoly agencies such as the Marketing Boards, which enabled capital to expropriate the peasant by paying him only a fraction of the value of his commodity in the world market. But a lot of the measures used for bringing the peasant into commodity relations and to control his conditions of production and exchange were very unpopular. Capital profited only by engendering enemies of the very system that enabled it to profit.

One more source of contradiction deserves mention. This is the monopoly power of the capitalist class which allowed it to pass on an inordinate burden to the peasant – paying for the prosperity of the capitalist in the form of the expropriation of surplus value from him, absorbing the impact of economic depression transmitted to the colony from the metropole, paying for the infrastructures which aided capitalist accumulation, paying to support the administrative system which legislated his oppression. We have already given an example of this inordinate burden in the case of Nigeria. In our examination of the Marketing Boards in that country we saw that the bulk of the domestic revenue for financing the development budget came from the surplus of the Marketing Boards. But this surplus was for all practical purposes surplus value appropriated from 'independent' producers. A further illustration of this point will be made briefly from Kenya.

In periods of financial crisis the colonial administration tended to increase the burdens of the Africans much more than that of the Europeans. For instance, in the face of the financial problem that the protectorate was facing around 1900, the poll tax was introduced and used very effectively to extract a greater contribution from Africans. The contribution of the tax to revenue rose very quickly from $4\frac{1}{2}$% in the financial year 1901–2 to 22% for the financial year 1903–4. By 1920, when Kenya was facing another financial crisis, the poll tax and hut tax (both paid by Africans) were each immediately doubled in May of that year. The measure engendered considerable consternation and opposition. An income tax on land directed at Europeans that was also introduced in this period was vehemently opposed, and it was quickly repealed in 1922. Again, between 1928 and 1933 when the Kenyan economy was depressed, there was an attempt to shift much of the burden on to Africans, for instance by cutting wages. As such burdens multiplied so did African discontent.

Contradictions of colonial ideology

We have seen that colonialism was a direct effect of the contradictions of capitalism in the West, and that the West's imperialist thrust into Africa which eventually led to colonisation was undertaken to aid the accumulation of capital. As might be expected, the coloniser's justification of colonialism did not run along these lines. Colonialism was justified on the grounds that it was to the mutual advantage of coloniser and colonised. The doctrine of the mutual benefits of colonialism is to be found in the *Dual Mandate in British Tropical Africa* published in 1922 by Lord Lugard, the former governor of Northern Nigeria, and *La Mise en Valeur des Colonies Françaises* published in 1923, by Albert Sarraut, a former Minister of the Colonies of France. It was argued that colonialism benefited the colonising country by providing a source of cheap raw materials, cheap labour and a market for exports, and by encouraging an international division of labour which made it possible for goods to be produced more cheaply to the benefit of all. The justification of the benefit of colonialism to the colonising country was as necessary as it was misleading. It was necessary because the government of the colonising power had to account to its electorate, and colonialism was a serious commitment which affected the interest of part of that electorate. For instance, some civil servants were uprooted from their familiar environment and posted to the colonies, part of the navy was deployed to protect the colonial trade, and soldiers were despatched to suppress rebellious 'natives'. It was misleading because colonialism was not undertaken to serve broader national interests, although it might have done so incidentally, but rather to serve the interest of the capitalist class in the colonising country.

Rather more emphasis was placed on the justification of colonialism as a service to the colonised people. What service? Essentially the service of civilising them. That is why colonialism was 'popularly' referred to by colonisers as a civilising mission. According to the theory, the civilisation of the natives entailed, among other things, bringing them Western education, the benefits of Western technology, bringing them into the stream of human history, getting them to discard their 'barbaric culture', and generally redeeming a way of life captive to ignorance, poverty and disease.

This justification of colonialism was full of contradictions, and we will discuss only the most important ones. The first is the question of reconciling the idea of the civilising mission with the barbarism of colonialism. As is well-known, the colonisation of Africa was a particularly brutal process: the military expeditions to liquidate dissident indigenes, and sometimes whole villages, such as happened during the Maji Maji and Mau Mau rebellions in East Africa, the merciless disruption of a people's culture, the use of force to make people toil under inhuman conditions sometimes leading to their death, the pillage of the resources of a powerless people, the devastation of the environment. How could all this be reconciled with the claim of a civilising mission? Was not colonialism brutalising rather than civilising?

For the coloniser this was not really a problem, for his claim was that the colonised was uncivilised. By brutalising the colonised, depriving him of a sense of self and pride and reducing him to utter wretchedness, the colonised became more of what he had to be to justify being colonised, with all that his colonisation entailed. In other words, the brutalisation of the colonised reduced him to wretchedness and his wretchedness became the justification for treating him as an inhuman creature. At the same time, the barbarity perpetrated on the colonised was shrugged off as means to the civilising mission. Thus Félix Chautemps, who was France's Minister for Colonies, wrote in 1913 that the colonised Africans 'will need some time to understand that we rob them and kill them to teach them to live an increasingly human life'. So the brutalisation no longer stands in contradiction to the civilising mission but in harmony with its claims. But only to the consciousness of the coloniser. To the colonised, it was otherwise. The barbarity of colonialism stood in stark contradiction to the idea of a civilising mission and created strong antipathies to the colonial system.

To turn to the other contradiction associated with the civilising mission: if the civilising mission was indeed to be pursued as theorised, it would have entailed a massive effort to develop the colony, a massive injection of resources from the mother country into the colony. What actually happened was quite to the contrary. The colonial regimes were not interested in developing Africa, as the statistics testify: only 2,850 miles of railway in British West Africa by 1957; only 2,300 miles of railway and 289 children in high school in all French West Africa in the same period. Far from putting resources into the development of the colony, the colonial power exploited it. This was as it should be. For as we saw before, Africa was colonised because European capital was seeking better opportunities to maximise capital accumulation, and as it maximised capital accumulation, it also maximised exploitation. So in the final analysis the African population was not helped but exploited. The ideology of colonialism had presupposed that Africans were somewhat less than human, and being somewhat less than human they could be brutalised and denied the right to govern themselves. This presupposition was implicitly racist. Quite often the racism was stated implicitly. For instance, Lord Lugard argued that the African 'lacks power of organisation and is conspicuously deficient in the management and control alike of man or of business'. This racism was a source of contradictions. The following passage from Lord Lugard's Dual Mandate gives us an idea of the nature of these contradictions. 'Here then is the true conception of the interrelation of colour: complete uniformity in ideals, absolute equality in the paths of knowledge and culture, equal opportunity for those who strive, equal admiration for those who achieve: in matters social and racial a separate path, each pursuing his own inherited traditions, preserving his own race purity and race-pride; equality in things spiritual, agreed divergence in the physical and material.' This passage is an excellent example of the contradictions of colonial ideology. The colonisers indoctrinated the African with the ideals of the white man's culture and yet expected him to remain compliant; they forgot that the ideals promised equal opportunity for those who strove and achieved, while the logic of the colonial system excluded Africans from such opportunities and frustrated their legitimate ambitions. Colonial racism only dramatised and forced on the popular consciousness the contradiction between social production and private appropriation. The racist isolation of the African in the miserable slums of the native reserve areas only brought home to him his alienation from the fruits of his labour and the parasitical character of the colonial ruling class. Missionaries and colonial administrators hoped that Africa would be content with spiritual equality and would tolerate 'the divergence in the physical and material'. They might have remembered that the enormous physical and material divergences were bound to register on the consciousness.

Conclusion

Such were the contradictions which generated and gave impetus to the wave of nationalist movements and liberation struggles in colonial Africa. They created the leadership of these movements, and also created the conditions which enabled them to mobilise the masses and politicise their grievances. Soon enough the nationalist and liberation movements emerged, quickly gathering momentum. The rest is familiar.

Bibliography

AKE, C., 'The Congruence of Ideologies and Economies in Africa', in P. Gutkind and I. Wallerstein eds., *The Political Economy of Contemporary Africa*, Beverly Hills, 1976.

BARNETT, D. AND MJAMA, K., *Mau Mau from Within: An Analysis of Kenya's Peasant Revolt*, New York, 1965.

BETTS, R., *Assimilation and Association in French Colonial Theory, 1890–1914*, New York, 1961.

CABRAL, A., *Revolution in Guinea*, London, 1969.

CLIFFE, L., 'Nationalism and the Reaction to Enforced Agricultural Change in Tanganyika during the Colonial Period', in L. Cliffe and J. Saul, *Socialism in Tanzania*, Nairobi, 1972.

COLEMAN, J., *Nigeria: Background to Nationalism*, Berkeley, 1958.

COHEN, R. AND GUTKIND, P., eds., *Peasants and Proletarians: the Struggle of Third World Workers*, New York, 1978.

CROWDER, M., *West African Resistance: The Military Response to Colonial Occupation*, London, 1978.

DESCHAMPS, H., *Methods of Doctrines: Coloniales de la France*, Paris, 1953.

FANON, F., *The Wretched of the Earth*, New York, 1963.

GANN, L. H. AND DUIGNAN, P., *Colonialism in Africa, 1870–1960*, Vol. 1, *The History and Politics of Colonialism 1870–1914*, Cambridge, 1969.

GERRY, C., 'African Responses to French Mercantilism and Colonialism 1700–1975', *West African Journal of Sociology and Politics*, 1, 1/2, 1976/7.

GOODE, K., 'Settler Colonialism', *Journal of Modern African Studies*, 14, 4, 1976.

GOULDBOURNE, H. ed., *Politics and the State in the Third World*, London, 1979.

HAMZI, ALAVI, 'The Post-Colonial State', *New Left Review*, 74, 1972.

HODGKIN, T., *Nationalism in Colonial Africa*, London, 1956.

HOPKINS, A., 'Economic Aspects of Political Movements in Nigeria and in the Gold Coast, 1918–1939', *Journal of African History*, 7, 1966.

ILIFFE, J., *Tanganyika Under German Rule, 1905–1912*, Cambridge, 1969.

INNES, D., 'Imperialism and the National Class Struggle in Namibia', *Review of African Political Economy*, 9, 1978.

KAKONEN, J., *The Political Economy of Colonialism in Ghana*, Cambridge, 1972.

KAY, G., *Development and Underdevelopment*, London, 1974.

KENYATTA, J., *Facing Mount Kenya*, London, 1938.

KILSON, M., 'Nationalism and Social Classes in British West Africa', *Journal of Politics*, 20, 1958.

KOSMIN, B., 'The Lukoya Tobacco Industry of the Shangwe People: A Case Study of the Displacement of the Precolonial Economy' *African Social Research*, 17, 1974.

LITTLE, K., *West African Urbanisation: A Study of Voluntary Organisation in Social Change*, Cambridge, 1966.

LUGARD, F., *The Dual Mandate in British Tropical Africa*, Edinburgh, 1922.

MAGUIRE, G., *Towards Uhuru in Tanzania*, Cambridge, 1969.

MAMDANI, M., *Politics and Class Formation in Uganda*, New York, 1976.

MEILLASSOUX, C., 'The Social Organisation of the Peasantry', *Journal of Peasant Studies*, 1, 1, 1973.

MILLER, R., 'Elite Formation in Africa', *Journal of Modern African Studies*, 12, 4, 1974.

MONDLANE, E., *The Struggle for Mozambique*, Harmondsworth, 1969.

MWASE, G., *Strike a Blow and Die: A Narrative of Race Relations in Colonial Africa*, Harvard, 1967.

PETRAS, JAMES, *Critical Perspectives on Imperialism and Social Class in the Third World*, New York, 1978.

POST, K., *On 'Peasantisation' and Rural Class Differentiation in Western Africa*, The Hague, 1970.

RANGER, T. O., *Revolt in Southern Rhodesia 1896–97*, London, 1967.

RODNEY, W., 'European Activity and African Reaction in Angola', in T. O. Ranger ed., *Aspects of Central African History*, London, 1968.

ROSEBERG, G. AND NOTTINGHAM, J., *The Myth of Mau Mau: Nationalism in Kenya*, New York, 1960.

RUDEBECK, L., *Guinea-Bissau: A Study of Political Mobilisation*, Uppsala, 1974.

SAUL, J., 'African Peasants and Revolution', *Review of African Political Economy*, 1, 1974.

SIMENSEN, J., 'Rural mass action in the context of anti-colonial protest: the Asafor movement of Akin Abuaka', *Canadian Journal of African Studies*, 8, 1, 1974.

WALLERSTEIN, I., 'The Colonial Era in Africa: Changes in Social Structure', in L. Gann and P. Duignan eds., *Colonialism in Africa, 1870–1960*, Cambridge, 1970.

WALLERSTEIN, I., 'Class-Formation in the Capitalist World Economy', *Politics and Society*, 5, 3, 1975.

WASSERMAN, G., 'Continuity and Counter-Insurgency: The Role of Land Reform in Decolonising Kenya, 1912–1970', *Canadian Journal of African Studies*, 7, 1, 1973.

WILSON, H. S., *Origins of West African Nationalism*, London, 1969.

YOUE, C., 'Peasants, Planters and Cotton Capitalists in Colonial Uganda', *Canadian Journal of African Studies*, 12, 2, 1978.

ZAKINE, D., 'Classes and Class Struggle in Devleoping Countries', *International Affairs*, 4, 1968.

5 The postcolonial economy

The expression 'postcolonial' could be misleading so it is as well to begin by clarifying it. The expression does not mean that an economy has been decolonised, i.e. that it no longer possesses the features of a colonial economy, which we have already described. The expression which follows conventional usage here is merely a convenient way of talking about the economy at a particular historical period – namely, the period following the winning of formal political independence.

Perhaps something should also be said about the periodisation implicit in the expression 'postcolonial'. By contrasting the structures of African economies in their colonial and postcolonial phases there is an implicit assumption that the winning of political independence was a watershed in the history of Africa, and that it was a change which could reasonably be expected to have had a major, if not decisive, impact on the future development of African economies. This assumption is not unreasonable. The nationalist petit-bourgoisie which fought for independence had insisted that political independence was the essential preliminary to a fundamental restructuring of the colonial economy, and many students of Africa seemed to agree that the political hegemony of the colonisers was a critical factor in the underdevelopment of African social formations. After two decades of political independence in Africa available evidence on the validity of this assumption is ambiguous. Revolutionary changes in the structure of African economies have clearly not occurred, and even their growth rates have been less than satisfactory. But some very significant changes have occurred – not necessarily for the better – particularly in the relations of production. The purpose of this chapter is to identify what features are changing and what are not, and to indicate why changes are occurring or failing to occur.

Disarticulation

Efforts to reduce the disarticulation of African economies have had a marginal effect at best. The major reason for the meagre progress is that the drive for economic development in the postcolonial era has followed the line of least resistance, which is generally the least desirable from the point of view of social benefits, balanced development and the long-term maximisation of development. By the time political independence came, the colonial economy had, so to speak, matured; its structure was firmly set and could not easily be changed. The new government no longer enjoyed the freedom of fabricating an economy from the start. The fully formed economy that it inherited imposed a certain logic and rigidity on the course of future development, and this logic was essentially one that favoured the persistence and even the reinforcement of the syndrome of disarticulation.

To begin with, enclave development continues, particularly in the sense that developmental activity and social ammenities are being concentrated in a few urban centres. This is reflected in the ratio of urban to rural incomes, which is quite often in the region of 4:1. There are many African socio-economic formations where one urban centre has become so economically and politically dominant that it could with some accuracy be described as a city state. The Ivory Coast is a good example of this phenomenon, as Table 5.1 shows.

TABLE 5.1 Ivory Coast: the economic dominance of Abidjan, 1974 (figures denote percentages)

Category	Abidjan	Bouaké	Others	Total
Production of value	64.7	8.8	26.5	100
Value added*	70.0	17.0	13.0	100
Wages and salaries	65.2	10.5	24.3	100
Employment	52.6	11.9	35.5	100

*The figure for value added for Abidjan is an estimate for 1973, while that for Bouaké is an estimate for 1971.

Source
Adapted from *Ivory Coast: The Challenge of Success. Report of a mission sent to the Ivory Coast by the World Bank*, Baltimore, 1978, p. 233

The government of Houphouet-Boigny, which came to power at independence, was aware of this 'problem' and seemed intent on doing something about it. But the trend continued all the time. According to the World Bank Mission Report just cited, 'throughout the 1960s, industry became increasingly concentrated in Abidjan. Despite some stabilisation in this trend since the early 1970s, the 1971–75 plan target of reducing Abidjan's share of total value added in manufacturing from 65 per cent in 1968 to 50 per cent in 1975 has not been met. Large projects such as the paper pulp and tyre plants, which were to be based outside Abidjan, could not be implemented, and the lack of effective incentives for decentralisation further affected this target'. The report of the Mission gives good economic reasons for the persistence: 'the city is an attractive industrial pole in terms of market, infrastructure, and services; infrastructure is less developed in the interior, regional markets are small, and minimum labour wages are the same in and outside of Abidjan'. All that is true. But the report of the Mission neglects to discuss what may well be the most important factor, namely that this enclave development is a manifestation of the class contradictions of postcolonial socio-economic formations. As we have seen, with few exceptions the petit-bourgeois leadership of the African nationalist movement was more interested in inheritance than in revolution, and it was inevitable that its policies would locate development and amenities to the convenience of the dominant class.

This has to be recognised in order to understand why it will be so difficult to deal with this aspect of disarticulation. Even when the government in office recognises the need to do something about the problem, it is restrained and sometimes discouraged by the prospect of impinging on the interests of the class in power. Thus development tends to follow the line of least resistance to the perpetuation of disarticulation, and in following this line of least resistance it creates economic conditions

TABLE 5.2 Principal exports of franc zone countries in Africa

Country	Year	Product	Percentage of total export earnings
Benin	1977	Palm-oil and products	22.0
		Cotton	20.6
		Cocoa	10.8
Ivory Coast	1978	Cocoa and products	33.0
		Coffee	25.0
		Timber	13.6
Upper Volta	1977	Cotton	39.7
		Livestock	29.0
Niger	1976	Uranium	64.0
		Livestock	15.0
Senegal	1977	Groundnuts and products	48.1
		Phosphate	9.4
Togo	1977	Phosphate	48.7
		Cocoa	25.8
		Coffee	14.1
Mali	1976	Cotton	50.4
		Livestock	12.6
		Groundnuts	16.4
Cameroon	1978	Coffee	28.7
		Cocoa	34.2
		Timber	12.3
Central African Republic	1978	Diamonds	37.5
		Coffee	29.6
		Timber	16.4
Congo	1977	Oil	53.3
		Timber	16.5
Gabon	1977	Oil	73.5
		Manganese	17.4
		Timber	7.8
Chad	1978	Cotton	68.6
		Livestock	10.1

Source
Adapted from *West Africa*, No. 3295, 15 September, 1980, p. 1751

which make it even easier to rationalise more concentration of amenities and projects in the urban enclaves.

Now let us look at the problem of disarticulation from a somewhat broader perspective. The discussion so far has given us an essentially geographical perspective of disarticulation, though, as we have seen, the geographical pattern is linked to the social relations of production. We will now look at disarticulation from a more structural perspective, that is in terms of structural differentiation and structural integration of the economy. Table 5.2 helps us to understand the persistence of the structural aspect of disarticulation. This table gives us a good picture of the narrow resource base of African economies. But it is also a good indication of disarticulation. The bulk of the export earnings comes from a limited range of economic activities, in most cases agriculture, in some, mining. Within this narrow range of economic activity the range of specific products is very limited, in most cases the bulk of earnings coming from just two products. The economies have already started to undergo the structural differentiation which will give them organic unity and resilience through complementarity.

This is all the more so because the linkages from these economic activities are largely external. It is also very significant that, with few exceptions such as palm-oil, the domestic consumption of these products ranges from insignificant to zero. This underlines the external orientation of the economics. In the event that the external demand for their products weakens considerably, they will be in very serious trouble. This contrasts sharply with countries such as Japan and the United States. For instance, Japan exports cars but the internal demand for cars in Japan itself is so strong that even a drastic reduction of external demand will not matter so much.

A further illustration of the persistance of disarticulation is provided in Table 5.3.

TABLE 5.3 Share of manufacturing in GDP and labour force in 1970 in six African countries (percentages)

Country	Manufacturing as percentage of GDP	Manufacturing as percentage of labour force
Egypt	20.6	12.3
Nigeria	6.1	0.4
Ghana	6.9	1.6
Kenya	11.4	1.7
Tunisia	15.9	4.2
Uganda	7.4	1.2

Source
Adapted from United Nations Department of Economic and Social Affairs, *Implementation of the International Development Strategy*, Vol. 1 E/5267, ST/ECA/178, New York, 1973, p. 128

The small share of manufacturing in Gross Domestic Product and the total labour force indicates that African economies have made very little progress towards overcoming disarticulation. For it is really the complex network of forward and backward linkages which comes from industrialisation that will make the postcolonial African economy an organic whole capable of self-sustained growth. It is not appropriate to go into a detailed explanation of why the rate of industrialisation is so sluggish, and a few basic points will suffice. The rigidity of the international division of labour has not allowed African economies to break out of the role of primary producers, for reasons which include lack of access to technology, the comparative advantage of the industrialised nations in manufacturing, and the constraints of the domestic market. These and other constraints were so powerful that the attempt at industrialisation has sometimes been self-defeating. For instance, the attempt to industrialise by import substitution led to very heavy importation of inputs, which created debt burdens and balance of payments problems, and this in turn encouraged the intensification of primary production to pay for imports. More recent efforts to promote industrialisation by enhancing export capacity have run into serious problems too. These problems include the increased importation of capital goods and their unfavourable effect on the balance of payments, restrictions of access to the markets of the industrialised countries, and the tendency for the competitive advantages of the developed countries to compel retreat from the idea of exportation to that of inefficient production for domestic consumption behind protective tariffs.

We have seen that in the final analysis the problem of disarticulation can only be removed by the development of productive forces or, to be more specific, by industrialisation. The question of the possibility of eliminating disarticulation tends to disappear into two other types of question. First, it could disappear into the question of whether capitalist development of developing countries is possible. This question has been argued at great length and with considerable passion, but the lengthy and tedious arguments have produced little enlightenment. The debate, though interesting, will not detain us here. What is reasonably clear is that very little capitalist development is occurring, and the indications are that the rate of development will not increase markedly in the foreseeable future. Another thing that is also reasonably clear is that if capitalist development were to occur it will be a development that comes with a considerable degree of dependency. So in a sense capitalist development will not fully solve the problem of disarticulation because in so far as there is dependence there is necessarily a considerable degree of disarticulation. Another problem with capitalist development is that it tends to increase the disarticulation of the socio-economic formation. By the disarticulation of the socio-economic formation I am referring to the developing contradiction of labour and capital in the course of capitalist development. Some may well argue with such premises that in the final analysis capitalist development does not solve the problem of disarticulation.

The question of eliminating disarticulation may also be assimilated into the question of the possibility of socialist development in Africa, a form of development that will, so to speak, short-circuit history so that socialism is attained without having to go through capitalism. Whether the socio-economic formation passes through a capitalist phase or not, socialism cannot be possible (unless it is confused with formations such as primitive communism) without a very high level of the development of productive forces. Because of the structure of the world economy, particularly the monopolistic character of the technology market, socialist development is also likely to entail a certain degree of dependency and so disarticulation. However, by its very nature, socialist development should avoid what we have called the disarticulation of the socio-economic formation.

Monopolistic tendencies

As is generally recognised, the nationalist movement which arose from the contradictions of the colonial economy achieved political independence and not economic independence. The change in the locus of political power was of course bound to have consequences for the locus and the distribution of economic power. But these changes (often subtle) took a long time to register, and it is only more recently that they are beginning to be clearly discernible. Market imperfections and monopolistic tendencies are economic features of the colonial social formation which have been very slow to change.

This is quite understandable. The capacity to survive is a necessary attribute of monopolistic enterprises and organisations. For, by definition, such organisations are strong relative to existing opponents, have a competitive advantage and are in a good position to prevent new rivals from emerging. Thus the great monopolies of the colonial era used their advantages to good effect and survived, as is evident from the strength of companies such as Leventis, United African Company, Elder Dempster, Union Trading Company, John Holt, K. Chelarams, G. B. Olivant and Paterson Zochonis. There are many reasons for the survival of the great monopoly enterprises of the colonial era and for the persistence of monopoly tendencies in the postcolonial situation. But the major one is that the monopoly concerns represented more than anything else the effective presence of international capital in Africa, to which the postcolonial economy remained and remains a client. The explanation of their persistence has to be subsumed under the general explanation of the persistent domination of the African economy by international capitalism, an explanation that will be dealt with later.

Even so, why should the effective presence of capitalism and even its domination take this particular form of monopoly? We have already touched on this point. But to repeat, the answer lies in the character of the historical process of capitalist penetration in Africa. Also, by the time capital is transplanted abroad as imperialism, particularly colonialism, it has already reached the monopoly stage, and its monopoly character distorts the development of indigenous capitalism. This 'monopoly character' of the nascent indigenous capitalism is reinforced by the essentially hostile political atmosphere in which the accumulation of capital occurs under colonialism.

If we bear this point in mind, it will be easy to grasp a related point which seems somewhat paradoxical, namely the fact of the persistence of the monopoly character of the economy despite the fading away of particular monopoly enterprises. The failure of particular monopolies to survive – and examples of this abound – does not mean that the pressures for competitiveness, real or potential, are strong in Africa. Rather, the rise and fall of particular monopolies reflected the objective conditions of the metropolitan economy, particularly the oligopolistic rivalries between the multinationals, the state of development of productive forces, and more generally the competition between imperialisms. These realities, which may be summed up as representing the pathological maturity of a colonial and postcolonial capitalism into a monopoly stage, tend to allow for the displacement or replacement of particular monopoly enterprises without allowing for the displacement of monopoly by competition.

In the postcolonial era a new dimension comes into the equation. This is the creation of a new type of monopoly resulting from state capitalism, that is the involvement of the state in an enterpreneurial role.

Tanzania presents one of the most striking examples of this development. The Tanzanian economy is now dominated by an elaborate system of state enterprises – the parastatal system. In a government publication entitled *Accounts of the Parastatals 1966–1974*, parastatals are officially defined in Tanzania as 'commercial enterprises owned by the government or with majority government participation and are run on commercial principles and whose accounts are not directly integrated into the government budget'.

The number of perastatals in Tanzania started to increase rapidly after the Arusha Declaration of 1967, which committed Tanzania to socialism. By 1967 there were only 43 parastatals, but by 1970 the number had risen to 85, and by 1974 it had risen to 139, and has continued to rise. The significance of the parastatal sector in the Tanzanian economy may be gleaned from Table 5.4 which shows capital formation in the country by sector. There are parastatals in every sector of the economy. In Agriculture there are the Bukoba Tea Company, Basuto Plantations Ltd., Tanzania Sisal Corporation, Arusha Plantations Ltd. and the Dindira Tea Estate. In mining there are the Nyanza Salt Mines, Tanzania Gemstones and the Tanzania Petroleum Authority. The numerous parastatals of the manufacturing sector include the National Milling Corporation, Friendship Textiles, National Cigarette Company, Tanganyika Portland Cement, Mtibwa Sugar Company, Ubango Farm Instruments, Tanzania Fertilizers, Tanzania Shoe Company, Tanzania Tanneries, and Tebora Msitu Products. The parastatals in the transport sector include, Zambia-Tanzania Road Services, Tanzania-China Shipping Line and Tachoshili. The commercial sector boasts a large number of parastatals which include the Tanganyika Pirethrum Board, Tanganyika Sisal Authority, Agricultural and Industrial Suppliers, General Food Company, National Pharmaceuticals, Building Hardware and Electronic Supplies, Tanganyika Cotton Authority and Serengeti Safari Lodges. There is also an impressive number of parastatals in finance and these include the National Bank of Commerce, the Bank of Tanzania, Tanzania Investment Bank, National Development Corporation, National Insurance Corporation, Tanzania Housing Bank and Tanzania Hotels Investments. The service sector is also well served with parastatals which include Tanzania Wildlife Safaris, Tanzania Tours, the

TABLE 5.4 Capital formation in the public and private sectors in Tanzania, 1965–73 (figures in millions of shillings at 1973–74 prices)

	1965	1966	1967	1968	1969	1970	1971	1972	1973*
Central government	148	182	215	276	356	426	408	412	626
Local authorities and EA Community	43	38	48	50	39	36	46	59	52
EA Community enterprises	28	78	119	78	62	115	136	152	229
Parastatal enterprises	34	91	283	214	165	659	1,084	1,186	1,170
Total public sector	253	389	665	645	622	1,236	1,674	1,809	2,077
Private – monetary**	383	443	393	486	431	472	517	461	531
Fixed capital formation – monetary	635	832	1,058	1,131	1,053	1,708	2,191	2,270	2,608
Increase in stocks	58	78	28	51	48	171	196	38	78
Capital formation – monetary	693	910	1,086	1,182	1,101	1,879	2,387	2,308	2,686
Non-monetary:									
Private fixed capital formation	154	150	174	171	160	170	177	202	220
Increase in stocks (cattle)	49	32	52	43	24	18	23	29	30
Total non-monetary capital formation	203	182	226	214	184	188	200	231	250
Total capital formation (monetary and non-monetary)	896	1,092	1,312	1,396	1,285	2,067	2,587	2,539	2,936

* Provisional
** includes cooperative and residual unidentified

Source
Republic of Tanzania Economic Survey, 1973–74, p. 12

National Board of Accountants and Auditors, Tanzania National Parks and the Tanzania Legal Corporation.

As has been indicated before, this tendency towards the development of state-owned enterprises is not limited to countries with socialist aspirations such as Tanzania. The trend is also very strong in countries such as Kenya which lean towards capitalism. For instance, Kenya has also developed a network of parastatals, and under the umbrella of the Industrial and Commercial Development Corporation of Kenya are Kenya National Properties, Kenya Industrial Estate Ltd., the Kenatco Transport Company, East African Fine Spinners Ltd., the Fluorspar Company of Kenya, Somerset Africa Ltd. and Kenya Mining Industries Ltd.

It would appear that state capitalism arises primarily out of the desire of the national petit-bourgeosie which inherited political power from the colonisers to create an economic base for its political power. The national bourgoisies which came to office in the wake of the independence movement soon found that they were in office only but not in power because they had very little control of the economy. But they also understood that political power offered opportunities for economic power, and that the opportunities inherent in their political power were the best and perhaps only way they had of creating an economic base for their political power. And they did not hesitate to use these opportunities. Essentially what they did was to extend the economic role of the state as widely and rapidly as possible. They set up state enterprises with public funds and sometimes in partnership with private investors. These enterprises were given privileges in regard to things such as import licences, credit, government guarantees of credit, tax concessions, government contracts, government patronage and preferred treatment in the granting of foreign exchange. Indeed some of them were given outright monopoly status in the very fundamental sense of having the sole right to operate in a particular line of business or to supply particular commodities or services. Why does the government establish such enterprises? First, it does so in order to promote industrialisation, economic growth and the development of productive forces. The assumption is that the interests of the private investors, which dominate the colonial economy, could scarcely be expected to be entirely harmonious with the national needs of development, particularly the need for industrialisation, the diversification of the economy, etc. Anyone who has read the development plans of African governments will easily recognise that such state enterprises were seen in every African country as a necessary part of the process of industrialisation, diversification, the development of productive forces and national economic independence.

The second reason for the growth of these state enterprises is that they were crucial in the struggle for the control of the economy as well as the struggle for economic independence. It was necessary to encourage the development of enterprises controlled by nationals which could compete with and, if possible, displace those controlled by foreign capital. However, since the discriminatory practices of the colonial regime had made it so difficult for nationals to accumulate wealth, the development of these national enterprises could not be left to indigenous entrepreneurs who hardly had the resources to compete with foreign capital. There was really not much choice but for the state to come into the picture and play the role of the entrepreneur. These state enterprises were needed not merely to compete with metropolitian capital for control of the economy but also to undertake some forms of investment which were considered necessary for development, but which the metropolitan capital would not be disposed to undertake.

A good proportion of these state enterprises were started as means to promote exports and to realise import substitution. It is also partly for these reasons that they were given monopoly privileges. The monopoly privileges were expected to help them to survive and eventually become competitive and even profitable.

Some of the state enterprises came into being as a result of nationalisations of foreign-owned private enterprises. Such nationalisations have been highly recurrent and popular in postcolonial Africa.

It is important to know that they are not necessarily motivated by ideological commitments. They have occurred with significant frequency in countries with socialist aspirations as well as those with capitalist aspirations, although more so in the former than the latter. To all appearances these nationalisations reflect the desire for local control of the economy. They also reflect the desire of the national petit-bourgeoisie which has come to power in the wake of the independence movement to create a material base for its political power. These nationalisations offered a particularly effective way of creating an economic base and for increasing their control of the economy in the shortest possible time. By nationalising, members of the petit-bourgeoisie brought more and more aspects of the economic sphere, and more and more wealth, under their political control, and so they were more able to control the process of accumulation to their own benefit.

The monopoly tendencies and market imperfections are highly significant features of the postcolonial economy. They affect the character of accumulation, the prospects of liquidating underdevelopment, the character of political competition and the prospects of political stability. But this is not the place to go into these implications.

A narrow resource base

There has been very little change for the better in the resource base of African economies since independence. For the most part African economies still remain undiversified, relying for their foreign exchange earnings (and by extension, their domestic source of development expenditure) on a few primary commodities, usually the ones which have been the mainstay of the economy since colonial days.

Table 5.5 gives an indication of the narrow resource base of African economies. When we disaggregate and look at particular countries the picture of a narrow resource base comes out in even sharper relief. Tables 5.6 and 5.7, on Nigeria and Kenya respectively, are indicative of the general trend of African economies, although the Kenyan picture is more typical of the rest of the continent.

TABLE 5.5 Exports of twenty commodities from developing Africa*, 1970–75 (total values expressed in millions of US dollars)

	1970	1971	1972	1973	1974	1975
Crude petroleum	3,925	4,828	6,006	8,788	22,600	19,300
Copper	1,473	1,069	1,155	1,680	2,290	1,250
Coffee	828	793	895	1,193	1,334	1,200
Cocoa	696	592	563	740	1,100	1,150
Crude phosphate	162	170	206	262	1,270	1,150
Cotton	780	848	851	1,039	1,240	1,000
Wood	256	265	340	647	654	560
Iron-ore	299	316	331	408	491	560
Sugar	153	174	214	288	532	480
Groundnuts and oil	230	175	228	248	250	270
Diamonds	270	236	252	295	321	260
Tobacco	82	102	119	154	188	230
Palm-oil and kernels	124	131	89	115	280	190
Citrus fruit	125	128	132	190	156	180
Wine	196	70	89	198	146	150
Tea	84	86	108	109	123	135
Rubber	85	73	63	108	158	100
Sisal	44	36	44	78	188	95
Olive-oil	23	51	124	85	206	90
Rice	92	68	61	75	112	80
Total	9,927	10,211	11,870	16,700	33,639	28,430
Total domestic exports	12,590	12,990	15,170	21,340	39,000	33,960

*Algeria, Benin, Botswana, Burundi, Central African Republic, Chad, Congo, Egypt, Ethiopia, Gabon, Gambia, Ghana, Ivory Coast, Kenya, Lesotho, Liberia, Madagascar, Malawi, Mali, Mauritania, Mauritius, Morocco, Niger, Nigeria, Rwanda, Senegal, Sierra Leone, Somalia, Sudan, Swaziland, Togo, Tunisia, Uganda, United Republic of Cameroon, United Republic of Tanzania, Upper Volta, Zaire, Zambia, and the East African Community.

Source
UNECA, *Survey of Economic and Social Conditions in Africa*, 1976, p. 92

It would appear that the task of widening the resource base of African economies has not really begun in earnest. An essential preliminary is the diversification and increase in the productivity of agriculture. The current trend is that agriculture contributes about 30% of the Gross Domestic Product of African countries but remains the means of livelihood for over 90% of the population. One implication of this is that the productivity of agriculture is very low. Another is that agricultural development had to be at the centre of any development strategy that seeks to bring the most benefit to the most people and in the shortest possible time. But more pertinent to the concerns of the present chapter is that if highly accelerated diversification and increase in the productivity of agriculture is not achieved, development in other areas, particularly industrialisation, cannot be achieved. What happens in the agricultural sector greatly affects the size of the Gross Domestic Product, the availability of inputs to other sectors, the cost of such inputs, the general level of public wealth, the availability of foreign exchange, the prospects of export promotion and import substitution etc. – factors

TABLE 5.6 Nigeria: export of major commodities by economic sectors, 1976–78

Commodity	Value (in ₦ million)			Percentage of total export value		
	1976	1977	1978	1976	1977	1978
Major agricultural, including fresh products	274.1	375.1	412.8	4.1	3.9	6.8
Mineral products	6324.7	7079.2	5402.8	93.7	92.8	89.1
Manufactured and semi-manufactured products	58.9	84.1	42.8	0.9	1.1	0.7
Other exports	86.0	82.7	193.7	1.3	1.1	3.2
Total domestic exports	6743.7	7621.7	6051.8	99.9	99.9	99.8
Re-exports	7.4	9.0	12.6	0.1	0.1	0.2
Total exports	6751.1	7630.7	6064.4	100.0	100.0	100.0

Note that the figures for 1978 are estimates.

Source
   Adapted from Central Bank of Nigeria, *Annual Report and Statement of Accounts for the year ended 31 December, 1978*

pertinent to the expansion of the resource base of the African economy.

What then are the prospects of the agricultural sector? In the decade of the 1960s the annual growth rate of agriculture was a disappointing 2.6%. According to the calculations of the United Nations Economic Commission for Africa, the growth rate of agricultural output at constant prices for the first five years of the decade of the 1970s was only 2.5%, well below the anticipated rate of 4%. Indeed, according to the calculations of the Food and Agricultural Organisation, the growth rate for the first five years of this decade had been only 1%. But the difference is due to differences in methodology, particularly classification, and by the fact that the United Nations Economic Commission for Africa used single general prices instead of sectoral deflectors as the Food and Agricultural Organisation had done.

We shall use the more optimistic estimates of the ECA because it is a more severe test of the argument made here, even though as Tables 5.8 and 5.9, which are also from the ECA, show, the estimated growth rate of 2.5% is too high; the growth appears to lie somewhere between the two.

TABLE 5.7 Kenya, domestic exports: principal commodities, 1964–73 (by percentage)

Commodity	1964	1965	1966	1967	1968	1969	1970	1971	1972	1973
Coffee, not roasted	32.7	29.9	32.3	29.3	22.2	26.6	31.1	26.8	27.3	29.2
Tea	12.9	12.9	15.0	13.8	17.4	17.8	17.7	16.2	18.1	13.8
Petroleum products	4.6	9.9	10.1	13.8	10.8	12.0	11.4	14.5	9.9	7.7
Sisal fibre and tow	12.8	8.2	5.8	3.9	3.2	2.7	2.6	2.1	2.3	3.9
Meat and meat preparations	4.6	5.2	5.2	5.3	5.2	4.1	4.0	5.0	5.4	3.1
Pyrethrum extract and flowers	5.2	4.7	4.9	5.4	5.3	4.4	3.0	4.6	5.0	3.0
Hides, skins and furskins, undressed	2.7	3.7	4.4	3.3	2.9	3.0	2.3	3.3	4.2	4.2
Cement, building	1.7	2.0	1.5	1.9	2.0	2.3	2.3	2.1	2.2	2.1
Copper and alloys, unwrought	0.9	1.9	0.7	–	–	–	–	–	–	–
Wattle-bark and extract	2.3	1.8	2.7	1.7	2.1	1.9	1.6	1.6	1.9	1.0
Sodium carbonate	1.5	1.7	1.9	1.9	2.0	1.4	2.3	2.5	2.1	2.3
Pineapples, tinned	1.9	1.6	0.9	1.0	0.8	1.1	0.9	1.3	1.0	1.2
Cotton, raw	1.4	1.6	1.5	1.2	0.7	1.2	1.7	1.6	1.3	1.1
Wool, raw	1.1	1.2	1.0	0.9	1.0	0.9	0.5	0.4	0.4	0.7
Cashew nuts	0.6	1.2	0.8	1.0	1.1	1.1	2.2	1.0	1.2	0.5
Beans, peas and lentils	1.1	1.0	1.0	0.6	1.4	0.8	0.7	0.6	1.2	1.0
Oil-seeds, oilnuts and oil-kernels	1.0	1.0	0.9	0.7	1.1	0.5	0.7	0.6	0.3	0.4
Scrap metal	1.0	0.9	0.8	0.7	0.5	0.6	0.7	0.6	0.5	0.4
Butter and ghee	1.6	0.6	0.7	0.5	0.6	0.4	0.3	0.1	0.8	0.6
Maize, unmilled	–	–	–	2.6	8.3	4.4	–	–	–	4.6
Other	8.5	9.1	8.0	10.5	11.4	12.8	14.0	15.1	14.9	19.2
Total	100	100	100	100	100	100	100	100	100	100

Source

Republic of Kenya, *Statistical Abstracts*, 1974, p. 63

The implications of the sluggish growth of agricultural output are very serious indeed. For one thing, Africa has now become a net importer of agricultural products as Table 5.9 indicates. In connection with Tables 5.8 and 5.9 the ECA points out that the increase in agricultural exports was due solely to the fact of increase in the prices of exported commodities. Attention should also be drawn to the fact that the volume of agricultural output in 1974 was the same as that of 1968.

There is little reason to expect that this situation will improve soon. As we have seen, for the period 1970–75, the annual growth rate of agricultural output was about 2.5%, probably less. For the same period the rate of growth of food production was about 2%, according to the estimation of the ECA. However, the rate of growth of population was about 2.7% and rising. So as food production lags behind the growth of population, Africa becomes increasingly unable to feed itself and is therefore likely to rely more and more on the importation of food. This trend weighs heavily against the prospects of diversifying the resource base of African economies. Diversification of the African economy will demand among other things heavy investment in agricultural extension services, in the development of new commodities and new techniques, in the importation of machinery, and in industrialisation. The chances of bringing this about are greatly reduced if the agricultural sector is too weak to reduce drastically the need for imported foods, or increase the incomes of farmers, and the rural population generally, and thereby improve the internal demand for manufactured goods and provide an export surplus to earn foreign exchange for development.

TABLE 5.8 Indices of agricultural food production per head in 18 selected African countries, 1970–75

	1970	1971	1972	1973	1974	1975
	Net agricultural production/head (1961/65 = 100)					
North Africa						
Algeria	88	83	82	76	69	64
Egypt	104	104	104	102	98	98
Morocco	119	119	120	106	114	97
Sudan	120	121	119	115	123	128
Tunisia	103	124	112	137	128	142
West Africa						
Ghana	100	103	94	89	91	93
Mali	94	99	78	61	63	67
Nigeria	98	93	89	80	84	84
Upper Volta	106	100	94	83	86	84
Central Africa						
Cameroon	123	123	127	118	121	124
Zaire	111	102	107	112	117	116
East Africa						
Ethiopia	102	99	99	94	83	82
Kenya	103	96	97	95	93	91
Madagascar	98	96	92	90	85	85
Malawi	109	120	130	124	126	113
Uganda	107	96	92	90	85	85
Tanzania	116	106	103	104	98	86
Zambia	97	96	97	93	99	94

Source
UNECA, *Survey of Economic and Social Conditions in Africa*, 1976, p. 38

TABLE 5.9 Indices of total African agricultural imports and exports, 1968–74 (1961/64 = 100)

Imports	1968	1973	1974	1968–73	1968–74
Total value	109	226	359	+102%	+229%
Unit value	98	156	223	+59%	+128%
Volume	114	143	156	+25%	+37%
Exports					
Total value	110	171	223	+55%	+102%
Unit value	104	151	215	+45%	+107%
Volume	105	113	105	+8%	Nil

Source
UNECA, *Survey of Economic and Social Conditions in Africa*, 1976, p. 51–2

The other aspect of the problem of a narrow resource base is the lack of industrialisation. As with the case of disarticulation, the problem of the narrow resource base of the African economy demands industrialisation whatever else is done. The performance in this respect since the winning of political independence has been anything but impressive. Africa's share of the manufacturing output of the world was a negligible 0.56% in 1972, and this has scarcely changed. According to the *World Bank Annual Report 1975*, in the period 1961–65 the annual average growth rate of manufacturing output in developing Africa was a promising 11.2%. But during the years 1966–67 the rate of growth fell to an annual average of 6.2%, but recovering slightly to a rate of 6.9% for the period 1971–74.

But to understand how far Africa is industrialising, or failing to industrialise, one has to look beyond the growth rate to the conventional indicator of industrialisation, namely the share of manufacturing in GDP. The share of manufacturing output in the GDP of developing Africa is estimated by the ECA to be 11.8%, which is very small indeed. According to the United Nations Industrial Development Organisation (UNIDO) guidelines, a country has not started industrialising when the share of the manufacturing sector of GDP is less than 10%. A country is said to be industrialising when the share of the manufacturing sector of GDP is between 10 and 20%. Now, according to ECA data, manufacturing output accounted for less than 10% in 20 out of the 47 countries of developing Africa, and between 10 and 20% in 25 countries. It accounted for between 20 and 30% in only 2 countries. If we refer back to the fact that for developing Africa as a whole the share of GDP accountable to manufacturing output is only about 11.8%, and if we make allowances for the fact that a large share of the manufacturing output is accounted for by a few countries such as Algeria, Gabon, Libya, Nigeria and Egypt, we find that, for all practical purposes, developing Africa falls into the classification of not having started industrialisation.

Finally, an examination of the relation of the development of manufacturing to the diversification of the resource base of African economies has to look at the structure of manufacturing activity in Africa, and not simply at its extent. This will be done briefly with an illustration from the industrialising effort of Nigeria, a typical example. According to Nigeria's *Third National Development Plan 1975 to 1980*, value added in manufacturing and craft grew at a compound rate of 10% per annum between 1962/63 and 1972/73. For this period the rate of growth of manufacturing alone was 12.2%. The contribution of manufacturing and craft to GDP rose from 5.64% in 1962 to 7.79% in 1972. Table 5.10 shows the structure of manufacturing as reflected in the relative shares of value added of different manufacturing activities. The structure of industralisation in Nigeria shows that the type of industralisation occurring is not very conducive to the diversification of the resource base of the economy, or even to the reduction of its disarticulation. In the first place, the bulk of the value added comes from light industries with a very low-level technology. Food beverages and tobacco accounted for 34.3% of the value added and textile and wearing apparels account for 17%. These are just about the two most elementary forms of manufacturing activity and they account for a total of 51% of value added. Table 5.10

TABLE 5.10 Nigeria: structure of manufacturing by share of value added

Industry group	1965	1971	1972
	% Value added	% Value added	% Value added
Meat products	0.9	1.6	1.4
Dairy products	0.3	0.4	0.4
Fruit canning and preserving	–	–	–
Vegetable oil milling	5.4	3.1	2.6
Grain mill products	3.3	2.4	1.7
Bakery products	1.4	1.3	1.0
Sugar and sugar confectionery	1.7	1.8	3.1
Miscellaneous food preparations and animal feeds	13.9	0.8	0.3
Spirits, distillery and beer	14.6	14.7	12.7
Soft drinks	1.3	1.3	2.4
Tobacco	–	9.7	8.7
Textiles	10.9	17.5	12.6
Made-up textile goods (except wearing apparel)	1.0	1.1	1.1
Knitted goods and woven carpets	–	0.4	1.8
Wearing apparel	0.4	0.3	1.5
Tanning	0.8	0.4	0.5
Travel goods	0.2	–	–
Footwear	1.3	1.1	0.3
Sawmilling	1.4	2.1	2.3
Wooden furniture and fixtures and other wood products	2.4	0.6	1.0
Containers, boxes of paper and paper board	–	0.7	1.0
Paper products	1.0	0.7	1.0
Printing	2.8	3.0	2.6
Basic industrial chemicals, fertilisers and pesticides	0.6	1.1	0.4
Paints	1.0	0.9	1.1
Drugs and medicines	–	0.4	0.8
Soaps, perfumes, cosmetics and other cleaning preparations	–	5.2	5.4
Other chemical products	6.4	0.9	0.9
Products of petroleum and coal	–	8.3	9.4
Tyres and tubes	2.3	2.3	2.4
Other rubber products	–	0.5	1.0
Plastic products	–	1.8	1.3
Pottery and glass products	0.3	0.5	0.3
Bricks and tiles	–	0.1	0.1
Cements	4.7	2.2	2.6
Concrete products	–	0.7	1.6
Basic metal, cutlery, handtools and general hardware	7.0	0.9	0.5

TABLE 5.10 continued

Industry group	1965	1971	1972
	% Value added	% Value added	% Value added
Metal furniture and fixtures	–	1.2	1.4
Structural metal products	–	2.0	2.3
Fabricated metal products	–	3.5	7.0
Manufacture of agricultural and special ind. machinery	–	0.1	0.2
Machinery and equipment except elect.	–	–	–
Manufacture of radio and TV and communication equipment	–	0.7	0.8
Manufacture of household electrical apparatus and supplies	1.0	0.3	0.4
Transport equipment, motor-body and ship-building and repairs	9.7	0.3	–
Manufacture of watches, clocks and jewellery	–	0.1	–
Manufacturing industry not yet classified	1.9	0.6	0.5
Total	100.0	100.0	100.0

Source
Adapted from Federal Republic of Nigeria, *Third National Development Plan*, Lagos, 1975, p. 148

also shows an almost total absence of an engineering industry in Nigeria. In the words of the *Development Plan*, 'although the aggregate share of this group of industry added up to 12.9% which compares fairly favourably to the average 16.4% for developing countries, a closer look at its composition shows that the three most elementary sub-groups, namely metal furniture and fixtures, structural metal products and fabricated metal, easily dominate the sub-sector. The real engineering sub-sectors: manufacturing of agricultural and special industrial machinery, machinery and equipment, household electrical apparatus, and transport equipment, account only for 2.3% of value added in manufacturing'. Finally Table 5.10 also reflects the weakness of intermediate goods, particularly in the areas of sophisticated technology. For example, basic industrial chemicals, fertilisers and pesticides only account for 0.02% of the total value added in the sector. On the other hand, the consumer-oriented chemicals group, which produces toiletries and household detergents, account for as much as 8.2% of the value added. Finally two more comments need to be made about Table 5.10. The first is that it indicates that industrialisation in Nigeria has been spurred on by import substitution as opposed to export promotion. The second is that the preponderance of light industries with low-level technology means a heavy dependence on imports, particularly machinery, chemicals, transport equipment, etc. This is clearly not the type of industrialisation which will greatly accelerate the widening of the resource base of African economies.

Dependence

A considerable amount of literature exists on the problem of dependence. This literature has arisen largely from dependency theory, particularly the debate over the relationship of dependence to underdevelopment. The availability of this literature obviates the need for going into a lengthy discussion here. We will limit ourselves to a few illustrations of the extent of the persistence of dependence and a brief discussion of aspects of dependence which are particularly salient to the general argument of this work.

In the first chapter we tried to underline the peculiar importance of the means of production in the labour process and the importance of its distribution in determining the character of the economy and the

TABLE 5.11 Technological dependence: selected socio-economic indicators: (averages expressed as medians for 1970 or latest year available)

Science and technology	Developed market economy	Developing countries		
		Africa	Asia	Latin America
Ration of total stock Engineers per 10,000 pop.	112	5.8	22.0	69
Ratio of Technicians per 10,000 pop.	142.3	8.8	23.4	72.2
Scientists & Engineers in R & D per 10,000 pop.	10.4	0.35	1.6	1.15
Technicians in R & D per 10,000 pop.	8.2	0.4	0.6	1.4
Expenditure on R & D as percentage of GDP	1.2	0.6	0.3	˙0.2
High-level manpower				
Professionals and Technicians as % of econ. active pop.	11.1	–	2.7	5.7
% of the econ. active pop. employed in manufacturing	25.4	3.5	10.5	14.1

Note that the size of the samples in every column vary by indication.

Source
Adapted from UNCTAD in *Africa Development*, Vol. 11, No. 2, June 1977

socio-economic formation. It was then pointed out how inequality in the distribution of the means of production reproduces itself endlessly in other inequalities. In this assessment of the persistence of dependence special attention will be paid to dependence involving two critical means of production, technology and capital, particularly the former, which is central to the all-important question of the development of productive forces.

Technology

Are African economies less dependent technologically today then they were during the colonial period? If so, to what extent are they less so? Technological capability is difficult to quantitify, but the crude indications in vogue are good enough for our limited purposes here. In Table 5.11 technology is defined in terms of high-level manpower in scientific, technical and engineering fields, and on expenditure on research and development as a percentage of Gross Domestic Product.

In Table 5.12 technological capability is defined somewhat differently – in terms of the technological innovation as reflected in patents granted. But the picture of technological backwardness and dependence which it presents is not dissimilar to that of the preceding table. The table does not specifically compare the technological capability of African countries with those of developing countries, so we

TABLE 5.12 Distribution of patents granted, 1920–70

Groups of Countries	1920	1940	1950	1960	1970
	In thousands				
Developed market-economy countries	119.6	114.6	131.01	221.4	313.6
Socialist countries of Eastern Europe	5.1	4.2	0.3	20.6	51.0
Southern European countries	5.8	0.2	5.6	9.3	12.7
Selected developing countries	2.5	2.1	2.5	11.6	15.1
Total	133.0	121.1	139.4	262.9	392.4
	As percentage of total				
Developed market-economy countries	89.9	94.6	94.2	84.5	80.2
Socialist countries of Eastern Europe	3.8	3.5	0.2	7.9	13.0
Southern European countries	4.4	0.2	4.0	3.2	3.2
Selected Developing countries	1.9	1.7	1.6	4.4	3.6
Total	100.0	100.0	100.0	100.0	100.0

Source
UNCTAD, *The Role of the Patent System in the Transfer of Technology to Developing Countries*, New York, 1975, p. 37

infer the technological status of Africa from membership of the group, developing countries. Two further comments are necessary on Table 5.12. First, it should be noted that for the purposes of the table only eight developing countries were surveyed. These were Brazil, Cuba, India, Israel, Morocco, Tunisia and Yugoslavia. But with data from these countries it was possible to generalise for the developing countries as a whole by assuming that the ratio between patent grants and manufacturing output which was found for these countries (the eight countries accounted for 60% of the total output of developing countries with patent laws) also held for other developing countries. The second comment is that the indications are that if data were available for African economies, it would show an even greater technological weakness than the aggregate data for developing countries.

On the assumption that the ratio between patents granted and manufacturing output for the developing countries surveyed also holds for other developing countries, UNCTAD estimates that the developing countries share of world patent grants was only 6%.

Even this plays down the technological weakness of the developing countries somewhat. In 1964 only 12% of the patents granted in developing countries went to nationals. In 1972 this figure was still only 16%. Indeed, according to UNCTAD, nationals of the developing countries 'hold in their own countries no more than about 1% of the world stock of patents'. To bring the point of technological weakness home, UNCTAD has compared the distribution of technology between developed and developing countries with other familiar data. 'Thus for instance the developing countries share in world population was around 75%; of world enrolment in Third level education (university equivalent), over 30%; in world income 20% to 30% (depending upon how net material product in socialist countries is converted into Western concepts); in world trade, 20%; in world manufacturing output, about 15%; in patent granting 6%; and in patent holding by their own nationals in the world total, 1%' (p. 42).

In technological, as in other areas, the pattern of dependence has not changed. African countries continue to rely on the industrialised capitalist countries for their technology. In his study which appears in the book *Multinational Firms in Africa* (1975), Helge Hveem shows that of the patents granted in independent African countries in 1971 between 90 and 99% were from the USA and the EEC. The most diversification of technological dependence was Egypt which had 2.1% from the USSR and 21.5% from the Communist countries as a whole. Most of the African countries covered in the survey had no patents whatsoever from Communist countries. For the few who did, the percentage was very small: Ghana had 9.1%; Mauritius 10%; Tunisia 0.6% from the USSR and 2.7% from other Communist countries; and Morocco had 2.5% from the USSR and 4.4% from other Communist countries.

This failure to diversify technological dependence might be related to the highly monopolistic character of the technology market – an important phenomenon which deserves some attention. The industrialised countries of the West enjoy an immense monopoly of world technology. As Table 5.12 indicates, in 1940 they had 94.6% of all patents granted, in 1950 they held 94.2%. Their share of patents fell only slightly to 84.5% in 1960 and 80.2% in 1970. Within the Western capitalist countries themselves the holding of patents is becoming increasingly concentrated in the hands of corporations rather than being dispersed as individual holdings. Table 5.13 illustrates the trend.

TABLE 5.13 Share of patent grants: individuals and corporations in France, USA and Canada (as percentage of total patent grants)

Country and year	Individuals	Corporations
France		
1964	23	73
1968	20	77
USA		
1908	81	19
1955	39	59
Canada		
1908	97	3
1968	37	63

Source
UNCTAD, *The Role of the Patent System in the Transfer of Technology to Developing Countries*, New York, 1975, p. 39

This trend reflects, among other things, the increasing role of corporations in research and development. As technology becomes increasingly sophisticated, forcing up the price of further technological development, the share of patent grants going to individuals as opposed to corporations will continue to decline. This trend is a matter of great significance, especially for the developing countries. First, as Clive Thomas has argued (*Dependence and Transformation*, New York, 1974), 'if technology is basically a monopoly of the capitalist centre, it follows from the dictates of the profit motive that its distribution from the capitalist centre must inevitably follow certain market norms. Among these are the need to balance the distribution of technology (ie. the gains from its use) in order to be assured that the monopoly is maintained, not in the static sense, but dynamically, through concentrating on the really strategic areas of technological leadership as they emerge. Thus the shifting pattern of resource exploitation by the metropolitan countries of the economies of the periphery (particularly from primary production to light manufactures) reflects a shift in the technological dependence of the periphery to the newer areas of computer and communications technology, etc. and the willingness of the centre to relinquish at a price, and for restricted uses, the technology of the light manufacturing of certain mass consumption goods'.

The possibility of the much desired transfer of technology on just about any terms remains highly problematic. Multinational corporations are generally regarded as the principal agents by which technological transfer occurs. It now seems that this notion is largely misplaced because the multinationals scarcely have the appropriate technology to transfer.

And what passes as transfer of technology occurs not because the technology transferred is appropriate but rather because it is available. Produced in response to needs and environments quite different from those of Africa, the transferred technology is not integrated into the local culture and system of production and so its ability to stimulate further technological development is severely limited. More often than not the transfer of technology – invariably inappropriate technology – encourages the production of goods which are irrelevant to the needs of the overwhelming majority of the people. With production divorced from need an essential condition for the development of indigenous technology is lost. Unfortunately there is little or no incentive for the multinationals to produce technology and goods more suitable for the needs of the masses in the developing countries. UNCTAD has put the reasons for this succinctly. 'First, although the gains to society from their doing so would be high, private profitability is low on account of the limited purchasing power of the income groups that would consume the products. Secondly, the specific production of appropriate goods tailored to the unique environments of individual developing countries would be inconsistent with the principle of efficiency based on standardisation and uniform specifications and quality characteristics. Modifications of product characteristics are rendered more difficult in the case of highly differentiated goods that are covered by trade marks or brand names identified in consumers' minds, rightly or wrongly, with a certain standard of quality. Finally such a policy would be inconsistent with the corporate ideology of achieving a "global structure of excellence" based on the Western model'. (UNCTAD *op. cit.*, p. 39)

To this should be added the observation that the very process of transferring technology is full of difficulties and often exposes the developing countries to more exploitation. This can be illustrated with the patent system. It seems beneficial for developing countries to grant patents and acquire patent licenses. The usual case for doing so is that this will enable the developing country to produce what it could not have produced otherwise, win foreign investment, gain value added and foreign exchange by encouraging import–substitution production. However, the case makes easy assumptions about the relationship between industrial property protection and foreign investment. Studies (eg. R. Vernon, *The International Patent System and Foreign Policy*, and E. Penrose, 'International Patenting and the less-developed countries', *The Economic Journal*, 83, 331, 1973) have shown that considerations of industrial property protection have little or no influence over investment decisions. But there is no need to dwell on this. The more pertinent point is to note the immense disadvantages that the developing country which enters a patent agreement usually has to face. To begin with such agreements entail royalty payments which can be inordinately high because of the monopolistic character of the technology market. They often entail obligations to restrict what they can do with the technology as well as management, marketing and production commitments, whose direct and indirect costs could be exceedingly high. To give just one example of the exploitative character of such obligations, in a well known study of the Argentinian pharmaceutical industry entitled *La Industria Farmaceutica Argentina Estructura y Compoxtamiento* (1973), J. M. Katz estimated 'the weighted degree of overpricing at about 680%'. An earlier study of the pharmaceutical industry in Colombia by C. V. Vaitos (published in *Revista de Planceacion y Desarrotlo*, 1971) found overpricing to the magnitude of 155% in excess of the world average. According to the author's calculation, if the finding is true for all pharmaceutical firms in the country, the overpricing would mean a balance-of-payments loss of over $20 million.

Such exploitation is only the symptom not the problem. The real problems are technological backwardness and technological dependence, which allow the developed countries to exercise control over what the developing countries produce and how, and over their general path of development. Because of their immense technological dependence, which tends to perpetuate itself, it is hard for African economies to make much progress in the fight against development because they are dependent on the industrialised countries and on the peculiar monopolistic character of the world technology market. It will be harder yet for them to deviate from the capitalist path of development.

Trade

In trade the old patterns of dependence largely remain, even though African economies have rather more room for manoeuvre. The bulk of the exports of African countries go to the former colonising powers and their Western allies. Very little has been achieved in the way of diversifying dependence by increasing commerce with socialist countries as Tables 5.14 and 5.15 indicate.

TABLE 5.14 Nigeria's foreign trade, 1966 and 1974 (millions of Naira)

	1966	1974
Western Europe		
Imports	328.8	1,119.1
Exports	442.8	3,056.2
United States		
Imports	83.0	213.2
Exports	44.6	1,589.9
Eastern Europe		
Imports	11.6	47.9
Exports	6.6	77.4
China		
Imports	10.0	30.4
Exports	–	3.6

Source
United Nations African Statistical Yearbook, 1975

When the statistics on the directions of trade are disaggregated to show particular countries, it is seen that on the whole African economies tend to depend more heavily in their commercial relations on the former

TABLE 5.15 Republic of Benin's foreign trade, 1966 and 1973 (millions of CFA Francs)

	1966	1973
Western Euope		
Imports	5,717	15,528
Exports	1,805	6,871
United States		
Imports	395	1,145
Exports	242	177
Eastern Europe		
Imports	525	678
Exports	–	491
China		
Imports	159	1,727
Exports	–	360

Source
  United Nations African Statistical Yearbook, 1975

colonising powers than on any other country. The statistics in Table 5.16 from Nigeria are indicative of this trend. It should be noted that the figures for 1976 are provisional. The table for exports shows more dependence on the United States than on the United Kingdom, Nigeria's colonising power. This is because of Nigeria's oil export to the United States. The situation in regard to financial dependence has hardly changed in the postcolonial era. African countries are heavily dependent financially on their former colonising powers and Western capital in general. What is surprising here too is not so much the persistence of dependence as the fact this dependence has not been substantially diversified by greater reliance on non-Western capital. Tables 5.17 and 5.18, which are quite typical, indicate the financial dependence of African economies on Western capital.

The story of Africa's continued dependence is not fully told by statistics on foreign aid and foreign investment. Dependence is much more pervasive than that. For instance, after about two decades of political independence the franc zone has still not managed to get its own internationally-recognised currency. The currency in use is the Communauté Française Africaine (CFA), which has international status only in so far as it is freely convertible with the French franc. To earn this dubious privilege the franc zone countries have to meet certain obligations to the French treasury, including the deposit of reserves in France. France is technically a guarantor, but it is a position that for all practical purposes entails neither risk nor sacrifice as the reserves from the African issuing banks are usually able to cover deficits. For the African countries the tie to the French franc has some serious disadvantages. It imposes very severe constraints on what they can do in the way of monetary policy; in particular it means that they are vulnerable to having their currency devalued, since it is fixed at parity with the

TABLE 5.16 Nigeria's foreign trade, 1973–76 (thousands of Naira)

Year and quarter	Common-wealth countries	Eastern Europe	Japan	United Kingdom	USA	West Africa	Western Europe	Others	Total
Imports									
1973	49,475	45,867	112,900	331,600	125,697	3,048	456,076	100,123	224,786
1974	69,858	73,092	160,185	402,167	213,194	6,580	704,418	107,830	1,737,324
1975	90,157	116,303	366,494	854,966	408,012	19,319	1,624,857	241,438	3,721,546
1976	130,806	89,841	493,118	1,204,375	599,106	24,775	2,284,636	307,388	5,143,045
Exports and re-exports									
1973	74,500	32,901	104,055	424,783	549,745	23,910	827,322	240,228	2,277,444
1974	126,066	105,800	238,042	978,124	1,589,891	81,701	2,010,822	664,291	5,794,837
1975	64,779	86,401	172,300	694,300	1,427,000	62,019	1,648,236	769,699	4,924,734
1976	34,960	14,249	191,133	814,281	2,001,548	94,591	1,834,944	714,427	5,700,133

Source
Central Bank of Nigeria, *Economic and Statistical Review*, 16, 2, pp. 114–5

TABLE 5.17 Kenya: sources of development aid, 1974-75 (estimated amounts in thousands of Kenyan shillings)

UK	1,617
IBRD	5,783
West Germany	1,203
IDA	6,661
Others	8,202

Note that both IDA (International Development Association) and IBRD (International Bank for Reconstruction and Development) are Western institutions and tools of Western capital.

Source
  Government of Kenya, *Statistical Abstracts*, 1974

TABLE 5.18 Nigeria: cumulative foreign private investment, 1970-76 (millions of Naira)

	1970	1971	1972	1973	1974	1975	1976
United Kingdom	444.4	592.0	769.7	860.9	832.8	857.5	942.0
United States	230.0	337.4	286.6	308.0	300.0	535.2	376.2
Western Europe (excluding UK)	224.8	261.0	367.0	415.5	459.8	590.1	653.1
Others	104.0	132.4	147.8	179.6	219.5	304.7	362.5
Total	1,003.2	1,322.8	1,571.1	1,763.7	1,812.5	2,287.5	233.8

Source
  Central Bank of Nigeria, *Nigeria's Principal Economic and Financial Indicators 1970-78*

French franc. In dealing with her own economic problems France is often unmindful of the effects of her policies on the African countries whose currencies are tied to hers; indeed she sometimes exploits the ties to her advantage. According to Alex Rondos (*West Africa* No. 3294, 8 September, 1980), 'there is evidence to suggest that in the last two years the French have considered monetary policies without adequately consulting the franc zone members. There are two other factors; French devaluations, especially in the early sixties, certainly strengthened the French position in the African countries and also compromised attempts by Francophone African governments to diversify their client, etc. Their efforts in trade are still limited because France remains by far the most dominant trading partner for all these countries. A French devaluation also influences the balance of payments by increasing the already considerable external debt of the developing countries'. Alex Rondos has also drawn attention to how the arrangement under review affects capital movements to the detriment of the African clients of France: 'The second important aspect of the franc zone is the free transfer of capital, made possible by the existence of fixed parity. There is therefore no control over the repatriation of capital abroad and this is a basic impediment to any accumulation of capital domestically. It has enhanced the position of foreign capital in the banking system and has naturally left an open path for French capital to leave the country. In Ivory Coast it is estimated that over $200 million leaves the country annually under the agreement. Given the structure of foreign capital present in all the industrial sectors of Francophone Africa, the free transfer has encouraged the investment by multinationals, based in France, through local subsidiaries and this has again stimulated the outflow of capital'. It says a lot about the problem of dependency that the CFA continues to be tied to the French franc despite these consequences.

Attempts to reduce dependence in Nigeria and Tanzania

It is useful to take a look at some of the attempts being made in Africa to reduce dependence, not only because they throw light on the persistence of dependence but also on the objective realities of Africa's postcolonial economics in general. We shall consider efforts at reducing dependence in two African formations, Nigeria and Tanzania.

Nigeria's nationalist leaders were very much preoccupied with economic dependence during their nationalist struggle. But it was not until the launching of the *Second National Development Plan, 1970—74* that a clear strategy for reducing economic dependence emerged. The document argued that it was necessary to localise ownership and control of the economy, that political independence without economic independence was an 'empty shell', that a 'truly independent nation cannot allow its objectives and priorities to be distorted or frustrated by the manipulations of powerful foreign investors'. The essential strategy for securing Nigeria's independence was outlined as follows: 'the government will seek to acquire by law if necessary, equity participation in a number of industries that will be specified from time to time. In order to ensure that the economic destiny of Nigeria is determined by Nigerians themselves, the government will seek to widen and intensify its position in industrial development.' This could be done, where necessary, by joint participation with private enterprises (foreign or indigenous) and as occasion demanded through complete government control and exclusive public ownership of strategic industries.

The Nigerian Enterprises Decree of 28 February, 1972 was the first major initiative for putting this strategy for independence into practice. The decree established a Nigerian Enterprises Promotion Board whose function was to 'develop enterprises in which Nigerians shall participate fully and play a dominant role'. The decree classified all enterprises into two schedules. The first schedule consisted of twenty-two items, including such enterprises as rice milling and newspaper printing and publishing, which were reserved exclusively for Nigerians.

A second schedule consisted of thirty-three types of enterprise in which aliens were permitted to participate provided that (a) paid up capital exceeded £20,000 or turnover exceeded £500,000, and (b) there was indigenous equity participation of not less than 40%. Several measures were taken to facilitate the implementation of the decree. For instance, in 1973 the government acquired a 40% share-holding in the three large alien banks which between them controlled approximately 70% of Nigerian banking; the percentage of government holding in these banks was eventually raised to 60%. The Nigerian Bank of Commerce and Industries was established with an authorised capital of ₦50,000 to provide equity capital and funds for Nigerians to invest in industry and commerce. An Agricultural Bank with authorised capital of ₦12 million was established to provide financing for entrepreneurs going into the agricultural sector.

The aim of localising control and ownership of the economy was pursued with more decrees; the Nigerian Enterprises Promotion (Amendement) Decree 1973, the Nigerian Enterprises Promotion (Amendment) 1974, and the Nigerian Enterprises Promotion Decree of 1976. These decrees brought relatively minor changes. The next major effort in the localisation of ownership and control of the economy was the Nigerian Enterprises Promotion Decree of 1977. This decree reclassified enterprises into three categories. The first category made up of enterprises requiring low technology and limited capital was reserved exclusively for Nigerians; there were altogether 40 types of enterprise in this category. Category two consisted of 57 types of enterprise in which aliens could be part-owners only if the equity participation of Nigerians was at least 60%. A third category consisted of 39 relatively capital intensive enterprises, such as ship-building and the manufacture of motor vehicles, and was open to aliens provided there was at least 40% Nigerian equity participation. What the decree essentially did was to increase the scope of Nigerian participation in the economy and also to improve the mechanism for the implementation of the policy of Nigerianisation. The decree ensured that Nigerian equity participation would vary from 40% to 100% depending on the character of the enterprise. In all critical enterprises, such as petroleum and banking, a minimum Nigerian equity participation of 60% was obligatory. Even within its limited purposes, the policy of pursuing economic independence by legislating for higher Nigerian equity participation in enterprises has not been very effective, though it has clearly increased Nigerian ownership.

Perhaps this approach to economic independence is one of the few options that the Nigerian government could realistically pursue, but it is not an answer to the problem of dependence. It does not address the problem in its essentials. First of all the state of Nigeria's technology is a critical aspect of her dependence, and this approach offers nothing relevant to this aspect of dependence. As long as Nigeria depends wholly on foreign technology, it cannot make significant progress towards economic independence. Thus achieving majority Nigerian equity participation in the petroleum industry does not say much about progress towards economic independence, for those who own the technology in fact control the critical means of production. If the technology is withheld then Nigeria's oil wealth, for all practical purposes, ceases to exist.

To be sure Nigeria has some choice of getting technology from more than one source. However, the cost of turning away from the old source of technology to a new one is virtually prohibitive. But that is only part of the problem. Nigeria is in a position similar to that of wage labour under capitalism, independent of a particular capitalist but a slave to the capitalist class. In reality even the analogy presents a rather optimistic picture because the international market for technology is highly monopolistic.

Second, this approach to the problem does not address itself of the fundamental causes of dependence. The approach concentrates on the redistribution of ownership and not on the widening of the resource base of the economy, nor even on changing the conditions and relations of production. Finally, the approach does not come to grips with the structural links of the economy to the metropole, which is another fundamental aspect of dependence. For instance, it deals with the ownership of enterprises without worrying about the nature of international exchange, which is a critical mechanism for the transfer of surplus to the metropole as well as for maintaining the international division of labour which underlines Africa's underdevelopment and dependence. Up to a point the strategy in question may be said to be reinforcing the dependence of the Nigerian economy. What it achieved was a limited indigenisation of capitalism, an indigenisation necessary to preserve it in the face of economic nationalism. While indigenising capitalism, this strategy also promotes accommodation between indigenous capital and foreign capital, for instance by demarcating areas of operation, clarifying the conditions of cooperation and reducing areas of conflict. In so far as the strategy succeeds in doing this it helps to perpetuate dependence.

Tanzania's effort to attain economic independence presents an interesting contrast to that of Nigeria. Tanzania is seeking self-reliance in the context of socialism and this is perhaps why the Tanzanian strategy addresses the problem of dependence much more fundamentally than that of Nigeria.

The Arusha Declaration was the first clear statement of Tanzania's strategy for simultanously achieving self-reliance, socialism and development. The Arusha Declaration held that the old approach to development, which relied heavily on capital and industrialisation, was inappropriate and led to neither development nor self-reliance. It argued that money and wealth are the effects and not the basis of development. The Arusha Declaration posited that emphasis should rather be placed on the land, the people and on good leadership. These ideas were developed and given specificity through a number of publications such as *Socialism and Rural Development, The Development Plan 1969–74*, and *Education for Self-reliance*.

Let us start with the agricultural sector. The problem here appears to have been how simultanously to maximise development, self-reliance and socialism. The Tanzanian leadership decided to do this by a system of village communities engaged in group work. These villages were subsequently called Ujamaa villages and the aim was to place the entire rural population in these villages. The villagisation programme was explained in *The Development Plan 1969—74* as follows: 'The objective is to farm the village land collectively with modern techniques of production and share the proceeds according to the work contributed. People who are farming together can obtain the economic advantages of large-scale farming, in the better utilisation of machinery, purchase of supplies, marketing of crops, etc. It becomes easier to supply technical advice through agricultural extension officers who can teach a group more easily in one place, rather than travelling from one small shambel to another. It is also easier to provide social facilities such as water supplies, medical and educational services, to farmers who live in groups rather than in scattered holdings.' The Ministry of Agriculture, Food and Cooperatives was to help the Ujamaa villages to accomplish these aims by providing technical services, and generally ensuring that they were given all the services and guidance which would make them an effective instrument for the modernisation of agriculture through large-scale production. In addition, the villages were to receive commercial advice from the Cooperative Development Division of the Ministry of Agriculture and irrigation services from the Water Development Division. To facilitate the realisation of self-reliance in the Ujamaa villages in the country at large, high-level technology and mechanisation were to be avoided and emphasis was to be placed on labour intensity and the development of simple tools.

The Ujamaa villages were to be supplemented by a system of state farms. It was thought that such farms were needed because certain lines of production need more complex organisation, larger farms and more mechanisation than the Ujamaa villages could cope with. This was particularly true of wheat and dairy products. The state farms would, in addition, serve as models for the diffusion of innovation, for experiments and training. *The Development Plan 1969—74* called for the establishment of 250,000 acres of new state farms over the period. These were to include 10 state farms for wheat farming covering 100,000 acres, 4 for rice production, and 2 for dairy products. The development of the cooperative movement in the rural areas was also to be encouraged in an attempt to promote development and self-reliance. Cooperatives grew rapidly from 172 in 1952 to 857 in 1961 and 1,696 in 1968.

There was a lot of sense in this rural strategy of self-reliance. If the rural population could in fact become self-reliant through the system of self-sufficient village communities the external dependence of the economy could be drastically reduced. There was a lot of sense in the notion that self-reliance could be furthered by collectivisation and by organising development around available resources, simple technology and the energy of the people. Unfortunately the promise of this approach did not quite materialise so that it contributed very little to self-reliance. In the first place the process of villagisation was poorly planned and hastily carried out. It would appear that government officials and party functionaries were more interested in the quantitative increase in Ujamaa villages to the neglect of the purposes for which villagisation was being undertaken in the first place. The rush to villagise caused considerable disorganisation and discomfort and the resulting hostility from this inevitably diminished the potential of the Ujamaa villages for realising their original aims, particularly the aim of increasing productivity.

The hostility arising from hasty villagisation was reinforced by emphasis on cash crops as opposed to food crops. The emphasis on cash crops led to food shortages. The shortages not only caused anger, alienation and opposition to Ujamaa, but also further defeated the original purposes of villagisation by compelling substantial food imports. In the face of these difficulties, the government of Tanzania felt obligated to spoon-feed the Ujamaa villages in an attempt to win legitimacy not only for the programme but also for the regime: free rations for one or two years, salaries comparable to urban wages for work on the collective farms, liberal dividends for settler families, pocket money of up to Sh. 30 a month, etc. There is a lot to be said for these incentives. For one thing they limited the role of force in villagisation. However, they constituted an immense financial burden on the economy. In some of the settlements such as Upper Kitete, it has been calculated that the government allocated as much as Sh. 30,000 per settler family for subsidies and capital.

The financial burden of villagisation was increased by too much mechanisation. This is somewhat difficult to understand because President Nyerere's writings, as well as Tanzania's official publications elaborating the idea of villagisation, had stressed that one of the ways in which they would help to achieve self-reliance would be to avoid dependence on mechanisation and to concentrate on the use of labour and simple tools. Yet there was too much mechanisation in some of the Ujamaa villages. In particular there were too many tractors. In his well-known report *Tanzanian Agriculture after the Arusha Declaration*, Professor René Dumont points out how the settlement at Upper Kitete 'was over-equipped, with its 10 tractors for 1,600 acres of corn'. Such mechanisation could hardly have helped the objective of self-reliance.

These difficulties seem to be relatively simple errors of tactic and judgement which could quite easily have been avoided. But this is not the case. They are symptomatic of fundamental difficulties. They are in fact embedded in the basic contradiction in the relations of production – contradictions which make it difficult for African leaders to get their priorities right and to effect the changes necessary to break out of dependence. It would appear that in the final analysis villagisation failed because of the vestiges of class exploitation. It was conceived and carried out with authoritarianism by a political class which demanded every sacrifice from others and little from itself. The attempt to steer efforts' towards the production of cash crops to the detriment of the production of food crops is indicative of the exploitative character of the villagisation programme as a way of manipulating production in the interests of the ruling class. The incentives to village settlement, which seem humane, also underline the failure to carry the people, and this failure is related to the fact that given the contradictions in the relations of production it was difficult for the leaders to carry the people with them. Let us now turn to the Tanzanian strategy for self-reliance in the industrial sector.

Tanzania's industrial strategy for increasing economic independence was essentially to change the structure of ownership of enterprises. The main thrust of this change in the structure of ownership was to nationalise assets and to set up parastatals. Elsewhere in this study we have already indicated the enormous growth of the parastatal system, which was seen not only as the means to economic independence but also as a necessary tool for the realisation of socialist Tanzania. The public sector has now become very dominant in the Tanzanian economy. To illustrate this, in 1973 public sector capital stock had risen to Sh. 2,077 million or 70.7% of the national capital stock, while the public sector's share of wage employment had risen to 64% of total wage employment. This enormous expansion of the public sector has meant a radical change in the distribution of ownership in favour of localisation. However, it should be noted that the statistics of the expansion of the public sector will exaggerate the extent of public ownership. This is because the government of Tanzania does not have 100% share equity in all public enterprises. For instance, the government (through the National Development Corporation) holds 60% equity in the Tanzania Fertilizer Company, 70% in the Tanzania Hides and Skins Limited, and 86.7% in Tanzania Tanneries.

This strategy for economic independence does not really address itself to the critical issues. It has furthered the localisation of control, but it has not started to effect those structural changes in her economy which will enable her to be independent – for instance, diversification, reduction of reliance on primary products, the eradication of dualism, a steep increase in the share of manufacturing in GDP. The extensive nationalisation of productive assets in Tanzania gives the illusion of economic independence and highly localised control. The impression is misleading because Tanzania is highly dependent, as Table 5.19 shows.

TABLE 5.19 Trends in central government finance in Tanzania, 1971/72–1975/76 (Sh. million)

	1971/72	1972/73	1973/74	1974/75	1975/76
Recurrent budget:					
1 Revenue	1,859	2,356	3,023	3,664	3,830
2 Expenditure	1,780	2,223	2,785	3,462	3,630
3 Surplus	79	133	238	202	200
Development budget:					
1 Domestic resources	389	438	961	1,007	1,160
2 Foreign loans and grants	359	325	481	1,192	1,430
3 Total Resources	748	763	1,442	2,199	2,590
(a) Ministries	519	374	982	934	1,390
(b) Regions	–	88	220	297	363
(c) Transfer to parastatals	229	301	240	969	848

Source
Ministry of Finance and Planning, Dar es Salaam

Attention should be drawn to the very large foreign share of development expenditure. Since development spending is associated with advancing and changing the economy, the dependence of Tanzania on foreign sources of development spending is unfortunate, since it will entail foreign influence over the articulation and implementation of development strategy. The situation represented in Table 5.19 does not appear to be improving.

According to the budget speech for the financial year 1977/78, (*Daily News*, 17 June 1977), estimated revenue for the year was Sh. 5,193 million, as against a recurrent expenditure of Sh. 5,461 million. For the same year the estimated development budget was Sh. 4,062 million, of which Sh. 2,227 was foreign aid commitments already made. But this foreign capital only brought the available development revenue to Sh. 3,625 million. For the financial year 1978/79 Tanzania would be depending for the bulk of her development expenditure on assistance from the World Bank, the International Monetary Fund, the United

Nations Development Programme, UNICEF, the Arab Bank for Economic Development in Africa, UNHCR, EEC, the OPEC Fund, Norway, Sweden, Holland, Denmark, West Germany, Canada, China, USA, Japan, India, Finland, Russia, Saudi Arabia, Cuba, the Kuwait African Development Bank, Australia, Rumania and Italy. The relation between dependence and lack of control was underlined in the recent Paris meeting between Tanzania and her creditors in which Tanzania had in effect to present her policies for scrutiny and approval.

The institutions which are supposed to represent Tanzania's expanding ownership and control of her economy, namely the parastatals, are themselves highly dependent on foreign funds and foreign management. Table 5.20 illustrates the financial dependence of the parastatals. Note should be taken of the fact that the table understates the financial dependence of the parastatals. A sizeable portion of the local borrowings of the parastatals comes from the investment banks, which receive a large percentage of their finances, most often over 50%, from abroad. When the accounts of some of the parastatals are analysed it is found that the central government of Tanzania might be controlling as little as 15% net of parastatal finance. This hardly puts it in a position to control or direct.

TABLE 5.20 Financing of investment in Tanzania, 1966–74 (Sh. million)

	1966	1967	1968	1969	1970	1971	1972	1973	1974
Loans from government	4.7	55.2	46.2	33.7	77.6	85.4	97.0	64.1	40.0
Grants from government	8.1	18.8	52.2	32.2	144.9	70.0	157.7	221.6	135.4
Loans from abroad	6.3	24.2	126.2	24.6	23.7	254.5	236.5	117.4	106.9
Grants from abroad	7.8	0.7	0.8	14.4	16.9	–	1.4	3.5	19.7
Local borrowing	4.5	62.7	76.7	97.6	438.7	359.5	481.8	913.6	894.6

Source
   Analysis of Accounts of Parastatals, 1966–74, Ministry of Finance and Planning, Dar es Salaam, 1976

This brief discussion of dependence has shown that dependence is a very complex phenomenon which is related to the monocultural character of the postcolonial economy, its disarticulation, class contradictions and the peculiar determinations and distortions of the colonial economy. If the examples of Nigeria and Tanzania are any guide to the strategies and policies which African countries are employing to deal with the problem of dependence, they are not very effective. They are directed at the symptoms rather than the underlying causes of dependence. But these ineffective policies are not due to ignorance of the nature of the problem on the part of those who make policy. While these policies are not what they ought to be, they are nonetheless all that they can be, given the interests at play and the prevailing domestic and international social forces. To be more specific, the monopolistic distribution of power in the global economy makes it extremely difficult for Africa to break out of economic dependence; class contradictions make it difficult for African leaders to get their priorities right and to engender the unity of purpose and the effort which is needed to tackle the problem of dependence.

Social relations of production

In our discussion of the social relations of production in the colonial economy we paid special attention to the following:

1 the relations and contradictions within the capitalist class;
2 relations between capital and labour;
3 relations between capital and the peasantry; and
4 relations and contradictions within the peasantry and between the peasants and labour.

Let us start with the relations and contradictions within the peasantry and between the peasantry and labour. On this score there appears to be very little change from the situation depicted in our discussion of the colonial economy. Rural society in Africa is still characterised by a juxtaposition of modes of production undergoing complex mutations and possibly producing new totalities. We can still properly characterise the mode of production in most of rural Africa as a primitive community mode of production with vestiges of petty commodity production. Capitalism is still making inroads into this mode of production, although we can reasonably conclude that its erosion or replacement by capitalism is proceeding very slowly. In so far as capitalism is making inroads, it has taken the form of individualisation of land holdings, the growth of large capitalist farms, the alienation of land by peasants to capitalist farmers and parastatals, and the growth of agricultural wage labour. It is important to repeat that these changes are taking place very slowly and on a rather limited scale in most African economies. The rate and scale of change vary from one place to another. For instance, they have been taking place on a greater scale and much faster in Kenya than in Nigeria.

The implications of these changes are reasonably clear. As part of the syndrome of capitalist development the general thrust of the changes will be towards homogenisation – homogenisation of relations of production, of the mode of exploitation and the modalities of the class struggle. The relations between the peasantry and labour do not appear to present serious problems or to have been undergoing any substantial change in the postcolonial era. There are potent contradictions, but they are essentially of a non-antagonistic nature. One is thinking primarily of the contradictions arising from the exploitation of the countryside in favour of the city and the differences in income and amenities between the city and the country. But these contradictions are mitigated by the persistence of primordial loyalties, the peasantisation of the proletariat who are forced to keep small farms in the country to supplement their incomes, and the depersonalisation of the process of exploitation involving the transfer of surplus value from the countryside to the city.

There is no reason to expect any significant changes in the relations between labour and capital and between labour and the peasantry in the postcolonial era. The former is the classic antagonistic relation of capitalist society. What is changing is not so much the quality of these relations as the quantities of the protagonists. In particular, it is to be expected that as capitalism gains ground in Africa the number of the proletariat will increase. The rate of increase appears to be slow. But indications of the process of proletarianisation can be seen, not so much in the growth rate of wage employment as in the immense and growing size of what is now conventionally called the informal sector. The informal sector consists of people in varying degrees of employment outside the official wage structure, such as roadside mechanics, hawkers shoe-shine boys, etc. The informal sector is, so to speak, a half way house in the process of proletarianisation. In a 1970 study, SETEF (Société d'Etudes Economiques et Financières) found that the employed population of the Ivory Coast was distributed as follows: 11.7% in the formal sector and 88.3% in the informal sector. African governments and international organisations such as the ILO, the World Bank and the ECA, seem very interested in institutionalising and stabilising the informal sector. However, it does not appear that they can stop or greatly slow down the process of proletarianisation. Now, in the case of peasants the expectation is that their number will decrease but the character of their exploitative relations with the capitalist class will remain the same. They will continue to be exploited through the complex mechanism described earlier. One might have expected class differentiation within the peasantry. To all appearances such differentiation is not occurring to any significant degree. The developing trend in class formation in rural Africa appears to be a growing economic gap between the peasantry and a small body of influential landowners and agrarian capitalists. The report of the ILO mission to Kenya, *Employment Incomes and Equality* (ILO, Geneva, 1972), seems to show that this type of class differentiation is occurring. Several other studies point in the same direction; for instance, in his study of rural Kenya (in *Africa Report*, 1, 2, 1972), Moody reaches the following conclusion: 'The more real class formation based on access to land in Kenya is taking place in relation to the differences between the exploitation of land in and out of the scheduled areas. For example, out of the total estimated areas of 6.7 million hectares of agricultural land in Kenya, 1.1 million hectares are still owned by only around 1500 owners. On the 0.6 million hectares of the settlement schemes, there are approximately 53,000 families, and on the remaining 5 million hectares of the "reserves" are approximately 1.3 million households. In others words, 0.1% of landowners share an average holding of 714 hectares, 96% of landowners have an average of 3.8 hectares.' The data is sketchy, but it appears that this tendency is more true of formations such as Kenya, Senegal, Cameroon, Malawi, Ivory Coast and Nigeria. It is far less true of formations such as Tanzania, Mozambique, Angola and Ethiopia, though they are the exceptions rather than the rule in Africa.

It is in the relations and contradictions within the capitalist class that the major changes appear to be occurring. The main point here, and it is a point of some significance, is that the capitalist class in African socio-economic formations has undergone some indigenisation since independence. This indigenisation of the capitalist class was brought about by three factors: the attempt by the colonial government to create an African 'elite' imbued with its values and tied to its interests and who would enable it to rule by proxy after independence; the attempt by the nationalists who came to power at independence to localise ownership and control of the economy; and the efforts of the nationalist leadership to consolidate its material base and to translate office into power. We will illustrate this process of indigenisation of the ruling class with reference to the Kenyan experience.

When the British saw that political independence for Kenya was inevitable they decided to choose their successors. Essentially they tried to create an African subsidiary bourgeoisie imbued with British values and with a vested interest in neocolonial dependence who would ensure that the new African government would be capitalist, docile and dependent. In Kenya the first major effort to create an African bourgeoisie and African landed gentry which would be sympathetic to capitalism and to British interests was made through various land settlement schemes, particularly the Million Acres Settlement Scheme, which was started in 1961. It was ostensibly undertaken to redress the injustice of reducing Africans to landlessness and to prevent the recurrence of the type of political violence which Kenya experienced during the Mau Mau rebellion. These schemes may well have served these purposes. But they were also intended to serve the purpose of creating an African landed gentry and to encourage agrarian capitalism. The Million Acres Settlement Scheme was the first in a series of such schemes. It settled 35,000 families on 470,000 hectares of land at a cost of approximately £30 million. The average size of the farms was about 12 hectares. Inevitably elites, or potential elites, were selected for the scheme. They were people who could inspire confidence that they could run such large farms. The people who qualified tended to be successful businessmen, politicians, high-level civil servants and wealthy farmers. The scheme was followed by several others, some of which accommodated people of more modest means. But the net effect of the wave of settlement schemes was to create a kulak class in Kenya and to give Kenyans a vested interest in capitalist farming, individual land ownership and political moderation. When a Kenyan nationalist government came into power in 1963 it continued to use land settlement in ways which reinforced the original intentions of the British, that is aiding class differentiation and fostering capitalism. This might be said to have been an unintended consequence. What they were really doing was to use land settlement to assuage land hunger, to increase Kenyan participation in the economy and to consolidate their material base.

Parallel developments occurred in commerce and industry. As independence approached, the British showed some concern with encouraging indigenous capitalism in order to moderate African radicalism and to ensure that some influential Kenyans would have a vested interest in neocolonialism. After independence, the nationalists who came to power contributed to the fostering of indigenous capitalism and class differentiation by their attempt to increase Kenyan participation in the economy and to create an economic foundation for their political power. One institution that was critical for these developments was the Industrial Development Corporation (IDC). This body was established in 1954 and intended to promote the 'industrial and economic development of Kenya through initiation, assistance or expansion of the industrial, commercial or other undertakings or enterpises in Kenya or elsewhere'. As independence approached and the British decided to groom successors who would be sympathetic to their interests and goals they started to use this organisation, as well as other means, to encourage indigenous capitalism. This trend was continued and accentuated by the Kenyan leadership which succeeded the colonial regime. In 1967 the Industrial Development Act changed the name of the Industrial Development Corporation to its present name, the Industrial and Commercial Development Corporation (ICDC). This was more than a change of nomenclature. While the Corporation was still concerned with the task of promoting economic development in Kenya, it was now to give serious attention to increasing Kenyan participation in the economy. Accordingly the Corporation provided the necessary support and facilities for Kenyan Africans to take over alien businesses or set up new ones. It developed a scheme for helping entrepreneurs to establish new small and medium-size businesses; an entrepreneur could borrow up to Ksh. 750,000 to buy equipment or to construct or buy a building in order to set up an industrial or commercial enterprise. The ICDC set up a scheme by which Africans who had savings were encouraged to register with the Corporation. The Corporation advised them on investment opportunities as they arose and ensured that their money was properly invested. The Corporation prepared feasibility studies on potential projects, disseminated this information to Kenyans as well as foreign investors, and assisted in meeting the long term loan requirements of such projects. The Corporation also promoted joint ventures with foreigners in the expectation that in the long run such ventures would be transferred to Kenyans when they could muster enough capital to take them over. The ICDC helped the development of indigenous capitalism by providing through its loan scheme credit to Kenyans taking over the businesses of non-citizen Asians who were barred by the immigration and trade licensing laws from operating industrial and commercial enterprises in Kenya.

From 1965 to 1971 the Corporation loaned about Ksh. 2.5 million to Kenyans, the vast majority of the loans going to the acquisition of non-citizen Asian businesses. These efforts to encourage indigenous capitalism were complemented by efforts to increase the intervention of the state in the economy, particularly the creation of parastatals. From the point of view of the interests of the new African leaders the extension of state participation in the economy was most desirable. The more of the economy they brought under the power of the state the more they increased their economic power and political leverage. The extension of state participation in the economy, which was often justified in the name of African socialism, the pursuit of economic independence and the rationalisation of the process of economic development, created opportunities for the enrichment of the ruling class by manipulation of the appointments of officers of the parastatals, by influencing how the parastatals conduct their business and with whom they do so, etc.

These then were the circumstances under which the ruling class was being indigenised. This indigenisation was among other things a response to the contradiction between economic and political power in the postcolonial socio-economic formation. The nationalist leaders who had just replaced the colonial regime had political power. But economic power was still largely in the hands of foreign capital, whose political power had been grossly diminished by the fact of political independence in the former colony. The pressure on the part of the nationalist leaders in office to translate their political power into economic power was one way of resolving this contradiction. But colonial capital, which had largely lost its political power, had to turn the new rulers into docile agents for promoting its interests. That was also one way of resolving the contradiction. Neither the nationalists nor colonial capital was in a position to have its way. But then again both sides succeeded to some extent.

In most African countries some accommodation was found between these two groups. Some of the nationalists now have a foot in the door of the capitalist class and have become appeased if not content. Foreign capital can feel more secure because of the vested interests of politically powerful African leaders in capitalism. All the same, contradictions still exist within the capitalist class despite this accommodation. For one thing the wider contradiction between political and economic power still remains as a source of frustration to both sides. And for another, the African bourgeoisie must be aware that the neocolonial structures which serve them so well also underline the dependence and underdevelopment which limit their power and undermine their political legitimacy.

It remains to examine some of the implications of this change in the relations of production under review, namely the indigenisation of the capitalist class. First it helps the development of class contradiction and class consciousness. For the most part indigenisation entails not the displacement of the metropolitian bourgeoisie but the broadening of the bourgeoisie by the inclusion of more indigenes. In the face of the slow development of productive forces and the sluggish pace of development, this in turn means that indigenisation has been associated with more intense exploitation as the surplus to be shared grows less than the number of people to share it. This in turn has, along with other factors, made indigenisation conducive to the widening of the gap between the ruling class and the subordinate classes. Income disparities in Africa have become exceedingly high. For example, in Ivory Coast in the year 1973–74 the top 20% on the income scale received 51.6% of total income, the middle 40% received 28.7% of total income, while the bottom 40% received 19.7%. It is not merely the intensification of exploitation or the growing inequalities that will aid the development of class consciousness and class conflict in this situation. In so far as the bourgeoisie is Africanised, class loses its old colonial association with race and the subordinate classes are better able to attain clarity.

The second implication of the change in the social relations of production under discussion is more important still because of the particular way in which this change has distorted capitalism and the role of the capitalist state in postcolonial Africa. The fact that the new nationalist leadership had to rely on political power as the means of creating their economic base is a fact of immense significance. It unfortunately created a tendency to make political power the means of accumulation. This tendency has persisted stubbornly for obvious reasons. Consider the situation in which certain enterprises are brought under state power, say by nationalisation, and state power is then used to appropriate surplus value through the nationalised enterprises. The situation seems to offer a particularly 'agreeable' type of exploitation. The relation between exploiter and exploited is totally depersonalised; the exploiter is able to hide behind a public enterprise which is ostensibly owned by the whole society for the benefit of the whole society. Also the exploiter takes little or no economic risks because he is not investing his own money; if there is a loss, it is borne by the taxpayer. And this arrangement saves the effort and all the trials of actually founding and managing a capitalist enterprise. The prospects for capitalist appropriation through political power are so attractive that some people who want to be wealthy and who would normally have engaged in productive enterprises have preferred to seek their fortunes by going into politics. With attention being directed to politics rather than to economics, and the emphasis placed on appropriation rather than production capitalism, this cannot be very conducive to the development of productive forces.

In a situation in which politics is the way to power as well as wealth, the premium on the acquisition of political power becomes inevitably very high. The further implication of this is that political competition becomes a grim battle in which winning is all important. Because winning is all important the competitors tend to use every means to win. This is part of the explanation of the high incidence of political violence and political instability in Africa. The high incidence of political violence and political instability in turn reduce the prospects of overcoming underdevelopment.

The massive intervention of the state in the economic sphere and the use of political power as the means of appropriation distorts the role of the capitalist state in Africa. For it means that the state gets too involved in the class struggle and begins to look like 'the executive committee for managing the affairs of the bourgeoisie'. Because it is so difficult for the state in Africa to rise above the class struggle and to mediate it, the struggle has become singularly crude and intense, and the contradictions are deepening and developing out of proportion to the state and to the development of the productive forces.

Social relations of production and the state

It is necessary to develop this discussion of the social relations of production some more by talking about the state if we are to understand how African socio-economic formations have changed in the postcolonial era as well as the future course of their development. This is a hazardous undertaking because questions such as what the state is, and how it relates to the economic system and to social classes, are very complex and rather confused. No one pretends that the confusions and complexities can be sorted out here. The point of treating the topic is to recognise that it should not be avoided, however difficult it is, and to indicate and clarify some of the assumptions that are made here in regard to the ongoing debates about the nature of the capitalist state and the postcolonial state.

To begin with, what is the state? What distinguishes the state from other social institutions is that, apart from being the ultimate coercive power, it makes exclusive claim to the legitimate use of coercive force. This definition does not tell us very much. It has to be supplemented by making clear what the state is not. First the state should not be confused with government. Strictly-speaking, government is the system of rule-making roles; these roles – at least the higher ones in the heirarchy – are then filled by political competition. The concept of government is often broadened in popular parlance to include the institutions which implement rules, namely the judiciary, the armed forces and the police, but this is to obscure the distinction between state and government. It is also important to make a distinction between the state and the ruling class, and between the ruling class and the government. The ruling class is the social class which by virtue of its control of the means of production is able to command a preponderance of social, political and economic goods and power. Strictly-speaking, it is really the ruling class that is in power, the government being merely in office. By virtue of its place in the social relations of production, the ruling class is usually able to ensure that those who occupy the high offices of government are sympathetic to its interests, and give it the necessary access to state power. But the leaders of government (we can call them the governing class) may not necessarily be members or the candidates of the ruling class, and a government may represent interests which are objectively in conflict with those of the ruling class. However, this is usually a transitional phenomenon.

What of the relation between the state and the ruling class? For a start, it should be noted that the government is essentially the formal link between the state and the ruling class, generally giving the former access to state power. In addition to this there are informal and more direct links between the state and the ruling class which give the ruling class leverage over state power, for instance the internalisation of the ideology of the ruling class by state officials. The relationship between the state and the ruling class is an extraordinarily complex one, being at once a relationship of fusion, complementarity, independence and contradiction. It is by the support of state power that existing property relations are maintained in the presence of the inevitable demand for redistribution. The growth of the coercive institutions which are the core of state power are related to the need for social control, which arises mainly from class differentiation and antagonistic contradictions. Those who benefit most from the 'stability' which the state maintains are the dominant classes. So the general affinity of state and ruling class is reasonably clear.

And yet the state and ruling class are separate and up to a point independent. Even when it is allowed that the coercive institutions of the state developed largely in the interest of the ruling class, the fact still remains that these institutions also have a dynamic all their own; the ruling class is not always able to control them and interests may develop within these institutions which are quite in opposition to those of the ruling class. Also, it should be remembered that the state is ideologically legitimised on the grounds of its service of universal interests. If this legitimation were merely a myth, the state could not be very effective, even for serving the interests of the ruling class; the concessions necessarily made to this myth enhance the separation and independence of state and ruling class. Finally it should be noted that the ruling class is hardly ever a monolith. While its members may have common interests they are not always conscious of these; they tend rather to be more conscious of the particular interests which are often competitive. From such considerations one must conclude that the control of the coercive power of the state by the ruling class is problematic. This is all the more so because the coercive institutions themselves are not passive but active foci of the class struggle (which is only counteracted in a limited way by coporate identity), so that their response to the particular demands of the ruling class cannot be predicted automatically but depend in part on the shifting constellation of class forces and the nature of their internal contradictions. No ruling class ever solves once and for all the problem of the mastery of state power.

The state cannot be understood by abstract definitions. The definitions have to be given concreteness by locating them in particular socio-economic formations. Since we are interested in Africa, where the capitalist mode of production dominates, albeit uneasily, it is useful to relate our discussion to the specificity of the state in capitalist socio-economic formations. What is it that gives the capitalist state its uniqueness? The distinction lies in the appearance of the capitalist state as being objective, representing universal interests of working for the benefit of all. To understand this we have to recall what capitalism is: pervasive commodification, a system geared to the production of exchange values rather than use values. With production so geared to exchange, capitalist society is a market society and as such is ruled (ideally) by the forces of supply and demand. The market is characterised by impersonality (often appearing to the consciousness as objectivity) and 'freedom'. Peoples' identities are masked as they confront each other as commodities and exploitative relations are hidden behind the mechanism of exchange. The exchange relations themselves appear as something into which people freely enter, and this often leads them to hold themselves responsible for their failure or success. Above the chaos of individual self-seeking in the capitalist market stands the state, enforcing contractual obligations 'for the benefit of all'. The objectivity of the state is underlined by the formal freedom and 'democratic' politics in the capitalist formation. Government is produced by a competition (analagous to the economic) in which all are formally free to enter. So it seems. This apparent objectivity reinforces the relative separation and independence of the state, and so it is able to some extent to rise above the class struggle and mediate it. Let us now turn to the postcolonial state.

What the African formation had at independence was a state which was (a) particularly developed and (b) immersed in the class struggle instead of rising above it. The development of the colonial state was due essentially to the overwhelming need of the colonisers for repressive force. The involvement of the colonial state in the class struggle was due to the fact that in the early colonial era most parts of Africa were for all practical purposes under the rule of companies, such as the Royal Niger Company, which acted as the state, and from this tradition the colonial state developed as a tool of capital. Also, in the colonial socio-economic formations of Africa state power was regularly needed for primitive accumulation.

These two characteristics of the colonial state were reinforced in the postcolonial era by the fact that the indigenous bourgeoisie which took over government at independence lacked a secure material base and used its political power for accumulation. Starting from here we can now characterise systematically the nature of the postcolonial state and its relation to the government, the ruling class and the process of accumulation.

To begin with, we have a state that is interventionist and involved in the class struggle, that is to say a state already dragged into politics and politicised. Partly because of this fact (whose significance is the perception of the state as being very partial), and partly because the state power in question is highly developed, there is a bitter struggle to gain control of it. A critical focus of this struggle is the control of government, which is the formal access to state power. Thus in Africa those in office do all they can to perpetuate their hold on it, and those out of office do all they can to get it; there is hardly any restraint beyond prudence as to permissible means for this struggle. That is one side of the equation.

We approach the other side by looking at the ruling class. The ruling classes of Africa are highly fractious; they are beset with contradictions arising from the state of development of productive forces, the juxtaposition of different modes of production in the socio-economic formation, the disarticulation of the economy, dependence, and the role of foreign capital. As always, contradictions make political competition intense, for the less a fraction of the ruling class feels it has in common with the others the less it is willing to allow that fraction to become politically dominant. The effect of the contradictions is to politicise the ruling class intensely. So we have a situation in which the ruling class is far less passive about who governs and becomes engaged in grim factional battles for hegemony through the control of the formal access to state power, namely the government. The battle for control of the government and for hegemony is all the more grim because, as we saw before, governmental and state power have tended to become the means of production for the African bourgeoisie. What picture emerges from all this? The boundry between the state, government and the ruling class is very blurred; a government tendentially used by the hegemonic faction of the bourgeoisie to manipulate state power, a state with limited potential for mediating the class struggle, and endemic political instability arising from too high a premium on political power.

The broader implications of this state of affairs are interesting and will be briefly noted. First, it means a crudely oppressive class rule; because the state and government are too involved in the class struggle, and because of the high premium placed on political power, the tone of politics is highly authoritarian and the hegemonic faction of the bourgeoisie adopts a seige mentality. Secondly, the existence of crude oppression and the involvement of state and government in the class struggle makes it more difficult to mask class contradictions and encourages the development of class consciousness. Thirdly, the potential of the state for making the socio-economic formation more coherent is limited. Fourthly, the tendency to accumulate through the use of state power rather than through productive activities makes postcolonial capitalism less conducive to the development of productive forces and the increase of surplus.

Bibliography

AKE, C., *Revolutionary Pressures in Africa*, London, 1978.
AKE, C., 'Tanzania: The Progress of a Decade', *The African Review*, 2, 1, 1972.

AKE, C., *A Theory of Political Integration*, Homewood, 1967.
AKE, C., 'Explanatory Notes on the Political Economy of Africa', *Journal of Modern African Studies*, 14, 1, 1976.
ALAVI, H., 'The Post Colonial State', *New Left Review*, 74, 1972.
AMIN, S., *Neocolonialism in West Africa*, Harmondsworth, 1974.
AMIN, S., *Unequal Development: An Essay on the Social Formations of Peripheral Capitalism*, New Yrok, 1976.
AWITI, A., 'Economic Differentiation in Ismani', *The African Review*, 3, 2, 1973.
BEER, C., *The Politics of Peasant Groups in Western Nigeria*, Ibadan, 1975.
BERNSTEIN, H., 'Notes on Capital and Peasantry', *Review of African Political Economy*, 10, 1977.
BERNSTEIN, H., ED., *Underdevelopment and Development*, Harmondsworth, 1973.
BUJRA, A., 'Technology and Development in Africa', *Africa Development*, 2, 2, 1977.
CLIFFE, L., 'The Policy of Ujamaa Villages and the Class Struggle in Tanzania', in L. Cliffe and J. Saul eds., *Socialism in Tanzania*, Vol. 2, Nairobi, 1970.
COHEN, R., 'Classes in Africa: Analytical Problems and Prospectives', *The Socialist Register*, London, 1972.
DUMONT, R., *African Agricultural Development: Reflections on the major lines of advance and the barriers to progress*, Addis Ababa, 1965.
ELKAN, W., 'Is a Proletariat Emerging in Kenya?', *Economic Development and Cultural Change*, 24, 1976.
FIELDHOUSE, D., *Unilever Overseas: The anatomy of a multinational*, London, 1979.
FOSTER-CARTER, A., 'The Modes of Production Controversy', *New Left Review*, 107, 1978.
GODFREY, M. AND LANGDON, S., 'Partners in Underdevelopment? The transnationalisation thesis in a Kenyan context', *Journal of Commonwealth and Comparative Politics*, 14, 1, 1976.
HARRIS, R. ED., *The Political Economy of Africa*, Cambridge, Mass., 1975.
HAYTER, T., *Aid as Imperialism*, Harmondsworth, 1971.
HVEEM, H., 'The global dominance system, *Journal of Peace Research*, 10, 4, 1970.
HELLEINER, G., 'Socialism and Economic Development in Tanzania', *Journal of Development Studies*, 8, 1972.
HILL, P., *Studies in Rural Capitalism*, Cambridge, 1970.
INTERNATIONAL LABOUR ORGANISATION, *Employment Incomes and Inequality in Kenya*, Geneva, 1972.
INTERNATIONAL MONETARY FUND, *International Financial Statistics*, October, 1976.
JUDD, E., 'The Changing Face of Foreign Business in Africa: Participation and Integration', *African Affairs*, 76, 1977.
KABUNDA, K., 'Multinational Corporations and the Installation of Externally-Oriented Economic Structures in Contemporary Africa: The Example of the Unilver-Zaire Group', in C. Widstrand ed., *Multinational Firms in Africa*, Uppsala, 1975.

KAMAU, C., 'Localising Capitalism: The Kenya Experience', in D. P. Ghai ed., *Economic Independence in Africa*, Nairobi, 1973.

KITCHING, G., 'The Concept of Class and the Study of Africa', *The African Review*, 2, 3, 1972.

KITCHING, G., 'Modes of Production and Kenyan Dependency', *Review of African Political Economy*, 8, 1977.

LANGDON, S., 'The Political Economy of Dependence: Note Towards Analysis of Multinational Corporations in Kenya', *Journal of East African Research and Development*, 4, 1974.

LEITNER, K., *Workers' Trade Unionism and Peripheral Capitalism in Kenya After Independence*, Verlag Peter Lang, 1977.

MEILLASSOUX, G., 'A Class Analysis of the Bureaucratic Process in Mali', *Journal of Development Studies*, 6, 2, 1970.

MEIR, G., *Leading Issues in Development Economics*, New York, 1964.

MERHAU, M., *Technological Dependence, Monopoly and Growth*, London, 1969.

MYRDAL, G., 'What is Development?', *Journal of Economic Issues*, December, 1974.

PAYER, C., *The Debt Trap: IMF and the Third World*, New York, 1974.

PETRAS, J., 'Class and Politics in the Periphery and the Transition to Socialism', *Review of Radical Political Economy*, 8, 2, 1976.

POST, K., ' "Peasantisation" and Rural Political Movements in Western Nigeria', *Archives Europeènes de Sociologie*, 13, 2, 1972.

PROCTOR, J. E. ED., *Building Ujamaa Villages in Tanzania*, Dar es Salaam, 1971.

RAIKES, P., 'Ujamaa Villages and rural socialist development', *Review of African Political Economy*, 3, 1975.

RANA, K., 'Class Formation and Social Conflict: A Case Study of Kenya', *Ufahamu*, 7, 1977.

REPUBLIC OF KENYA, *Economic Survey*, Nairobi, 1975.

ROBSON, P., AND LURY, D. EDS., *The Economies of Africa*: Evanston, 1969.

RWEYEMAMU, J., 'The Political Economy of Foreign Private Investment in the Underdeveloped countries', *The African Review*, 1, 1, 1970.

SANDBROOK, R., *Proletarians and African Capitalism: The Case of Kenya 1960–72*, Oxford, 1974.

SANDBROOK, R. AND COHEN, R. EDS., *The Development of an African Working Class*, London, 1975.

SANTOS, T. DOS, 'The Structure of Dependence', *American Economic Review*, 60, 2, 1970.

SHAW, R., AND GRIEVE, M., 'Dependence on Development: International and Internal Inequalities in Africa', *Development and Change*, 8, 3, 1977.

SHAW, R., AND GRIEVE, M., 'The Political Economy of Resources: Africa's Future in the Global Environment', *Journal of Modern African Studies*, 16, 1, 1978.

SHIVJI, I., *Class Struggle in Tanzania*, London, 1975.

SILVER, J., 'Class Struggles in Ghana's Mining Industry', *Review of African Political Economy*, 12, 1978.

SWAINSON, N., 'The Rise of a National Bourgeoisie in Kenya', *Review of African Political Economy*, 8, 1977.

TARABRIN, E., *The New Scramble for Africa*, Moscow, 1974.

UNITED NATIONS ECONOMIC AND SOCIAL COUNCIL. ECONOMIC COMMIS-SION FOR AFRICA, *Survey of Economic and Social Conditions in Africa*, 1976 E/CN.14/654, February, 1977; *Applications of a Unified Approach to Development Analysis and Planning Under African Conditions*, E/CN.14/CAP.6/4; *A Critique of Conventional Planning in Africa in Relation to the Unified Approach*; *Report on a Unified Approach to Development Analysis and Planning*, E/CN.5/519, December, 1974.

WEEKS, J., 'Employment, Growth and Foreign Domination in Underdeveloped Countries', *Review of Radical Economies*, 4, 1972.

WORLD BANK, *Ivory Coast: The Challenge of Success*, Baltimore, 1978.

6 The dynamics of African socio-economic formations

In the preceding chapters we have been concerned mainly with delineating the salient features of African economies. In this chapter we will focus attention on trying to understand their dynamics, bearing in mind that we cannot understand an economy, much less its dynamics, without being interested in its contextual socio-economic formation.

The question of how African economies might develop should not be confused with the question of how African economies might liquidate underdevelopment or achieve development. The first question is interested in what might be, the second question is interested in realising what is desired. The first question is concerned with the laws of motion of African economies, the second question subordinates the laws of motion to a teleological concern.

Before proceeding further, it is necessary to explain why we should be interested in the first question rather than the second. If existing practice is any guide, it would have been expected that we should be interested in the second question. Almost without exception scholarly writings on the economies of Africa, and indeed of the developing countries, take the prospect of development (that is overcoming underdevelopment) as their central theme. Increasingly the political economy curricula of academic institutions in the developing countries are also making the problem of achieving development their point of main interest. These academic tendencies are in turn merely reflections of the preoccupation with the problem of underdevelopment on the political level. The political leaders in Africa and other developing areas are clearly preoccupied with the problem of underdevelopment. If government documents and pronouncements of leaders and officials are any guide, the problem of underdevelopment is for them by far the most fundamental problem. They see it as the basis of all other problems – the social disorganisation of their societies, the military and political weakness in the international system of states, poverty, etc. It is also clear that they see their societal evolution primarily in terms of the possibility of achieving development. It is possible and even likely that this consciousness was foisted on them by their former colonial masters, who want to maintain their domination by making them think of their history in terms of the possibility of fashioning their societies in the image of the West. No matter. The pertinent fact is that the consciousness in question exists.

In the light of this existing state of consciousness it would seem highly appropriate – one might almost say mandatory – for a book of this nature to go into a long discussion of the prospects of overcoming underdevelopment. However, we have chosen otherwise and are concentrating our interest on the nature and laws of motion of African

133

economies. To avoid misunderstanding, it should be stated right away that we are not discounting the necessity of coming to grips with the prospects of overcoming the underdevelopment of African economies. This question has already received considerable attention in the preceding chapters. Even in this chapter some attention will inevitably be paid to this question, but indirectly and as an aspect of a wider concern. It is not possible to throw light on the laws of motion of the African economy without also illuminating its prospects of achieving development. But the question cannot rest at that. It is useful to explain why we are not focusing attention on the prospects of development.

The explanation is simply that if we did so, our perspective would be too narrow and too blurred. If we focus narrowly on the prospects for development we will be imposing limitations which will impair our understanding of the present realities in Africa. Understanding of the realities must come first, no matter whether we conceive our interest in the study of Africa as a scientific concern or as the practical interest of one who seeks to bring about a particular state of being. Unless we first understand the world we cannot be effective in the enterprise of changing it. But we cannot understand the realities of the African situation fully if we confine our interest to the problem of underdevelopment, important as it is. It is quite possible that there may be important aspects of the situation which may not be specially relevant or interesting from the point of view of the prospects of development. If the prospects of development monopolise our criteria of relevance then these aspects may well be neglected or under-appreciated. And yet they may be critical for understanding the society in its totality. Indeed there may also be aspects of the situation in Africa which may be highly pertinent to the problem of development, but whose relevance may be currently obscure, perhaps because of the way the problem of development is phrased or because of the deficiencies in our perception or analytical tools. That is reason enough for caution in assimilating discussion of African societies or even African economies too exclusively to the prospects of development, as is the current practice.

There is the additional problem that if we focus our interest on the prospects for development, our perspective on the present realities in Africa may be too blurred. This blurring of focus arises from the confusion associated with prevailing conceptions of underdevelopment. A brief illustration of this confusion is in order. Some see underdevelopment and development as two sides of the same coin, both arising from the contradictions of world capitalism. Some see development as capitalist economic growth; within this usage there is considerable disagreement on the indices of growth. The definition of underdevelopment which complements this usage is the absence or retardation of growth. Some who reject this notion of underdevelopment prefer to think of underdevelopment not in terms of lack of growth but in terms of distortions of capitalist growth processes such as dependence. This notion of underdevelopment is, however, very problematic, since it is not clear what the standards are against which distortions are being measured. There are usages of development and underdevelopment which equate them with industrialisation or lack of industrialisation respectively. There are also those which limit the concept of development to the development of the productive forces. This list of usages is by no means exhaustive. It is only a sample of a large number of existing definitions and conceptions.

This confusion casts doubt on the usefulness of talking generally of the prospects for development of a particular socio-economic formation. It is more useful to talk in terms more specific than development, and to do so in the context of an analysis that concentrates on understanding what is happening in the socio-economic formations of Africa rather than what ought to happen. That is of course what this study has been trying to do all along. Preceding chapters identified the main features of African economies and tried to show how they have come to be what they are. The present chapter assesses the potential of African economies for change, the probable directions of change and their implications. Our point of departure is the main structural feature of African economies which we have already outlined. We have to look at their relatedness in order to understand their propensities for change or persistence.

Relations of the main structural features

When the main structural features of African economies delineated in this study are seen in their relationship, one immediately sees a picture of enormous inertia. Each of the structural features has a built-in resistance to change and they tend to be mutually reinforcing in their state of equilibrium.

Disarticulation

Let us start with disarticulation. Disarticulation tends to be self-perpetuating. The preceding chapters indicated some of the reasons why this is so. To recapitulate, private investors more interested in profit than in intersectoral integration naturally tend to concentrate investments in the enclaves which offer economies of scale and also the availability of infrastructures, support services, and easier access to markets. The policy-makers often have a vested interest in further development of the enclaves because of personal convenience and also because of the pressure to show results quickly. The need to secure foreign exchange earnings for development projects is another powerful pressure for the maintenance of the African economy in the state of disarticulation. Also, all the obstacles to industrialisation in Africa perpetuate disarticulation for the complex network of linkages and reciprocities which come with industrialisation, and will need to be tackled if the problem of disarticulation is to be dealt with in a fundamental way. To this may be added the fact that disarticulation perpetuates itself by making the planning process, or at any rate the conventional planning processes, difficult. These rely heavily on mathematical equations which describe relationships of the different macro-variables and sectors of the economy. Such equations become relatively useless in a disarticulated economy in which the relationships of the different elements is either non-existent or obscure.

Dependence

Now let us bring in dependence. We will not discuss its stubborn persistence which is well known. We will rather confine ourselves to its relation to disarticulation. That the two features are closely related and prone to be mutually reinforcing is easy to see. As is implicit in our discussion of the integration of Africa into the world capitalist system, disarticulation and dependence might be said to be aspects of the same thing as far as African economies are concerned. It was in the process of the integration of Africa into the world capitalist system that both dependence and disarticulation became features of African economies. Colonial policies oriented the different sectors and regions of Africa to the metropole. Each sector had a strong tie with the metropolitan economy, in most cases so much so that they might be said to be an integral part of the metropolitan economy. It is precisely because of these vertical ties between sectors of the periphery economy to the centre that African economies have become so disarticulated. Dependence and disarticulation not only arise from the same source, they mutually reinforce each other. For instance, dependence entails external control, which inhibits the ability of the national leadership to undertake the restructuring of the economy necessary to reduce disarticulation. The dependence of African economies perpetuates their disarticulation by making it easier for metropolitan economies to maintain the international division of labour which consigns Africa to primary production and retards her industrialisation. Disarticulation in turn reinforces dependence in ways that are readily apparent. The oil boom in Nigeria illustrates the tendency of disarticulation and dependence to be mutually supportive. Oil greatly increased Nigeria's dependence, both technologically and financially, particularly the former. Apart from technological dependence the oil industry had very few backward linkages and virtually all the forward linkages were external. Of course the bulk of the demand for the oil was also external. All this meant that the oil industry was externally-oriented. Since it is so completely dominant in the economy (it now accounts for about 94% of export earnings), it has tended to influence the subsidiary sectors towards an external orientation, thereby exacerbating the disarticulation of the Nigerian economy. The oil boom itself diverted attention away from some sectors of the economy, particularly agriculture. Nigeria has grown progressively incapable of feeding herself and dependent on food imports from the West. To sum up, to the extent that an economy is disarticulated its capacity for independence is diminished, and to the extent that an economy is dependent it is more prone to disarticulation.

Narrow resource base

Let us now bring in the third feature of African economies, namely their narrow resource base, particularly foreign exchange resources. When this element is considered the picture of inertia looks even worse. Not surprisingly. For dependence tends to perpetuate a narrow resource base. It greatly inhibits the ability of African policy-makers to effect the policies which are needed to integrate their economies, such as localisation of ownership and control, export promotion, import substitution, restrictions on foreign investment, imports and repatriation of profits. Such policies are against the interests of metropolitan capital.

The dependence of African economies on external demand for primary products imposes severe constraints on the ability to diversify and to reduce disarticulation. Foreign exchange is needed to carry out development aspects, but to earn foreign exchange countries are obliged to continue along lines of production which reinforce their unenviable role in the international division of labour. The narrowness of the resource base of African economies in turn deepens their dependence. For one thing the resources from this narrow base are usually too meagre, so that external borrowing has to be resorted to and foreign investment sought, etc. Also the narrow base is invariably made up of a primary commodity. The supply of primary commodities is highly inelastic in the short run and its demand is fairly elastic because of the multiplicity of sources of supply and the increasing availability of synthetic substitutes, and the international market for primary products is subject to acute price fluctuations. All these encourage dependence of both a political and economic nature, for instance on international arrangements to stabilise import earnings for primary producers, such as the arrangements made between the ACP countries and the EEC under Lomé I and II, particularly Stabex.

The relation of the narrow resource base to disarticulation is easy to grasp. The fact that most African economies are essentially monocultural export economies is itself a form of disarticulation. Disarticulation and narrowness of resource base spring from essentially the same causes, including dependence and lack of industrialisation. Disarticulation impedes the effort to diversify the resource base of African economies. It limits the spill-over effect from one sector of the economy to another. Those are some of the ways in which these three features interlock and perpetuate themselves.

Monopolistic tendencies

The relation of the fourth feature, monopolistic tendencies, to the others is rather less obvious. We will consider the two important aspects of the monopoly tendency. First is the intrusion of Western capital into the African economy as a monopoly enterprise. Much of Western private investment into Africa comes under the auspices of the all-powerful multinationals such as International Business Machines, General Electric, General Motors, British Petroleum and ITT. These multinationals are part of the mechanism of dependence, and the disarticulation of African economies. It was hoped that the multinationals would be useful tools for developing the productive forces in Africa by investing in research and development, manpower training, the transfer of technology, the local manufacture of components for export, etc. However, these expectations have not materialised, for many reasons which include fears of African economic nationalism and political instability, the state of the infrastructures and the limited size of the market in most African countries, and the preference of those multinationals in extractive industries to integrate backwards into mining rather than forward into processing. The power of the multinationals within the African economy as well as the world economy has made it very difficult for African governments to domesticate them and make them a real asset to the enterprise of building a coherent economy capable of self-sustaining growth.

The effect of the monopoly enterprises owned by African governments is, as to be expected, rather more salutory. As we have seen, the parastatals were established expressly to combat the dependence on foreign enterprises, to reduce the export of capital, and most importantly· to engage in those enterprises which are not so attractive to foreign investors but which are nevertheless necessary for the development of productive forces. Some of these parastatals have had some success in breaking the monopoly of foreign enterprises, or in the limited processing of primary products, or in the production of consumer goods requiring low-level technology such as textiles, footwear, furniture, cement, tobacco, beer and soft drinks. In these ways they have contributed to the reduction of disarticulation and dependence. But their contribution has been very modest at best. Their capacity to challenge the multinationals is limited and, despite the efforts of the parastatals, industrialisation in Africa has not come anywhere near the diversification needed to deal effectively with the problems of disarticulation and the narrow resource base of African economies. The parastatals can hardly have a significant impact on the reduction of dependence since many of them are dependent on foreign management and on foreign capital. All the same they have potential for changing the status quo.

Social relations of production

It remains to consider one salient feature of the African economy, namely the social relations of production. This is the feature which appears to contain the strongest impulse towards change, partly because it is so full of contradictions. The contradictions arise from the existence of several precapitalist modes of production at different stages of decomposition, the advance of capitalism, the increasing differention within the capitalist class, the contradictions between Western capital and indigenous capital, the process of proletarianisation, the opposition of the capitalist mode of production to the small commodity and primitive community modes of production, and the lack of symmetry between political and economic power.

The implications of the relations of production for the maintenance of African economies in their present conditions is rather ambivalent. Some aspects of the productive relations are clearly conducive to inertia. Up to a point the indigenous capitalist class in many African countries are really agents of Western capital and by extension part of the structure of the imperialist exploitation of Africa. In so far as they fall into this role, they are unable to champion effectively those changes which will liberate African economies from their exploitative dependence and diversify her economy. The conflict of interests between indigenous capital and Western capital quite often resolves itself partly in an accommodation resting on the delimitation of spheres of influence and collaborative arrangements. The process of indigenisation in Africa, for instance in Zaire, Nigeria, Kenya and Ghana, was essentially interesting not so much as economic nationalism but as the articulation and institutionalisation of this accommodation. The effect of this type of accommodation is to arrest a development which has great potential for fundamental change. In this sense the contradiction between local and Western capital aids the forces of inertia.

The indigenisation of capitalism in a period of relative stagnation has caused a great deal of alienation between African leaders and the masses. The African leaders face the dilemma that they are not able to stem the deepening contradictions or the mutual alienation of leaders and masses in a manner compatible with the maintenance of existing relations of production. Some of them such as Mobutu of Zaire and Bokassa of the Central African Empire increasingly had to rely on Western capital and Western governments for their survival. Such a situation does not allow leaders to do very much by way of reducing dependence, disarticulation and the monocultural character of their economies, because a serious effort to deal with these issues is bound to bring them into grave conflict with Western capital.

There are also aspects of the relations of production which are more conducive to disequilibrium. In the first place, the national bourgoisie is well aware that dependence, disarticulation and the narrow resource base of their economies underlie the underdevelopment which threatens the credibility of their leadership. They are clearly anxious to do something about it. So an impulse to change exists here, although the realisation of the requisite change will be limited by fear of confrontation with Western capital on which the African bourgeoisie depends so heavily for their prosperity and security. They have tried to deal with this dilemma by making an ideology of development. By their incessant elaboration of this ideology they are able to convey to their people the impression of immense concern with their poverty and the economic backwardness of their country, as well as their determination to tackle the problem of getting out of this backwardness with the utmost sense of urgency. This wins them some legitimacy.

They have not merely talked, they have also tried to take measures to realise development. Judging from what they are doing, as opposed to what they are saying, it turns out that their notion of emerging out of economic backwardness amounts essentially to Westernisation and industrialisation. At any rate, apart from a few exceptions, the general trend is to try to stimulate economic growth within the context of the existing neocolonial economic structure. In short, with varying qualifications of a largely insignificant nature, most of them are pursuing essentially capitalist development. And so it was relatively easy to avoid some kind of confrontation with Western capital. Indeed a partnership has emerged, a partnership in development. Western capital encourages the propagation of the ideology of development and gives some aid to ensure a barely credible performance, as well as the persistence of existing exploitative ties between African economies and Western economies. However, the dilemma is not removed; it is merely relocated. On the part of Western capital they face the problem that economic problems and political sensitivities at home do not really allow the mobilisation and deployment of aid to Africa which will really give credibility to the current strategies and performance of development.

African leaders feel humiliated by having to beg constantly and for never getting enough. They feel frustrated by the havoc that economic forces originating from the industrialised countries does to their economies. These feelings lead to occasional outbursts of hostility and conflict. Behind this is the more ominous dilemma of being locked into a path of development which produces marginal improvements at best without offering any real prospect of breaking out of underdevelopment.

Another aspect of production relations which has potential for stimulating change is the contradiction between economic power and political power. At independence there was clearly a state of disequilibrium because a national leadership had just captured political office while economic control of the economy still remained in the hands of Western capital. This disequilibrium has been moderated by the natural play of social forces. Western capital has tried to translate its economic power into political control with some success. Equally African nationalist leaders have tried to translate their political power into economic power by means which we have already indicated. And they have met with some success too. So the two factions of the bourgeoisie have moved closer together and in some cases one can talk of the emergence of a new equilibrium. This equilibrium (perhaps accommodation is a more appropriate word), though representing a new and higher synthesis, is at the same time a conservative force in that it is blocking at least for the time being the development of a more radical realignment of social forces. But some possibilities of this more radical realignment of forces remain. To give an example, one such possibility lies in the contradictions within the African bourgeoisie. Some of them accumulate wealth through their positions as bureaucrats, some through commerce, some as agents or subcontractors to Western capital, particularly the multinational companies. Some have become prosperous by mobilising indigenous sources of capital, some by producing goods and services on a modest scale but with considerable independence from Western capital, except perhaps in technology. These factions are not equally dependent on Western capital, and the relations of the interests of each faction to the interests of Western capital varies. The relationship of the African bourgeoisie to Western capital depends to some extent on which of these factions becomes hegemonic in a particular country. It is conceivable that the struggle for hegemony will bring to the top factions which will be inclined and able to effect a more radical realignment of social forces and change fundamentally the existing economic system.

The contradictions between the capitalist class on the one hand and African workers and peasants on the other is another source of change in African economies. As capitalism becomes indigenised and develops, the contradictions between capital and these other classes have grown deeper, all the more so because of the very poor performance of African economies since independence. Because of the intense politicisation of African society during the nationalist struggle, the development of these contradictions has been quite out of proportion to the development of productive forces. The revolutionary pressures from below arising from this situation have significant implications for political and economic change in Africa. But to avoid repetition, we will refrain from discussing the likely effects of these revolutionary pressures at this point.

This concludes our brief survey of the relation between the main structural features of African economies. In the course of this survey we have tried to determine the potential for change in the economic system inherent in these structures and in their relationships. We have seen that the potential for change is very limited and that the more general tendency is towards inertia. This is of course a very incomplete picture. Because we were looking at structures we have not adequately taken account of human volition, which is after all a critical engine of change. We cannot get a clear and accurate picture of the prospects for change in African economies until we have taken full account of the volitional element. That is not to say that preceding discussion of structural features was misleading or misguided. It was a necessary and useful exercise. The structural characteristics of African economies is an important aspect of the realities which define what kind of change is possible and how much. We cannot merely focus on what people would like to do, we must also try to understand the circumstances that determine what human will and effort can achieve. Will always has to be balanced against possibility. We now turn to the volitional element, namely how African leaders wish their economies to change, what they are doing about bringing such changes into being, and how far they are able to effect change.

The desire for development

One important impulse for change in African economies is the desire of African leaders, apparently shared by their followers, for development. The desire for development might be described with equal accuracy as a passion or an ideology. The informal and formal pronouncements of African leaders give one the impression of an unshakeable commitment to the idea that they must try to achieve development, perceived as the primary condition for their own welfare, the legitimation of their leadership and the well-being of their countries. They are convinced that there is a link between the underdevelopment of their countries and the most fundamental problems which plague their states, such as poverty, the high incidence of disease, unemployment, military weakness, ignorance, technological backwardness, cultural deprivation, short life-expectancy, social disorganisation, and the high incidence of political instability. They see development of their economies as the necessary condition for dealing decisively with these problems. That is how development has come to be an obsession in Africa, even though few are clear what development is.

As suggested earlier in this work, development is also an ideology. It is an ideology in so far as African leaders tend to visualise progress towards a better society in terms of development, see their historical evolution in terms of the possibility of achieving development, and base the possibility of the good life on the primary necessity of overcoming underdevelopment.

Development has become such an obsession that it is easy to forget that the idea of development is relatively recent. In Africa the idea really started coming into vogue after the early 1960s when many African countries had become independent. The colonial governments were not much interested in development and did not talk very much about it. They were interested in keeping order and maintaining the political and economic conditions for the exploitation of the colony. During the period of nationalist agitation for independence the African leaders did not talk much of development either. With few exceptions they were immersed in a bourgeois revolution. They wanted to inherit a system rather than to revolutionise it, and their platform was remarkably silent about what they would do with power, and even more so on what they intended to do about changing the inherited economic system. But somehow by the late 1960s the idea of development had been elavated to the level of ideology in virtually every African country. And it would appear that this change occurred on account of the initiative of the Western world to redefine its relationship with the former colonies in the light of new realities. First, the categories developed and underdeveloped countries were used in the place of the old classification of metropolitan countries and colonies. Instead of the old partnership of the colonial days expressed in the 'Dual Mandate', a new partnership in development was proposed. And this was propagated intensely in the United Nations, through its agencies and in the launching of successive development decades. The interest of the Western world in all this lies in the fact that the fundamental concept in this ideology of development was generally some variety or permutation of the notions of Westernisation, industrialisation or capitalist economic growth. Thus wanting development became virtually the same thing as wanting to be like the West.

It is this Western notion of development which prevails in Africa today. At the same time there is some evidence of considerable uneasiness with the notion among African leaders. Some of them can see its Western affiliation and the implications of this acceptance for the perpetuation of the domination of the West; some can sense that it cannot take them very far on the road to achieving development, much less a good society. But somehow even the sceptical have found it difficult to do away with the notion of development. Nowadays many of them, including people with substantially different philosophies such as Julius Nyerere of Tanzania and the late Jomo Kenyatta of Kenya, have said repeatedly that they intend to reject the Western idea of development and instead evolve an original idea of development which will do justice to the uniqueness of their historical experience. Nevertheless analysis of their development policies and development plans shows that they lean heavily on the Western idea. When one goes beyond the ritual equivocations, development for them comes down to Western-style industrialisation and the problems of development can be reduced to mobilising more capital, improving technical know-how, increasing the productivity of labour and stimulating entrepreneural drive. A typical example of the operational meaning of development is to be seen in the development plan of Lesotho for the period 1974/80. The plan's objectives are to increase GDP, encourage new productive investment in industry, increase national motivation to achievement, crop production, private investment, employment, the Africanisation of positions, and the diversification of the sources of foreign finance. Operationalised in this way, the plan fosters the continuation of capitalist development, the confusion of development with economic growth, and indifference to the causes of economic backwardness which are rooted in the integration of their economy into the Western capitalist system. The example of Somalia's development plan 1971/73 is more interesting, coming as it does from a country which had loudly renounced its colonial past and proclaimed itself socialist. The plan claims to reflect 'The Somali People's aspirations for a just and forward looking society based on the principles of socialism'. Accordingly, it seeks to establish 'new trends in economic organisation and function'. When we read on to find what these are, we discover to our surprise that we are once more confronting the Western notion of development. Here is the plan's enumeration of the major elements of the new trend.

1   Determined effort to rationalise government finances by increasing revenues and reducing government expenditure;
2   Tightening up government administration in order to assure the smooth implementation of development projects;
3   Mobilising the self-help potential of the people by government participation in development projects based on self-help;
4   Transforming the productive potential of the unemployed into economically useful activities;
5   Broadening the base of the socialised sector of the economy in the fields of agriculture, industry and banking in order to enable the public sector to dominate the commanding heights of the economy;
6   Initiating processes to correct lacunae in legal requirements essential for supporting economic development.

These are hardly bold new departures or the way to build socialism. There is nothing here that is incompatible with the Western idea of development. From the point of view of our present concern, which is the implications of the quest for development as an impulse for change in African economies, the significance of the acceptance of the Western notion of development is that it limits the effect of this impulse to the promotion of marginal change. The Western notion of development does not encourage attention to the revolutionising of existing social relations of production as a likely or even possible stimulant to development. It does not encourage the disengagement of African economies from the exploitative structural links with Western capitalist economies. It encourages the perception of the process of development as the gradual solution of limited and technical problems within the context of the existing order. That is the sense in which the notion of development under review limits the scale of change of African economies. But this is all rather theoretical and hypothetical. Let us now take a look at what African countries are actually doing about promoting development in order to improve our understanding of how far African economies can change and in what direction.

Strategies for development in Africa

It is quite hazardous to talk of development strategies in Africa, not because there is anything inherently problematic about the concept in the African context, but because it is not in the least clear that many African

143

countries have a strategy which is identifiable. They have goals of economic development and sometimes these goals are clear enough; they have policies which are sometimes clearly articulated and operationalised. But it is difficult to encounter anything that can properly be called strategy. This is in itself an important cause of their ineffectiveness in changing their economy in the way they would like to. It will be interesting to go into an explanation of why strategies of development seem so elusive in Africa. However, that will take us too far beyond the concerns of this study. But a few general comments are in order. Part of the problem is that some African leaders assume that once one is committed to the goal of achieving development or liquidating underdevelopment it is fairly clear what to do. This state of mind carried too far leads to fuzziness in strategy, and is reinforced, too, by political sensitivity if not caused by it in the first place, for many African leaders are very impatient with disagreement and ideological debate on the plea that the problems of their countries, and what to do about them, are quite clear.

A second aspect of the problem is a tendency to focus on one or two problems in vogue, such as indigenisation, and allow the elaboration of the character of this problem and the policies and procedures for dealing with it to assume the status of a development strategy in the absence of a real strategy. A third aspect is the tendency to forget that goals which are individually desirable may not necessarily be collectively compatible. More often than not development is thought of in terms of discrete and substantive goals, and when each of these goals is treated systematically it is readily assumed that they constitute a master plan for dealing with the problems of society. This tendency is obvious in the development plans of African countries. More often than not, the plan is really not a strategy for development but an aggregation of projects and policies, which may sometimes be incompatible. One must hasten to add that, from the point of view of our present purpose here, this lack of clarity in regard to development strategy is not in itself a serious problem. It would be if we were interested in the achievement of development. But as it is, we are only interested in the possibilities of change from the present state of African economies. From this point of view this lack of clarity in development strategy is an uncomplicated fact whose significance is quite clear. It indicates that African aspirations are not likely to be realised, and that their economies are not likely to undergo rapid and profound changes. Having said all this, we must now be more specific and return to a consideration of the implications of some of the things which pass for strategy in Africa.

In the last two decades in Africa several ideas of the overall thrust of development have been in vogue at various times – these include expansion and diversification of agricultural export commodities, import substitution, export promotion, integrated rural development and a basic needs approach. These strategies were not necessarily spelled out clearly, nor were they always pursued systematically. More often than not they were one feature, albeit a prominent feature in a mixed bag of approaches. Nevertheless, it is instructive to look at them briefly. We wish to get some impression of how they were practised if at all, and their real or likely effect on the transformation of African economies.

1 Increase and diversification of export commodities

One development strategy which was popular during the earlier years of independence, and which continues to recur in development plans, is the expansion and diversification of agricultural export commodities. The appeal of this strategy comes mainly from two sources. First, it was a 'realistic option' – some would argue one of the few realistic options available in the immediate postcolonial era – in that it involved directing the development effort along the line of least resistance. Under colonialism African economies had been geared to the production of agricultural commodities. They relied on this pattern of production for sustaining the population, for government revenue and for foreign exchange earnings. Under pressure to earn foreign exchange for development projects, African countries were tempted to turn to the expansion of output of agricultural export commodities. Also the expansion of agricultural export commodities seemed a viable point of departure for dealing with the problems of disarticulation, narrow resource base and industrialisation. The other source of appeal of this strategy was the international economic situation, notably the unfavourable terms of trade for primary producers caused by the rise in the prices of manufactured products relative to primary commodities. This development put a severe constraint on the availability of foreign exchange and the availability of capital for development projects.

We know that this strategy met with only very modest success. To begin with, the developed market economies were very reluctant to allow free access to the commodities of agricultural producers in Africa. This reluctance has been gradually overcome over the years, as is evident from the Lomé conventions between the African-Caribbean-Pacific group of countries and the European Economic Community. Though the problem of access contributed to the frustration of the strategy, it is doubtful that an immediate and liberal response by the industralised countries would have made much difference. The experience of the 18 African countries which have enjoyed over ten years' of association with the EEC is indicative here. The products of the countries which received preferential treatment in the EEC did not expand their market share; rather their share of the EEC market shrank.

Access to Western markets was certainly not the only cause of the failure of strategy under review. There was also the problem of demand, which arose in part from the shift in the consumption patterns of developed countries towards a preference for consumer durables, from the availability of synthetic substitutes, and from the slow rate of increase of population in the developed countries.

The strategy also suffered from the fall in export earnings caused by international economic forces which could not be counteracted by attempted stabilisation schemes. The slow response of agricultural products to changes in demand, and the differences in the elasticity of the supply of tree crops and annual crops relative to the changes in export demand, contributed to the failure of the strategy.

But even without these difficulties, the strategy would still have been a failure from the point of view of the most fundamental objectives of the development effort as stated by African leaders. Indeed the success of the strategy would have strengthened the existing international division of labour and helped to stabilise Africa in her role of primary producer. That apart, the strategy had great potential for perpetuating the exploitative dependence of African economies on the metropolitan economies. It encourages a perspective of development which links the prospects of development to the nature of the vertical links between the African economies and those of the metropolitan countries. And it sees the solution to the problem in terms of export gaps, export earnings stabilisation arrangements, and access to the markets of industrialised countries, and discourages attention being paid to the self-reliant evaluation and exploitation of local resources and local capabilities. This type of perspective on the problem of development fosters dependence, disarticulation and ultimately the limitation of Africa's resource base.

2 Import substitution

Import substitution was a very popular approach to development in Africa in the late 1950s. This was due perhaps to the decline in the demand and earnings of primary products at this time. With the fall of demand for primary products came a fall in foreign exchange earnings. The curtailment of foreign imports and the production of local substitutes seemed a natural and sensible reaction to this situation.

But development by import substitution was not simply something which arose out of sheer necessity. The necessity was complemented by popular arguments about the desirability of import substitution. First, it was argued that in the course of foreign trade the underdeveloped country had already established a market, although this market was currently supplied by foreign entrepreneurs. By import substitution the country could, by supplying the market from local sources, save foreign exchange and promote domestic industrialisation. Second, import substitution was held to be necessary to correct the differences in the income elasticities for imports and exports. Third, import substitution was said to have some potential for decreasing underemployment. Fourth, import substitution was credited with the ability of making more goods available than foreign exchange constraints would normally allow in the absence of import substitution. Fifth, it was said to aid industrialisation and the diversification of the economy. These were some of the considerations which seduced Africa into industrialisation based on import substitution. To encourage import substitution, African governments gave all sorts of incentives to indigenous and foreign capital, such as tax holidays for a certain number of years for pioneer industries, tariff protection, accelerated depreciation allowances, import duty relief for imported inputs industries, the provision of industrial estates, and the provision of equity capital and debentures.

The drive for import substitution-led industrialisation was rather disappointing. To begin with, even on the level of economics there was perhaps not enough critical understanding of the limitations of import substitution as a means of generating development. First, a concerted effort to achieve import substitution means in effect rapid industrialisation. It will create a demand for imported inputs and for capital goods, and probably lead to balance of payments problems. Import substitution may have inflationary effects on price levels as the newly produced goods are likely to be more expensive, producers not yet having maximised from economies of scale, and since they are likely to depend on protective tariff barriers. Import substitution may also create inefficient monopoly enterprises.

But of course we cannot decide this type of issue on the strength of theoretical arguments, for so much depends on how the tendencies mentioned in these theoretical arguments are concretised and mediated in particular historical circumstances. The evidence is available. We know from the extensive research of organisations such as the United Nations Economic Commission for Africa and from the admission of African governments themselves that the pursuit of import substitution-led industrialisation has not been very rewarding. (See, for instance, the UN Economic Commission for Africa's *Survey of Economic and Social Conditions in Africa for 1976 and 1977*.) In particular the evidence is that the policy of import substitution has had at best a marginal effect on the promotion of industrialisation, on diversification, and on the reduction of dependence, the major changes that African leaders wanted to effect with it.

The Nigerian experience is typical of the African experience of import substitution efforts in Africa. In a careful study of this process in Nigeria, Peter Kilby concludes as follows: 'Because the industrial surveys do not distinguish imported input purchases and so do not show profits, it is impossible to determine whether Nigeria's import substitution has resulted in a saving or organisation of the foreign exchange requirements per unit of consumption. On the basis of the specific evidence presented . . . and upon the general importance of (a) foreign investment – approximately two-thirds of the total, (b) foreign managers and technicians – accounting for 30% of total labour costs, and (c) substantial import requirements of capital equipment and intermediate inputs, one is inclined to estimate that import substitution has resulted in a slight increase in imports per unit of consumption' (*Industrialisation in an Open Economy: Nigeria 1945–1966*).

We have already seen in an earlier discussion that Nigeria has made very little progress in industrialisation and the diversification of her economy. We have seen from our passing glimpse of the structure of industrialisation in Nigeria that she has been confined to low technology input and highly elementary processing. In so far as import substitution was taken as a major tool of industrialisation and diversification in Nigeria, the evidence shows that it has not been a success. Let us briefly move beyond these generalities and see some of the ways in which import substitution failed.

In the period of independence when the policy of import substitution was launched, the Nigerian economy was dominated by a relatively small number of merchant companies particularly Société Commerciale de l'Ouest Africain, John Holt, Compagnie Française de l'Afrique Occidentale, The Union Trading Company, The United Africa Company and Peterson Zochonis. These enterprises made the Nigerian economy highly monopolistic because of the immense capital requirements of the international merchandise trade, government-initiated import quota rationing, cartel arrangements, and the wide range of products they catered for. These were precisely the enterprises that were in a position to mobilise the capital, know-how and contacts to spearhead the policy of import substitution. However, their contribution was greatly limited by their conservatism arising from their privileged position. The companies often had financial investments in the home countries from which they imported and did not wish to encourage the development of manufacturing in Africa to harm these interests. In addition to this, the import trade made their export trade more profitable by reducing overheads. So these companies were not very enthusiastic about import substitution, and when they tried it they went about it very timidly and selectively, always mindful of their merchant interests. Peter Kilby's study contains an interesting analysis of the investments of the biggest of the Nigerian merchant companies, the United Africa Company, between 1948 and 1965. His analysis shows that all but one of 28 projects in which the United Africa Company invested were projects connected with marketing activities. According to him 'as a rule of thumb, UAC will only consider an industrial investment if it represents the protection of an established merchant interest, which is both sizeable and profitable. Production-wise the industry must be within the competence of the company, the Unilever organisation, or a principal supplier who can be persuaded to join the venture as a technical partner'. These types of constraints did not allow the merchant companies to contribute very much to the achievement of the goals which import substitution was supposed to achieve.

This is one aspect of the divergence of the interests of African governments and those of foreign capital in regard to import substitution. There was also a conflict of interests between African governments and overseas suppliers. These overseas suppliers had considerable potential for aiding import substitution, but once more their own interests got in the way. They undertook some production in Africa instead of exportation, but only in order to protect the market they already had, and in the course of this they carried their rivalries to Africa to the detriment of the aims of import substitution. One example which rapidly comes to mind is the rivalry between two exporters to Nigeria of asbestos cement products, who between them accounted for 95% of the import of Nigeria. These were Turner and Newall of Britain and Eternit of Belgium. As soon as Eternit formed a partnership with the Western Nigerian Development Corporation to build a plant in Nigeria in 1960, Turner and Newall immediately embarked on a similar project even though it was quite clear that the market could only support one of these plants. Similarly, rival overseas exporters of paint to Nigeria built five paint production plants in one year because they were struggling to protect their market. There is also the example of Michelin and Dunlop who between them supplied about 80% of Nigeria's tyre imports. Each of them established a tyre manufacturing plant within a year of each other, even though it was clear that the market could only support one such plant. The tendency for overseas suppliers to respond to the pressure for import substitution by market protection investment helped to frustrate the achievement of the goals for which the African leadership undertook import substitution in the first place. It limited the potential of import substitution for achieving diversification and even independence. It caused inefficiency and waste, especially as the enterprises were able to obtain from government very high protective tariffs inflated by the cut-throat competition.

African governments were realistic about the contribution which foreign capital could make towards the achievement of the goals which they wanted to realise through import substitution. That was why some of them decided to go into business alone or in partnership in order to promote their goals. It is familiar knowledge now that the performance of the parastatals in Africa has been dismal. Much of the responsibility for running them was given to civil servants who knew little or nothing about business and who were quickly taken advantage of by foreign business managers and partners of the government. There was also the problem of the politicisation of these investments. In the location of industries, and even in their selection, political considerations were often put above economic rationality. Important positions and subcontracts were given as political patronage, often to people lacking the ability to play these roles. Finally there was the problem of corruption, caused especially by the promotional activities of unscrupulous firms, some of whom encouraged useless industrial ventures in order to sell plant and machinery. These useless industries were often promoted in collusion with local politicians. Examples of such useless ventures are the glass factories at Port Harcourt and Ughelli. Such ventures invariably cost money and worsened the country's balance of payments problems. They were often tied to exploitative management agreements which not only threatened their economic viability but also their ability to promote self-reliance. These were some of the circumstances which led to the failure of the 'strategy' of import substitution.

3   Export promotion

The desirability of export promotion is another approach to development which has enjoyed considerable popularity in Africa, although this popularity does not appear to have been justified by the practical commitment to it or by its effects in solving the problems it was supposed to solve. These are the same problems which import substitution was supposed to solve, namely industrialisation, self-reliance, a better balance of trade, savings in foreign exchange and the diversification of the economy.

Export promotion clearly has some advantages over import substitution. Unlike import substitution it is not limited by the size of the domestic market. It is less prone to lead to subsidisation of inefficient production and it tends to require less imported intermediate inputs. But it also has some notable disadvantages. It is limited by the external demand, a limitation which is all the more serious because it is difficult for developing countries to remain competitive in manufacturing. It offers a less flexible and perhaps more limited scope for the expansion of linkages. For instance, in the case of import substitution a start can be made from a little value added through finishing touches such as the assembling of automobiles and the manufacture of a few simple accessories such as tyres. But again these points are mentioned just to put the discussion in clearer perspective. Nothing rests on the pros and cons of these theoretical arguments. What is really of interest is how the policies of export promotion in Africa fared in encouraging industrialisation, diversification, self-reliance and better terms of trade. Here again we may say that the evidence is available. It is oblique and circumstantial but it will do. From the numerous data about the performance of African economies available in government publications such as Development Plans, as well as in publications from agencies such as the World Bank and the United Nations Economic Commission for Africa, it is clear that on the whole the export promotion strategy has not worked well. With the exception of a few countries such as the United Arab Republic, African countries are not yet in a position of exporting significant quantities of manufactured goods. Table 6.1, based on information from the United Nations Economic Commission for Africa, sheds light on the situation.

TABLE 6.1 Exports from developing Africa, 1970–75 (in millions of US dollars)

	1970	1971	1972	1973	1974	1975
Foodstuffs	2,853	2,672	3,053	4,196	5,342	5,484
Drink and tobacco	240	219	300	437	520	510
Raw materials	2,287	2,385	2,568	3,293	4,723	4,823
Fuels and lubricants	4,074	4,971	6,132	9,069	22,653	19,821
Vegetable oils	206	211	327	331	471	626
Chemicals	89	108	127	178	247	252
Manufactured goods	2,261	1,849	1,970	2,542	3,694	2,765
Machinery and transport equipment	254	278	375	505	575	578
Misc. manufactures	107	118	146	198	250	251
Others	29	52	50	86	121	120
Total	12,400	12,863	15,048	20,835	38,596	35,229

Source
ECA, *Survey of Economic and Social Conditions in Africa, 1976*, part I, p. 97

According to the ECA, manufactured products made up 12.3% of all exports of independent Africa in 1974, and 10.9% in 1975. Africa remains the weakest region in the developing world in terms of manufacturing output. In 1972 its share of manufacturing ouput of the developing world was a mere 8.1% compared to 54.6% for Latin America and 37.3% for Asia.

In order to understand the significance of this it is necessary to bear the following comments in mind. According to the Economic Commission for Africa, the price index of manufactures exported by developed countries increased from 100 in 1970 to 105 in 1971, 113 in 1973, 162 in 1974 and 182 in 1975. Applying these index numbers to the numbers of exports in value, it will be seen in Table 6.1 that the value of manufactured exports in four categories from developing Africa increased only marginally between the three years 1970–72 and the three years 1973–75. The ECA goes on to say that manufactured products made up 12.8% of all exports in 1974 and 10.9% in 1975.

It is instructive to look at some of the causes of the poor results of the pursuit of export promotion in Africa. To begin with there was the usual problem of breaking into a highly competitive international market.

The disabilities imposed by the underdeveloped state of African economies – the high capital-output ratio, the rudimentary development of infrastructures, the limited opportunities for linkages and economies of scale, etc. – made it difficult for the policy of export promotion to succeed. To make up for their uncompetitive production conditions, African countries are often obliged to make unrealistic claims on the generosity of the countries whose market they wish to break into or to resort to very burdensome subsidies to their own manufactures. These were hardly the conditions conducive to the expansion of exports. The international atmosphere has not been helpful to the African quest for export promotion. To begin with, there is the shift of demand in industrialised countries from cheap primary semi-processed goods to high quality goods. The disparity in the rate of increase of the prices of manufactured goods relative to primary goods, debt servicing, etc. created serious balance of payments problems for African countries. This pushed them to take drastic steps to restrict imports. This protectionism was unfortunately unfavourable to export promotion (although it favours import substitution). In some cases the policies necessary to support export promotion have not been properly worked out and applied efficiently, with the result that they have failed to achieve the purpose for which they were intended. In particular, the mix of restrictions on imports and subsidies for export production intended to aid export promotion sometimes distorted the relative magnitudes of profit in domestic and home markets, encouraging exports to be diverted into home markets. Export promotion has also been frustrated by the necessity of relying too much on imported inputs. Many African countries really had very little option but to start with the kinds of export promotion which meant the increase of value added to semi-finished goods imported from abroad, for instance in the case of automobile assembly. But it proved difficult to move on from assembly and the addition of a few accessories and finishing touches. The requirements for this marginal value added in terms of skill, etc. were quite different from that needed to go into the production of components in a serious and comprehensive way. Besides, the breakthrough into substantial manufacturing would require the overcoming of great bottlenecks of manpower, as well as the provision of chemical and base metal industries. The anticipated gradual and painless move from assembly and a few finishing touches to manufacturing has proved quite elusive.

Finally and most importantly is the problem of entry to the markets of the industrialised countries. The developed countries have been very reluctant to allow Africa and other underdeveloped countries access to their markets. They themselves are already having difficulties marketing their own products to each other. These difficulties of marketing their products to each other are causing considerable tension in their relationships. They have tried to deal with this by urging self-imposed restraint in production, and encouraging countries such as Japan to absorb more imports to reduce the balance of payments problems of their partners, such as the USA. The availability of large quantities of manufactured goods seeking markets has led to increasing concern about the outburst of protectionism among the industrialised countries. Their problems have been compounded by the influx of goods from fairly competitive developing areas such as Korea, Taiwan, Hong Kong and India. It is to these Western countries already so hard-pressed that African countries expect to liberalise the entry of African manufactured goods. Although such expectations seem so unrealistic, there has nevertheless been an effort to mobilise international opinion and an effort to encourage it. Examples of such efforts are the Lima Declaration and the Programme of Action adopted at the Second Conference of UNIDO in March 1975. Sometimes matters have gone beyond intentions into some arrangements between the industrialised and African countries in respect of access to the markets of the former countries, for instance the Yaoundé Conventions and more recently Lomé I and II.

But all that has not helped much. It is doubtful whether the efforts that have gone into the Lomé Conventions between the EEC countries and the 58 ACP (African, Caribbean and Pacific) countries were a good investment. By the conventions the EEC countries have promised free entry to virtually all the products of the ACP countries. However, this is hedged with qualifications and of course there is the mechanism of covert protectionism. In any case such concessions seem somewhat irrelevant in the face of the difficulties that the developing countries are experiencing to make their manufactured goods competitive. More worrying is the effect of some of the arrangements in the Lomé conventions supposedly designed to promote industrialisation and the export of manufactures in the ACP countries. In particular, under Lomé I industrialisation, diversification and economic integration are to be encouraged by a system of linking small firms to medium sized firms and to large firms. This complex network is then tied to patron Community firms for the purposes of financing, technology and management inputs, etc. As one United Nations document (E/CN.14/ECO/90/Rev.3, of June 1976) rightly commented: 'It is possible to interpret this pattern as one which will have the effect of tightening vertical relations between the ACP States and the Community far more efficiently and far more extensively than at any time in the past. The results may well be to extend the number, variety and scope of enclaves and the strengthening of the position of foreign transactions in the economies of the ACP countries.'

4   The unified approach

The unified approach to development was really an outcome of the disappointment with the conventional approaches to development described above. The actual event which immediately occasioned it was resolution 1494 (XLVIII) of the Economic and Social Council of the UN and resolution 2681 (XXV) of the General Assembly. These resolutions pointed to the need for an approach to development planning which would integrate the economic and social components in the formulation of policies and programmes at the national and international levels. The broad objectives of the unified approach were stated as follows:

1   To leave no sector of the population outside the scope of change and development;
2   To effect structural change which favours national development and to activate all sectors of the population to participate in the development process;

3　To aim at social equity, including the achievement of an equitable distribution of income and wealth in the nation;

4　To give high priority to the development of human potential.

Following the resolutions, a unified approach was subsequently elaborated in a report prepared by the United Nations Research Institute for Development (E/CN.5/519, December 1974). As a follow up to this another document was also prepared jointly by the United Nations Economic Commission for Africa and the United Nations Research Institute for Social Development. The document, presented to the Conference of African Planners in Addis Ababa in October 1976, was called *Applications of a Unified Approach to Development Planning Under African Conditions* (E/CN.14/CAP.6/4). This paper defined the unified approach as follows: 'We define Unified Approach for this study as a systematic attempt to deal with the problem of uneven growth and involve the total economy and society in development. The Unified Approach is not a matter of an emphasis in allocative planning upon the social services as distinguished from economic growth; it is an emphasis upon the general style of development affecting the various aspects of development and their interrelationships, including participation, cross-sectoral, and spatial aspects. Development is viewed as involving various kinds of structural and institutional change and social and individual transformations which build up the capacity of the society and of its members to realise higher levels of production and welfare.'

Under the unified approach development is 'conceived not as the increase of an aggregate quantity like GNP but as growth and change of a pattern or complex of social and economic factors. It implies observed progress towards a set of goals or values; but it also implies the objective changes taking place which underlie the observed progress'. Development strategy of a unified approach would aim primarily at 'changing the existing style of development into a more desirable style as judged in terms of cross-sectoral linkages, spread effects, participation, distribution, and like criteria'. The use of a unified approach entails preoccupation with 'questions of kind or composition within the different fields of developmental activity; the *kind* of industrial growth, the *kind* of agricultural growth, the *kind* of imports, the *kind* of technology, the *kind* of educational development, the *kind* of health programme, etc.'

The unified approach encourages planners to think in terms of what is called capacitating operations, 'which do not try so much to define and control the future as to establish present conditions or capacities which will permit a given society to meet its problems in the future'. 'An example of such a "capacitation" activity would be the undertaking of structural or institutional change, which conventional planning does not readily deal with; through its technical methods various structural and institutional conditions tend to be taken as given in planning procedures. . . . social transformations such as the abolition of class constraints on mobility also fall outside the scope of orthodox planning techniques.'

The thrust of the unified approach towards mass need and mass participation and institutional change gives it great potential for changing African economies in a fundamental way. But these aspects of the approach which make it so useful, unique and progressive are also the factors which make the unified approach little more than a statement of intentions. Examinations of development plans and development policies of African countries reveal that the unified approach has had little or no influence on public policy. In the development plans of the more progressive countries such as Guinea-Bissau, Angola and Mozambique, there are policies which take types of stances that the unified approach recommends. But the plans of most African socio-economic formations display no awareness of this approach, except the occasional cliché about the determination of the government to reduce inequality and to make resources serve basic needs and so on – declarations of intention which are soon contradicted by substantive policies.

The economists and the United Nations agencies who are promoting the unified approach appear to be fully aware of the problems of making it acceptable as a strategy of development in Africa. For instance the report of the United Nations Institute for Social Development (E/CN.5/519 of 5 December 1974), elaborating the unified approach had this to say: 'The basic decisions on development policies are largely political decisions, and political ideologies and derived policies are often cited as reasons for uneven patterns of development in various developing countries. Where political regimes reflect power structures based on wealth and inequality, these regimes will not be inclined to legislate out of existence the base of power. Some regimes have sought to build up an urban middle-class as a major instrument of development, to the neglect of the rural poor, while others have concentrated on promoting the interests of landed wealth. Political leadership that is oriented towards unified development goals may have limited options if it is to remain in power, and very often has limited effectiveness in executing the policies it does adopt. . . . The idea of "unified development", with its structural and distributional implications, presents many more difficulties of a political nature than does the idea of development as growth of the national product-growth measured in aggregative terms that conceal distribution and differentiation.'

What is being talked about here in the characteristically 'clean' vocabulary of United Nations documents are class contradictions and revolutionary change and their relation to the liquidation of underdevelopment. The passage poses the classic dilemma of the quest for development in Africa. When the quest is made within the constraints of the existing relations of production it tends to lead nowhere. But it cannot be expected to transcend these constraints because those who have the power to make the critical decisions are also those who stand to lose by carrying the quest for development to the point of breaking the existing barriers of the existing relations of production.

5   Integrated rural development

This approach to development appears to be better known among politicians and policy-makers than the unified approach, and it might have had marginally more influence on economic policies and development plans as well. The application of integrated rural development to Africa was elaborated in a United Nations publication,

Integrated approach to Rural Development in Africa (E/CN.14/SWSA/8). It was also elaborated in great detail at the African Regional Conference on the Integrated Approach to Rural Development, held at Moshi in Tanzania in October 1969. First, what is integrated rural development? As the phrase suggests, it involves the focusing of development effort on the transformation of rural society in Africa. The focus on rural life is justified by the fact that about 75% of Africa's population live in the rural areas, and also by the fact that agriculture is the mainstay of Africa's economy. It assumes that the focusing of development on rural society is necessary to ensure the maximum benefit to the most people as well as the growth of the entire economy.

'The word integrated in the phrase suggests that "all aspects of development are co-ordinated and flow together to form an unbroken whole. In some respects this type of development is analogous to assembly line production, where all the parts and sub-assemblies must arrive at the right place at the right time if the production of the finished product is to be facilitated". The need for an integrated approach is demanded by the conditions of rural society which do not favour conventional planning methods. For instance the rural population is dispersed over a wide area in relatively isolated pockets; these dispersed populations have to be integrated to some extent so that certain minimal infrastructures necessary for promoting development can be viable. To increase productivity in the rural areas it is necessary to upgrade health services, improve tools and techniques of production, combat some superstitious attitudes, etc. In short, the nature of the process of rural development and the magnitude of the problem of promoting economic and social progress in rural areas requires that inter-related action be taken on several fronts simultaneously. Thus, programmes for the promotion of agriculture, education and training, health and nutrition, community development and the like must be planned and executed in a co-ordinated fashion with account being taken of the effect that development programmes in one area are likely to have on other areas.' (E/CN.14/CAP.6/2).

The general meaning of integrated rural development is clear enough, but unfortunately the concept lends itself to a wide range of operational definitions. Almost any system of welfare measures undertaken in the rural areas can be called integrated rural development, and any system of extension services or agricultural improvement programmes, especially when they are tied to the improvement of some social amenities, can be called integrated rural development. In several African countries all sorts of projects of rural development are called integrated rural development, although they are widely different. The manifesto of one of the leading political parties in the Nigerian elections of 1979 had a proposal for integrated rural development which is effectively a programme for the capitalisation of agriculture. The only feature that all the agricultural development schemes which go by the name of integrated rural development in Africa appear to have in common is their focus on the rural areas.

It is perhaps the vagueness of the concept of integrated rural development and its suggestion of a progressive bent which accounts for its popularity among African policy-makers. It is clearly progressive to focus development in the rural areas where most of the population lives and where the most elementary necessities are lacking. But having taken advantage of the suggestion of being 'progressive' by using the concept of integrated rural development for political legitimation, the idea is trivialised by the types of programme designated as integrated rural development schemes. So in a sense the idea of integrated rural development becomes something of an ideology which at once confers legitimacy and conserves the system, by acknowledging the need for change while promoting only marginal change. Since the point of this review of development strategies is to determine the magnitude and direction of change of African economies it should be stressed that the implications of the ideological character of integrated rural development is that it is not likely to inspire fundamental change in African economies.

Having said this, the following qualification should be made. The point about African leaders taking advantage of the progressive implications of the idea of integrated rural development, while trivialising the idea in practice, is more true of some leaders than others. To obtain a clearer idea of the implications of integrated rural development for the possibility of change in Africa it is necessary to take note of the nature of some integrated rural development programmes in Africa.

Tanzania

Tanzania is one of a handful of progressive countries who have taken the idea of integrated rural development fairly seriously. She took it seriously in the sense of really making an effort to give attention to the development of rural Tanzania, and to introduce into the countryside changes that were fundamental and comprehensive and which if successful would have meant a significant improvement in the welfare of rural people. For the most part these changes were not made in the name of integrated rural development but rather in the name of the promotion of socialism and self-reliance. But it does not really matter. The important thing is that the substantive changes ran along the lines that exponents of integrated rural development were suggesting. The cornerstone of this policy was the promotion of the Ujamaa villages, a policy to which the government of Tanzania became committed in 1967. In his speech on the occasion of the tenth anniversary of Tanzania's independence, the President of Tanzania, Julius Nyerere characterised Ujamaa villages as follows.

'For these are or will be the cooperative farms which are under the direct control of the producers, who will themselves decide what to grow, how much, and so on. Further, these are not just economic units; an Ujamaa village is, or will become, an economic, a social and a political unit. Its people will not only produce their crops together, so that they talk of "our shamba" [Swahili word meaning farm] and "our output"; they will also run their own affairs, supervise their own schools, organise the improvement in their own living conditions and become a community for all purposes.'

Steps taken to implement this idea included the consolidation of the rural population of Tanzania into bigger villages – called the villagisation programme. By June 1971 there were already 2,700 Ujamaa villages in existence with a total population of about 840,000 people. By 1974 about 20% of the rural population of Tanzania was living in Ujamaa villages. Effort was made to support the villages with extension services, infrastructures such as water, agricultural equipment, field personnel and credit. The point of all this was simultanously to improve the productivity of rural labour, and the quality of life in rural society.

The results of the villagisation policy have been rather ambiguous. The consolidation of the rural population into villages was often hastily and crudely done by overzealous officials, with the result that it caused considerable alienation. The expectations of an increase in productivity have not materialised. The growth of agricultural production in the years 1968–73 was only 2.4%, somewhat below the population growth rate of 2.7%. In the 5 years 1963–68 the annual growth rate of agricultural production was 3.9%. But it is easy to exaggerate the failure of the villagisation programme. What might have registered as failure was the fact that the government put emphasis on greater equality in income and social conditions. All the same the Tanzanian government has had to retreat from the Ujamaa idea. The idea of collective farms is being replaced by cooperative farming in which individual plot ownership is permitted.

The Tanzanian experiment in integrated rural development is interesting. It shows the possibilities of the idea for bringing fundamental and beneficial change if taken at all seriously. But at the same time it shows the force of the contradictions which make it so difficult for African economies to change in fundamental ways. In spite of being quite progressive, the political class in Tanzania could not quite make the leap to the types of commitment which would have made integrated rural development a truly effective assault on the underdevelopment which it was supposed to overcome. The political class was not quite prepared to give enough to rural development. In 1969/70, 36% of development expenditure went to agriculture. This is very high by African standards but it is still far from the radical reallocation of resources between the agricultural and other sectors which is required. Even then the share of agriculture fell to 33% in 1970/71, 29% in 1971/72 and to 27% in 1972/73, according to estimates of the United Nations Economics Commission for Africa.

In an excellent analysis of Tanzania's policy of 'Ujamaa Uijijini' (Socialism and Rural Development), Mapolu and Phillipson, writing in *Africa Development* (Vol. 1, No. 1, 1976), have shown how class contradictions marred the policy's good intentions. They note an unfortunate 'trend away from participation and initiative at grass-roots level and the ever greater concentration of power in the hands of the bureaucracy', despite the fact that official policy puts considerable emphasis on peasant initiatives in the formation and management of Ujamaa villages. According to Mapolu and Phillipson, the authoritarianism of the bureaucracy was justified by their perception of themselves as experts who possessed forms of knowledge from which the peasants are 'radically estranged'. It is necessary to quote Mapolu and Phillipson (p. 47) at greater length.

'New agricultural practices, new implements, etc. are presented from above to the "ignorant" peasants as steps which are progressive in themselves, with little prior study of local conditions. Tractors, for instance, are the object of a bureaucratic display of "modern agricultural techniques" and sent to villages which have for one reason or another met the favour of the district officials or appear to them as being particularly deserving. . . . Very often costs are not taken into consideration, returns are very low due either to the nature of the crop or to the lack of other inputs which would be necessary to achieve higher yields. . . . This use of means of production as prizes or "rewards" to villages which the bureaucracy favours can have as its only result the further estrangement of the villages from modern technology – always received from above – and planning since information on costs and productivity are never made available beforehand. For instance, a village which has been allocated, say, ox-ploughs, will find itself penalised in comparison with its neighbours who would have "enjoyed" the benefit of having a tractor at their disposal, even if the use of the tractor brought a loss in financial terms. . . . This vertical relationship, which always places the peasants at the receiving end in a passive dependence, must be considered the major obstacle to any rural development strategy in Tanzania, and it is certainly a more important one than environmental constraints or the low ideological level of the peasant masses'.

There is much greater awareness of these problems now in official circles in Tanzania, but it is not clear yet whether they can be overcome.

Malaŵi

The second example of integrated rural development, that of Malaŵi, is interesting too, but for a different reason. The case of Malaŵi is a case of the trivialisation of the concept of integrated rural development. What was loudly hailed as Malaŵi's exercise in rural development was really a programme of enclave agricultural development with high capital intensity. The projects concerned here were the Lilongwe Land Development Project, the Shire Valley Agricultural Development Project, the Karonga Rural Development Project, and the Lakeshore Development Project. One of the largest of the projects, the Lilongwe Land Development Project, was scheduled to cover an area of 500,000 acres when completed. The project, launched in 1968, was to be completed in three phases stretching over 13 years. These projects seem to be essentially large demonstration projects in rural development. They were intended to increase agricultural productivity and to inculcate better farming methods. To this end they were to be backed by infrastructures, extension services and credit.

The Lilongwe project has received much praise. It has been said that its implementation was 'one of the best in East Africa', and that the first phase of the project was 'extraordinarily successful by almost any standard' (E/CN.14/CAP.6/2). But it would appear that the praise has been earned because the project developed roughly on schedule, carried out the projected infrastructure development, and in the case of crops such as maize it brought about an increase in yield quite close to target. However, this praise is typical of the confusion, or deception, surrounding Africa's development effort. The project may have performed well in terms of the limited concerns and values of the IDA

(International Development Agency) which founded it. However, it was promoted as an example of integrated rural development and should be judged in those terms. And on these terms it is unquestionably a failure. If it is supposed to be an exercise in integrated rural development, then it should be judged not just in terms of the building of infrastructures and in the increase of productivity; even more importantly it has to be judged in terms of its distributive effects, the participatory possibilities generated for rural people, its general impact on welfare, and its comprehensiveness in terms of the linkage of the development of the economic, social and political, etc. The concept of integrated rural development is trivialised by ignoring these criteria and an evaluation which ignores these criteria becomes largely irrelevant.

Alifeyo Chilivumbo has made a more comprehensive evaluation of rural development projects in Malaŵi including the Lilongwe Land Development Project, (*Africa Development*, Vol. III, No. 2, 1978), and has the following to say.

'The pattern of fund distribution in the land development shows that relatively little amounts are allocated to very few selected peasant farmers. In the Lilongwe Land Development Project, for example, one of the largest and costliest projects, in 1974, out of half a million peasants, only 5% obtained credit facilities amounting to just K586,000, averaging about K20 per farmer. In another major project, the Karonga Project, credit facilities were extended to only 4% of the total population, each one receiving about K30. In the Shire Valley Project only 19% of the total funds were reserved for revolving peasant farmers' and fishermen's credit funds, while 81% of the funds were allocated to capital development and management costs. Rather than redirecting the funds to the peasantry in the form of credits to eradicate proverty, the projects spend the bulk of their funds on capital development, luxury offices, accommodation and salaries of a top heavy bureaucracy. Thus in 1974 the Shire Valley Development Project was able to give credit facilities averaging K20 per person to only 3% of the total population. The patterns of expenditure show reluctance to improve the lot of the peasantry. Though a few are assisted the majority of the peasantry is left out.'

Behind the talk of integrated rural development is a very exploitative agricultural development which will at best encourage growth without development. For instance, there is much authoritarianism, oppression and exploitation in relations of production. The peasants who participate in the different development projects are subject to the very strict authoritarian supervision of project managers; they do not have any security of tenure and can be easily thrown out of the project. For the few farmers who received loans the terms were very harsh. The loan was simply deducted at the end of the crop season so that the farmer had little left. The peasants are ruthlessly exploited through the marketing mechanism. They must sell to the Agricultural Development and Marketing Corporation which pays them much less than the value of their crops, the enormous gain going not to peasant welfare but to the government treasury, through which it is used mainly for the interests of the political class. (By contrast estate owners are allowed to sell their products individually.) The wealth from agriculture is very unevenly distributed. As Chilivumbo shows, 'in 1975 the peasantry, making up

95% of the entire population, earned only K14 million out of a total of K120 million of agrarian generated wealth. . . . In that year, 1975, tobacco generated or brought into the country K44 million. Out of the total value of K44 million only K3 million was earned by the peasantry, the bulk, K41 million, went to a few estate owners, who account for less than 1% of the entire population and to ADMARC'.

To sum up, a development effort following the integrated rural development approach has considerable potential for changing African economies fundamentally and in a progressive direction. We have seen indications of this potential in the case of Tanzania, where an attempt was made to take the idea of integrated rural development seriously, though in the final analysis the government appears to have recoiled from the logic of the idea. Any attempt to take the idea seriously as a development strategy, and to implement it, comes up against the formidable obstacle of the class contradictions of Africa's fledgling capitalist economies. It is not at all surprising that the socio-economic formations which have taken the idea more to heart happen to be those which already had a progressive bent. The general tendency is for African governments to take advantage of the aura of enlightenment of the concept of integrated rural development to buttress their legitimacy without really pursuing integrated rural development in substance. Behind the slogan of integrated rural development they pursue policies which at best offer some minimal economic growth, while contributing little or nothing to development or to changing Africa's neocolonial economic structure.

Even with the best of intentions African leaders cannot effect the changes they need for development by relying exclusively on the internal manipulation of their economy. This has become increasingly clear to African governments and development agencies and institutions over the last two decades. It is now accepted that the internal effort has to be supplemented by forms of international cooperation, or at any rate by changes in aspects of international economic relations. In this connection two types of changes are most often talked about, namely regional cooperation among African countries and the improvement of Africa's economic position through the pursuit of a New International Economic Order. These are major motivations for action and change and since we are considering the possibilities of change in African economies it is necessary to give them some attention, however brief.

5 Regional cooperation in Africa

The case for regional cooperation in Africa is easy enough. Cooperation among African formations is needed to enable them to be strong enough to deal with the powerful multinational companies operating in Africa and to exert better terms from their economic relations with international organisations, development agencies and other regional organisations such as the European Economic Community. Regional cooperation is needed because the internal markets in Africa are generally too small. Cooperation will facilitate the expansion of markets which in turn will aid industrialisation. The constraints of the size of the market on industrialisation and development which African countries face can be seen from the following: 26 out of the 47 countries of developing Africa have a population of between 5 and 10 million; only 9 countries have a population of between 10 and 30 million, and only 2 countries have a population of over 30 million. Regional cooperation will help to mobilise more capital for development to operate certain projects on a scale which make them economic, to achieve product specialisation which is needed to increase inter-African trade and to improve efficiency in the use of human and natural resources.

African leaders and economic planners are well aware of these benefits and several regional organisations for economic cooperation have been formed at various times. These include the Customs Union, (Swaziland, Botswana, Lesotho and South Africa); the East African Community (Kenya, Tanzania and Uganda); the Arab Unity Council (Egypt, the Sudan, Morocco); the Central African Customs and Economic Union (Central African Republic, the Congo, Gabon, the United Republic of the Cameroon); the Mano River Union (Liberia, Sierra Leone); the Union of Central African States (Chad and Zaire); the Magrhib Permanent Consultative Committee (Algeria, Mauritania, Morocco and Tunisia); the West African Economic Community (Benin, the Ivory Coast, Mali, Mauritania, Niger, Senegal, Upper Volta); the Economic Community of West African States (Cape Verde, Benin, Gambia, Ghana, Guinea, Guinea-Bissau, Ivory Coast, Liberia, Mali, Mauritainia, Niger, Nigeria, Senegal, Sierra Leone, Togo, Upper Volta).

The difficulties in the way of regional cooperation are well-known. The vertical integration of African economies upwards to the metropolitan socio-economic formations creates serious problems for the fashioning of horizontal ties between African states. The attempt to forge these horizontal linkages have not sat well with the former colonial powers, who see them (quite correctly) as a threat to their hegemony. The French have been noticeably hostile to ECOWAS.

The present organisation of Africa's production for export is another serious obstacle to regional cooperation. One United Nations source (E/CN.14/ECO/O/Rev.3, of June 1976) has noted that production in African states 'was organised to meet extra-African needs. Not only was there a monotonous similarity in the pattern of export production, the whole machinery of marketing, transportation and communication, banking and insurance and even business information and specialised skills was geared to serve this end. The development of intra-African trade requires a massive orientation of part of that machinery or a newly designed machinery to match supply and demand, to exert influence on production patterns, to make feasible the movement of goods and persons among the countries of the Region, to facilitate dealings in intra-regional currencies and enable inter-country balance to be cleared or managed.' The seriousness of this obstacle to regional cooperation in Africa is reflected in the statistics of trade between African countries. The Economic Commission for Africa estimates that inter-African trade as a proportion of total African trade was only 4.3% in 1975. Even though there was an increase of 146% in the value of inter-African trade between 1970 and 1975, its proportion of total African trade was actually declining, having been 5.5% in 1970.

The experience of regional cooperation in Africa indicates that they can be and have been successful in achieving certain objectives of regional cooperation. In particular, they have been quite successful in effecting the common defence of African interests as producers and in facilitating the improvement of communications between members in order to improve trade. There has been a surprising willingness to give assistance to poorer regions within the cooperating countries. But the success and the prospects of success in these objectives do not go very far. They will make only a very limited contribution to the reduction of the disarticulation and dependence of African economies, to their transformation from monocultural export economies to diversified and industrialised economies capable of autocentric growth. Regional cooperation will contribute much more significantly to these goals through a very high degree of coordination of the economic policies and programmes of African countries, as well as arrangements to make their economies more complementary through product sharing and production specialisation. However, these are precisely the areas in which regional cooperation in Africa has made little progress and shows no signs of future improvement. African leaders are too insecure in their power, too jealous of national sovereignty and too tied to their former colonial masters to take the kinds of measures which are needed to realise the coordination of development policies and the complementarity of their economies. Under pressure from the political implications of economic stagnation, and the chronic crisis of legitimacy, African leaders are desperate to produce results quickly. The gains from the really fundamental changes, such as product sharing and specialisation within cooperating countries, will take too long to be visible – far too long for the timespan of most African leaders. One must conclude that despite the understanding of the need for regional cooperation and even the evidence of the political will to do so, regional cooperation is not likely to bring fundamental changes in African economies and even in their position in the international economic system in the foreseeable future.

6   The New International Economic Order

A lot of the responsibility for transforming African economies for the better has been pinned on the New International Economic Order. According to a United Nations source the New International Economic Order is 'the restructuring of international economic relations in such a way as to make it feasible for countries of the Third World to initiate or accelerate internally located and relatively autonomous processes of growth, diversification and integration'. This has become necessary because 'neither the policy of increasing production of one or two major agricultural products for export, nor import substitution industrialisation has laid the foundations for viable self-sustaining socio-economic systems or removed substantially the geographical and commodity constraints on Africa's external trade'. The idea of the New International Economic Order was developed through a body of United Nations resolutions particularly, the General Assembly resolution 3201 (S-VI) of 16 May 1974 and resolution 256 (XII) which was adopted in Nairobi on 28 February 1975. The implications of the resolutions on the New International Economic Order are discussed in a United Nations document (E/CN.14/ECO/90/Rev.3 of 25 June 1976). This document is also an excellent general exposition of the concrete application of the New International Economic Order to the African experience. The document states that the New International Economic Order seeks to initiate autonomous processes of growth, diversification and integration in African economies in order to 'mount effective attacks on emerging internal crisis, principally mass poverty, mass unemployment and growing food deficits. Emphasis is therefore placed on ways and means of ensuring, through trade and aid, increased net-inflows of real resources to the developing countries.' The document then goes on to define the New International Economic Order in terms of a concrete set of policy measures.

1 *The restructuring of international trade*: 'One of the objectives is the restructuring of international trade to enable developing countries to export increasing quantities of traditional (agricultural) products to advanced countries at remunerative prices in what are implicitly conditions of potential oversupply. The removal of these barriers could be extended to agricultural products processed locally and to manufactures. On the part of developed countries, this would require the removal of tariff and non-tariff barriers against imports, including imports of manufactures from the developing countries; the expansion of the Generalised System of Preferences (GSP) and the restructuring of the internal economies of the developed countries to accommodate an increased volume of imports from the developing countries.' These measures are to be supplemented by price indexation arrangements, commodity management and stabilisation schemes.

2 *Processing and manufacturing for export*: The point here is that processing and manufacture for export by African and other developing regions of the world is necessary for the development of their industry, and agriculture as well. The reasons for this assumption are fairly obvious. The internal markets of most of the countries in Africa are too small to provide a market suitable for industrialisation. They need to break out of their specialisation in primary production and they need more means of earning foreign exchange, in order to buy the capital goods and the services they need for their development.

3 *The transfer of real resources from developed countries to developing countries*: This transfer of resources from developed countries to developing countries is supposed to be accomplished through three mechanisms, namely indexation, technical assistance and the transfer of technology.

4 *Economic cooperation*: Particular emphasis is placed on cooperation between developing countries. The expectation here is that such cooperation will yield benefits through outcomes such as product sharing and specialisation arising from the development of complementarity and producer associations.

Does the quest for a New International Economic Order have much potential for changing African economies? How fundamental might these changes be? In what direction will they point? In approaching these questions it is helpful to bear in mind that there is very little that is new in the New International Economic Order. It is really a hodge-podge of elements of development strategy which are familiar, and which have left no impact on dependence, disarticulation and economic stagnation. Let us briefly look at each of the main policy objectives.

The restructuring of international trade

The first calls for the reconstruction of international trade to enable developing countries to export increasing quantities of traditional agricultural products. This is clearly an echo of the commodities strategy of the 1960s with additional emphasis on the need to secure markets for commodities and for minimising the fluctuations of earnings from commodities. Some progress has been made towards the implementation of these policies. The group of 77 developing countries called African Caribbean and Pacific countries (ACP) worked out concrete proposals in their Manila Charter of February 1976. This Charter was a comprehensive expression of the positions of the developing countries regarding the implementation of the New International Economic Order. In the fourth session of UNCTAD held in Nairobi in May 1976 the idea of an Integrated Programme for Commodities along the lines proposed by the Manila Charter was adopted. This integrated programme covered, among other things, coordination of national policy on commodity stocks, management of supply, funding of the scheme of stabilisation of export earnings, and access to markets. The industrialised countries and the third world countries have been renegotiating the implementation of these objectives. Perhaps the best known and the most far-reaching outcome of these negotiations so far are the Lomé Conventions between the EEC and the ACP countries. Essentially, the Conventions enable the ACP countries to make marginal improvements in their world trade while reaffirming the existing global economic order.

To illustrate this, let us consider the achievements of the Lomé Conventions. Under the first Lomé Convention (popularly referred to as Lomé I), the most important achievement by all accounts was Stabex, the scheme for the stabilisation of export earnings. This was hailed not only as the great achievement of Lomé I but as a breakthrough to a New International Economic Order. The Stabex scheme works like this: if the price of commodities of the participating developing countries falls by 7.5% or more, the affected developing countries become eligible for compensation from a fund set up by the EEC. The amount of compensation is tied to the average price of the preceding four years, and it is payable only if the fall in prices is due to the free play of market forces. The commodities covered by the agreement are bananas, cotton, coffee, cocoa, coconuts, groundnuts, hides and skins, iron-ore, palm-oil, palm-kernels, raw sisal, tea and timber. For the purposes of paying compensation the EEC has established a fund of $375 million to cover the five years of the agreement. Only one-fifth of the available fund can be disbursed in payment of compensation each year, but in exceptional circumstances an additional 20% could be borrowed from the next year's compensation quota. So the maximum compensation payable for any given year is $90 million. The compensation is not really a grant in aid or a gift, it is really a repayable loan, although its repayment is waived for the countries which fall under the classification of 'least developed countries'.

Stabex is clearly not the type of measure that can make any significant difference to the plight of the developing countries. As we have seen, the maximum compensation payable each year is $90 million. This sum is utterly negligible when account is taken of the number of developing countries involved in the agreement and also the number of commodities involved. All minerals were excluded from the scheme except iron-ore, and minerals are of critical importance to many African economies. For the EEC, Stabex is virtually a cost-free token gesture because current prices are likely to be higher than the average prices of the preceding four years due to rising production costs. Finally, Stabex does not make any provision for counteracting the adverse effects of import inflation.

Has Lomé II of 1979 made any difference? Not much. One of the major advances of Lomé II over Lomé I is the scheme which attempts to bring to mineral production some of the 'benefits' which Lomé I brought to agricultural commodities – hence the name 'son of Stabex'. The scheme is made to assist participating countries when their mineral export capacity declines substantially due to price collapse, natural disaster, political events or the accidents of nature. In the event of such a significant price drop, the affected country gets a loan to finance a project it has proposed for restoring its export. The fund for backing this scheme amounts to only $372 million. This is very small. If a mineral producer such as Zaire were to be hit by a serious drop in mineral export earnings, the entire amount would be inadequate for dealing with Zaire's problem.

Stabex itself was extended under Lomé II. Originally only 26 commodities were affected. The number had grown to 34 before Lomé II. Now ten more commodities have been added, namely shrimps, prawns, pepper peas, squid, cotton, cakes, oil-cake, rubber, beans, lentils and cashew nuts. The terms of the loans given under Lomé II are more flexible and the terms for qualification for the loans have become more lenient.

The main negotiating point, and the one that caused the most acrimony, was over the total amount that the EEC was to make available to the ACP countries. Under Lomé I the amount was 3,466 million units of account. At Lomé II the ACP countries demanded 10,000 million units The EEC countries conceded only 5,600 million units of account, which was only 500 million units of account higher than Lomé I after adjustment for inflation. These were the major changes of Lomé II. Besides them there were several utterly inconsequential changes: for instance, a declaration of intent to help ACP countries with their sea transport problems; a declaration of intent on the coordination of effort on the use and conservation of fishing resources; and a declaration to the effect that workers from ACP countries legally residing in EEC countries will be granted the same conditions of work as EEC nationals. This is clearly not the kind or the scale of change that is going to make any significant contribution to the struggle against underdevelopment and dependence, or facilitate Africa's liberation from her present place in the international division of labour.

It is not really surprising that these conventions have made only marginal concessions to the needs of the ACP countries; nobody has really advanced a persuasive argument as to why the EEC countries should proceed to change the balance of economic forces in the world to their own detriment. What is perhaps surprising is that the ACP countries have settled for concessions which are not merely virtually useless but possibly opposed to their original objectives of promoting an 'internally located and relatively autonomous process of growth, diversification and integration'. In a previous reference to Lomé I we mentioned the arrangement by which industries and firms in the ACP countries will be tied to Community firms (Article 26b). This can only extend and tighten the vertical integration of the ACP economies to those of the EEC, and it is bound to increase the role and the power of multinationals in the economies of the ACP countries. That is surely not the way to go about these struggles for independence and development. The implications of the schemes for stabilisation of earnings from minerals and agricultural commodities are equally disturbing. The most disturbing thing about them is that they are prone to freeze the ACP countries in their present role as primary producers in the international division of labour.

Promoting processing and manufacturing

The other policy objectives and modes of implementation of the New International Economic Order are equally unpromising. The second objective, mainly the promotion of processing and manufacturing for export, has been quite difficult to translate into effective policies that would be acceptable to the developed countries. Emphasis has been placed on securing access for the processed commodities and manufacturers of developing countries in the markets of the industrialised countries. The industrialised countries have made considerable concessions on market entry, for instance under Lomé I and II. But any sense of achievement that the developing countries nurture in this regard would be an illusion. For the problem is really their ability to process and to manufacture in the first place, and then competitively. It is really only when these fundamental problems are solved that the question of markets becomes important. The EEC countries are making concessions that cost them little and make an insignificant contribution to furthering the goals of the ACP countries.

Transfer of resources

How about the third major objective, namely the transfer of real resources from the developed to the underdeveloped countries? Here again the struggle is over concessions which fall far short of what is needed to deal with the problems for which the concessions are being sought. One area in which attention has been directed has been the problem of debt burden and balance of payments. There was a lot of debate about monetary reform, the reduction of the debt burden by waivers, cancellations and postponement. The developing countries have made numerous proposals but the developed countries have understandably been reluctant to make concessions, even concessions that cost them little. This reluctance has been evident in the failure of the negotiations being conducted under the auspices of UNCTAD, a notable example being the failure of the UNCTAD conference of 1976 to deal with debts, balance of payments deficits and other related issues. Another area in which the problem of transfer of real resources has been dealt with concretely is the sphere of technology. One of the decisions made at UNCTAD was on the improvement of the institutional infrastructures to facilitate the availability of technology. The most notable import of this for Africa was the decision to establish an African Centre for the transfer and development of technology. It is still not clear whether this will really take off and what it will accomplish. In 1971 there was a *World Plan of Action for the Application of Science and Technology to the Third World: Targets of investment of industrialised countries in science and technology assistance to the Third World.* The targets were about 0.05% of GNP at 1970 levels and 5% of research and development expenditure. But the targets were happily ignored. Now, eight years afterwards, the United Nations Conference on Science and Technology, which met in September 1979, has come up with similar targets and there is no reason to expect that there will be a greater success this time. Indeed this very concern that the conference might be another waste of time was expressed at the gathering. A Tanzanian delegate, Dr Chagula, worried about the proposals of UNCTAD suffering the fate of the World Plan, referred to the latter as 'a document destined to gather dust on the shelves of librarians'.

Regional cooperation

The fourth objective regarding cooperation, particularly among developing countries, has a better potential for furthering the goals of the African countries on development in the long run. And it represents a more interesting departure from previous tendencies in development. But as we saw in an earlier discussion of this option, there are many difficulties in the way of realising its potential.

We must conclude that the New International Economic Order cannot offer very much. In the first place it offers few ideas that are new. It is largely an aggregation of elements of development orientations that have been largely discredited in the past. There is a very great gap between the goals which it is designed to achieve and the actual policies which are being used to fulfil the goals. The goals entail fundamental changes in the international system and in the role of the developing countries, the means are puny and can at best only achieve marginal changes while reaffirming the fundamentals of the status quo. The question now is not whether the practical policy measures emanating from the idea of the New International Economic Order are working or not working. The question is whether the potential dangers of the New International Economic Order can be mitigated.

In the pursuit of the New International Economic Order, the developing countries are getting bogged down deeper into illusions and misconceptions which might be compounding their problems. They are asserting and politicising the contradictions between them and the developing countries, while at the same time expecting that the developing countries will voluntarily improve their competitive position in the world at their own expense. They are appealing to charity rather than to self-interest, and yet expecting to get results. They are confusing the symptoms and causes of underdevelopment. Perhaps the options for realising the goals of the New International Economic Order are too limited by existing constraints. All the same, that is no excuse for making simplistic assumptions about the means to the goals. The developing countries have set about the pursuit of the New International Economic Order in ways that are quite self-defeating. The policies associated with the New International Economic Order put too much stress on the vertical links between the developed countries and the underdeveloped world. Diversification, self-reliance and industrialisation, etc. are made to depend on the ability of the developing countries to get access to the markets of the developed countries, to get more lenient loans, more and better technical assistance, to encourage the governments of developed countries to protect the investments of their citizens in the developing countries with suitable guarantees, to contribute more to mineral development, to fund schemes for the stabilisation of export earnings, to give more money for research and development in the developing countries, etc. This is precisely the type of thinking and the types of policies which will perpetuate the existing international division of labour, increase dependence and freeze the economies of the developing countries in their monocultural and disarticulated modes.

7 Regional integration and collective self-reliance

The last development strategy to be considered in this survey is collective self-reliance through regional integration. The idea of regional integration as a means to collective self-reliance has been around in Africa for a long time and some regional groups for promoting economic cooperation and integration, such as the East African Community, existed before independence. In the past, regional integration was regarded more as a supportive measure rather than as a development strategy. What is new now is that regional integration is being talked of rather more seriously as a grand strategy for breaking out of underdevelopment and dependence. As the favourite development strategies failed and the competitive position of the developing countries, particularly in Africa, continued to deteriorate, the idea of regional integration for collective self-reliance has become more attractive. In the last decade United Nations development agencies have put more emphasis on collective self-reliance as a way out for developing countries. As far as Africa is concerned, this has been reflected especially in the publications of the Economic Commission for Africa.

But the most interesting indication of the current status of the idea of economic integration for collective self-reliance in Africa is the OAU (Organisation of African Unity) special Economic Summit, which was held in Lagos in 1980. The idea was by far the dominant theme and commitment to it reflected a rare unanimity for the OAU. There was much concern about going beyond rhetoric, and a plan of action was adopted which called for the establishment of an African Common Market by the year 2000. The Conference also declared its firm commitment to the action plan for the implementation of the Monrovia

Strategy, an economic document adopted at a preceding OAU Conference in Monrovia, Liberia. In both the action plans adopted in Lagos and Monrovia the operative words are collective self-reliance, self-sustaining development and economic integration. Among the measure mentioned for the realisation of these goals are the promotion of more inter-African trade (horizontal links), an African energy policy, self-sufficiency in food production, improved transport communications in Africa and the establishment of an African Monetary Fund to supplant the International Monetary Fund.

Judging from the difficulties experienced by more regional groups, such as the East African Community and the Mano River Union, and indeed the general history of regional integration in Africa, it is difficult to be optimistic about the chances of an African Common Market. However, it is more likely that the goal of collective self-reliance will be sought through more limited regional groupings such as the Economic Organisation of West African States; the Organisation Commune Africaine et Mauricienne, OCAM, (Benin, Central African Republic, Gabon, Ivory Coast, Mauritius, Niger, Rwanda, Senegal, Togo, Upper Volta); and the Communauté Economique de l'Afrique de l'Ouest, CEAO (Ivory Coast, Mali, Mauritania, Niger, Senegal and Upper Volta).

The basic problem with the strategy of collective self-reliance is that it presupposes a considerable degree of regional economic cooperation and integration which Africa has tried for a long time to promote with very limited success. The difficulties in the way of even limited regional economic integration in Africa are considerable. First are the political differences, which include the differences in the development ideologies of member countries and their fear of compromising their control over their territories. Second is the fear of metropolitan powers that new regional groups will reduce their influence over their clients (France has been hostile to ECOWAS). Third is the disparity of the size and economic development of members, which tend to cause monopolisation of the benefits of economic integration. For instance, it is the more developed members who benefit most from trade liberalisation and preferential treatment. For the poor members the main effect of trade liberalisation is likely to be a deteriorating balance of payments. This tendency towards the monopolisation of the benefits of integration was one of the problems which led to the collapse of the East African Community. In this case Kenya was where the benefits polarised much to the dismay of Tanzania and Uganda. The same problem is now threatening CEAO, in which Ivory Coast is monopolising the benefits. The same problem is bound to plague ECOWAS, in which Nigeria is so much more powerful than every other member. Where the political will is strong such problems can be counteracted to a large extent. Whether such political will now exists in Africa remains to be seen. Fourth, members of regional groups would be export-oriented primary producers whose primary products are in very little demand within the regional group. This reduces the incentive for practical commitment to economic integration. To try to remedy the primary export orientation of African economies will entail the willingness of members to import crude, inefficiently produced goods from member states and even to protect them with high tariffs. In the past it has been difficult to accept this type of obligation.

All this is still only the conventional level of looking at the strategy of collective self-reliance through economic integration. The strategy can be looked at from the level of the fundamentals of the problem of underdevelopment and imperialism. And when it is examined on this level the strategy looks even less hopeful. The fact of the matter is that there is a good chance that the strategy will only lead to the collectivisation and deepening of dependence and underdevelopment. We have to bear in mind the significance of the dependence of African formations on international capital, which has been documented in this study. How do the multinationals, which have such a firm control of African economies, come into the question? They are so powerful that if regional integration seriously damages their interests they will try to ensure its failure, and they may well have the power to do this. At the very least they can make economic cooperation very difficult and reduce its benefits. On the other hand, they might decide – and this is the more likely option – that African economic cooperation is in their interest and support it. But then it will be an economic cooperation which will continue their exploitative activities in Africa. The way that the idea of economic cooperation is being developed indicates that it will not greatly threaten the interests of international capital; in fact the implementation of the strategy is supposed to depend greatly on foreign capital. None of the official writings and pronouncement on the strategy are grappling with the fundamental problem of the conditions of production, particularly their control. The level at which the problem of collective self-reliance is being discussed will likely lead to absurdities (masked as progress) such as a situation in which Ivory Coast imports French cars assembled in Nigeria, while Nigeria imports from the Ivory Coast building materials manufactured by French companies in Abidjan. It is not likely that the renewed attempt to realise collective self-reliance through economic cooperation will be more than marginally more successful than past efforts. So much for African development strategies.

Conclusion

This chapter has tried to understand the dynamics and possibilities of change in African economies and socio-economic formations. We have found a strong tendency towards inertia, especially in the sense that there is very little potential for moving out of underdevelopment. We have seen that the interaction of the main structural features of African formations underlie this inertia; we have also seen that the attempts by African leaders to overcome this inertia have largely been unsuccessful; in some ways they have reinforced it.

It is important to appreciate this failure. In our analysis we have tried to illustrate this failure, but we have been more interested in showing on formal grounds the necessary consequences of structural features, and the necessary consequences of development strategies and policy; in short, we have been interested not so much in evidence of failure as in the logical necessity of failure. This is of course the way to proceed in order to avoid confusing empiricism with science. All the same it seems necessary to add that the fact of failure is established and widely

TABLE 6.3 Prospects for growth during the 1980s (average annual percentage growth, 1977 prices)

	Population 1980 (millions)	GNP per person 1980 (dollars)	Growth of GNP High case		Growth of GNP per person Low case			High case	
			1980–85	1985–90	1970–80	1980–85	1985–90	1980–85	1985–90
Subsaharan Africa	141	186	3.1	3.8	0.2	-0.3	0.1	0.1	1.1
Industrialised countries	671	7,599	3.3	4.0	2.4	2.5	2.5	2.8	3.5

Note that there are two types of projections, designated high case and low case respectively. The high case projection is based on more optimistic assumptions about the ability of economies to adjust to certain problems. The low case assumes an inability to adjust to these problems.

Source
Adapted from *World Development Report, 1980*, The World Bank, Washington, 1980

accepted; and there is increasing alarm at the extent and possible consequences of this failure. This is easily ascertained by referring to three authoritative studies published recently: *World Development Report*, 1980 (The World Bank, Washington, 1980); the *Brandt Commission Report*, 1980; and *The World Economic Crisis; A Commonwealth Perspective*, (Commonwealth Secretariat, 1980). *The World Bank Report* is particularly instructive because its growth projections indicate that there is very little chance of better performance in the near future, as Table 6.2 indicates. The World Bank Report notes that 'Subsaharan Africa has the most disturbing outlook. Even in the high case, its growth in 1985–90 would be a meagre 1% per person – far below the average for the oil importers; and in the low case average incomes would actually be lower in 1990 than they were in 1980', as can be seen from Table 6.2, which shows that growth GNP per person for the period 1980–85 in the low case will actually be negative, −0.3%.

The past failures and depressing prospects have caused a great amount of concern. The policy-makers themselves are at a great loss as to what to do. The African bourgeoisie and international organisations such as the World Bank and the United Nations agencies which inspire their development strategies appear to have run out of ideas. This is not surprising because they have tried to 'solve the problems' within the context of maintaining existing relations of production on the domestic level, and even on the international level. With that kind of constraint the options are naturally very limited. The exhaustion of ideas is evident in the types of development strategies and policies the African bourgeoisie is adopting. They are now reduced to dusting up old ideas and piecing together odds and ends from development strategies that have been tried and discredited in the past. The exhaustion of ideas is well illustrated by the report of the high-powered committee set up by the United Nations to outline a new international development strategy for the 1980s. The report, *Development in the 1980s: Approach to a New Strategy* (New York, 1978), could find no new strategy to present, and it contents itself with repeating familiar clichés such as urging 'structural change to ensure a more rational balance within and between countries', 'strengthening of institutions of international economic management' – but it repeats them with less conviction.

Bibliography

ADEDEJI, A., 'Prospects of Regional Economic Cooperation in West Africa', *Journal of Modern Africa Studies*, 8, 2, 1970.
AKE, C., 'Ideology and Objective Conditions', in J. Barkan ed., *Politics and Public Policy in Kenya and Tanzania*, New York, 1979.
AKE, C., 'Explaining Political Instability in New States', *Journal of Modern African Studies*, 2, 3, 1973.
AKE, C., 'Charismatic, Legitimation and Political Integration, *Comparative Studies in Society and History*, 9, 1, 1966.
ALAVI, H., 'Peasants and Revolution', *Socialist Register*, 1969.

ALLEN, C., 'Tanzania: Les Illusions du Socialisme', *Espirit*, 26, February 1979.

AMIN, S., 'Self-Reliance and the New International Economic Order', *Monthly Review*, July–August, 1977.

ANYANG-NYONGO, P., 'Liberal Models of Capitalist Development in Africa: Ivory Coast', *Africa Development*, 3, 3, 1978.

ARRIGHI G., AND SAUL J. EDS., *Essays in the Political Economy of Africa*, New York, 1973.

AWITI, A., 'Class Struggle in the Rural Section of Tanzania', *Maji Maji*, 7, 1972.

BARNETT, A., 'The Gezira Scheme: Production of Cotton and the Reproduction of Underdevelopment', in I. Oxaal, T. Barnett and D. Booth eds., *Beyond the Sociology of Underdevelopment*, London, 1975.

CHILIVUMBO, A., 'On Rural Development: A Note on Malawi's Programmes of Development for Exploitation', *Africa Development*, 3, 2, 1978.

CLIFFE, L., 'Rural Class Formation in East Africa', *Journal of Peasant Studies*, 4, 1977.

COULSON, A., 'Agricultural Policies in Mainland Tanzania', *Review of African Political Economy*, 10, 1977.

DAVIDSON, B., 'African Peasants and Revolution', *Journal of Peasant Studies*, 1, 3, 1974.

ESSEKS, J., 'Economic Dependency on Political Development in the New States of Africa, *Journal of Politics*, 33, 1971.

FRANK, A. G., *Crisis in the Third World*, New York, 1980.

FURTADO, C., 'Development: Theoretical and Conceptual Considerations', *Polish Economic Society Round Table*, Warsaw, June 1978.

FURTADO, C., 'Le Mythe du "development economique" ', *Anthropos*, Paris, 1976.

GALTUNG, J., 'Poor Countries versus Rich: Poor People versus Rich – Whom will NIEO benefit?, University of Oslo, Paper 63, 1977.

GALTUNG, J., 'International Monetary Fund', *International Financial Statistics*, October 1976.

GALTUNG, J., *Integrated Approach to Rural Development in Africa*, E/CN/14/SWSA/8.

JEWSIEWICKI, B., 'L'anthropologie economique et les modes des production', *Culture et Development*, 9, 2, 1977.

KILLICK, T., *Development Economics in Action*, London, 1978.

KILBY, P., *Industrialisation in an Open Economy: Nigeria 1945–1966*, Cambridge, 1969.

LAMB, G., 'The Neocolonial Integration of Kenyan Peasants', *Development and Change*, 8, 1977.

LEBRUN, O., AND GERRY, C., 'Petty-Commodity Producers and Capitalism', *Review of African Political Economy*, 1, 1975.

LELE, U., *The Design of Rural Development: Lessons From Africa*, Baltimore, 1975.

LEYS, C., *Underdevelopment in Kenya: The Political Economy of Neo-Colonialism*, London, 1975.

MALIMA, K., 'Planning for Self-Reliance: Tanzania's Third Five Year Development Plan', *Africa Development*, 4, 1, 1979.

MANDELEY, J., 'Third World Pressures at Nairobi: the Political and

Economic Significance of UNCTAD IV', *Round Table*, 264, 1977.

McINTIRE, A. ET AL., *Towards a New International Economic Order, A Final Report by a Commonwealth Expert Group*, Commonwealth Secretariat, 1977.

MIHYO, P., 'The Worker's Revolution in Tanzania', *Maji Maji*, 1974.

MITTLELMAN, J. H., *Underdevelopment and the Transition to Socialism: Mozambique and Tanzania*, New York, 1981.

MOSS, A., AND WINTON, H. EDS., *A New International Economic Order: Selected Documents 1945–1975*, 2 Vols., Munich.

OLOWO, B., 'ECOWAS: Some Unsettled Issues', *The Journal of Business and Social Studies*, June 1978.

O'KEEFE, P. ET AL., 'Kenyan Underdevelopment: A Case Study of Proletarianization' in P. O'Keefe and B. Wisner eds., *Land Use and Development*, London, 1977.

PAYER, C., *Commodity Trade and the Third World*, London, 1975.

PHILLIPS, A., 'The Concept of "Development" ', *Review of African Political Economy*, 8, 1977.

PREBISCH, R., 'The Economic Development of Latin America and Its Principal Problems', *Economic Bulletin for Latin America*, February 1962.

ROXBOROUGH, I., 'Dependency Theory in the Sociology of Development: Some Theoretical Problems', *The West African Journal of Sociology and Political Science*, 1, 2, 1976.

SANDBROOK, R. AND COHEN, R. EDS., *The Development of an African Working Class: Studies in Class Formation and Action*, London, 1975.

SAUL, J., 'African Peasants and Revolution', *Review of African Political Economy*, 1, 1, 1974.

SCOTT, J., 'Hegemony and the Peasantry', *Politics and Society*, 7, 3, 1977.

SEIDMAN, A., *Comparative Development Strategies in East Africa*, Nairobi, 1972.

SEIDMAN, A, 'Import-Substitution Industry in Zambia', *Journal of Modern African Studies*, 12, 4, 1974.

SEIDMAN, A., *Ghana's Development Experience*, Nairobi, 1978.

SLOVO, JOE, 'A Critical Appraisal of the Non-Capitalist Path and the National Democratic State in Africa', *Marxism Today*, 18, 6, 1974.

SZENTES, T., *Interpretations of Economic Underdevelopment: A Critical Study*, Centre for Afro-Asian Research of the Hungarian Academy of Sciences, Budapest, 1968.

THOMAS, C., *Dependence and Transformation: The Economics of the Transition to Socialism*: New York, 1974.

UKPONG, I., 'Structural Changes in Value Added in Manufacturing in Nigeria, 1960–1974', *Journal of Business and Social Studies*, 1, 2, 1978.

UNITED NATIONS ECONOMIC AND SOCIAL COUNCIL: ECONOMIC COMMISSION FOR AFRICA, *Public Works Programmes and Integrated Rural Development for the Alleviation of Mass Poverty, Unemployment and Underdevelopment*, E/CN.14/CAP.6/2, August 1976; *Social Development Planning in Africa within the Framework of the Principles of the Unified Approach to Development Analysis and Planning*, E/CN.14/CAP.6/3, August 1976; *A Critique of Conventional Planning in Africa in Relation to the United Approach* E/CN.14/CAP/6/5, September, 1976; *Applications of a Unified Approach to Development Analysis and*

Planning under African Conditions, E/CN.14/CAP.6/4, September, 1976; *Survey of Economic and Social Conditions in Africa*, 1976, E/CN.14/654 Part I and II, February, 1977; *Africa's Strategy for Development in the 1970s*, E/CN.14/Res/218(x), 1973; *Integrated Approach to Rural Development in Africa*, E/CN.14/SWSA/8; *The Indigenisation of African Economies 1978*, (includes case studies of Nigeria, Ghana, Tanzania and Kenya); *Revised Framework of Principles for the Implementation of the New International Economic Order in 1976, 1981, 1986*, E/CN.14/ECO/90/Rev. 3, June, 1976.

WARREN, B., 'Myths of Underdevelopment: Imperialism and Capitalist Industrialization, *New Left Review*, 81, 1973, (see also discussion of thesis by others in *New Left Review*, 85, 1974).

WORLD BANK, *World Tables, 1976*, Baltimore, 1976.

7 Contradictions and syntheses

In the preceding chapter we tried to look at African economies in dynamic terms. We identified and analysed likely sources of change in order to determine what might reasonably be conjectured about how African economies might change and why. In the course of this analysis we saw that the very types of change which African leaders are so passionately and vociferously seeking, particularly economic growth, are hardly occurring. Instead the more general picture in Africa is one of economic stagnation and the decline of Africa's competitive position relative to the developed economies, and even to most other underdeveloped regions of the world. This failure to achieve economic growth, or to make any tangible impact on the liquidation of underdevelopment, is the point of departure of this chapter. This particular failure has serious consequences for the development of the contradictions of African socio-economic formations and for the types of new syntheses by which the contradictions might resolve themselves.

Failure and the development of consciousness

The failure to achieve a reasonable measure of economic growth is contributing to the development of contradictions and consciousness in African socio-economic formations. To appreciate this point it is necessary to take note of the particularly conspicuous circumstances in which this failure has occurred. African leaders have been singularly vociferous about the disabilities connected with underdevelopment and their determination to liquidate it. Development has been elevated to the level of ideology, thereby filling an ideological vacuum which existed from the time when political independence was achieved. In the colonial era the political mobilisation of the African masses by the nationalist leadership rested simply on the antipathy against colonial domination. When political independence was won, anti-colonialism naturally lost much of its force and something else had to be found. Eventually most African countries settled for the idea of development, although development was often a cover for the pursuit of capitalism. The metropolitan countries had also promoted very aggressively the idea of development as an overriding concern of public policy in Africa so as to forge a new accommodation which would allow them to maximise their political and economic influence in Africa in the post-independence era. These were some of the circumstances under which development came to be a central element of the *raison d'être* of state power in Africa and by extension a major – perhaps the major – criterion of regime performance in Africa. The intensive propagation of the ideology of development organised and focused expectations on fairly clear criteria of regime performance, and the failure to fulfil the much advertised expectations bred disillusion, critical attitudes and prepared people's minds for induction into more radical political attitudes.

In a sense the failure of the development effort might be said to be accentuating an effect which was already created by the nationalist movement. The nationalist movement itself promoted not merely the politicisation of the masses but also the radicalisation of their consciousness. It politicised them by mobilising them into politics, many of them for the first time. The nationalist leaders had to base their political power on the support of the masses, and accordingly stirred them into being politically active. But they were mobilised into politics in circumstances which also gave them an essentially progressive if not radical political consciousness. For behind the antipathy of the nationalist movement was a system of progressive ideas. For instance, the nationalist leaders argued that they were against colonialism because it was the negation of self-determination; they argued that colonialism negated freedom, that it impeded the development of the colonised peoples and that it was brutally oppressive and exploitative. The nationalist leaders engaged in a struggle for liberation had to represent themselves as champions of the cause of equality and freedom and as enemies of exploitation.

As soon as political independence was won the ideas which aided the politicisation of the masses by the nationalist leadership became a fetter to the purposes of this very leadership. For the demands for equality, freedom, self-determination, and freedom from poverty and oppression which they had taught the masses to make on the colonial government was inevitably directed at them, now that they were at the helm of affairs. The difficulty was that the nationalist leadership – with a few exceptions such as in Mozambique and Angola where nationalism was ultimately transferred into an essentially revolutionary struggle – was interested in inheriting the coloniser's powers and not in implementing the progressive ideas which had helped it to come to power. And this has created a serious contradiction between the nationalist leadership and the African masses. The masses have been socialised into ideas and expectations which seem subversive now that the nationalist movement, having brought its leadership into power, has moved into its reactionary phase. Equally they have been socialised into expectations which cannot be met in a manner compatible with the maintenance of existing relations of production. The failure of the development effort, which denies the leaders of Africa even the opportunity to buttress their legitimacy with the material betterment of the masses, has deepened the contradictions caused by the ideological thrust of the nationalist movement.

It is important that the failure of the development effort has occurred against a background of hopes of material betterment. During the days of the nationalist agitation there was much talk about the possibilities of material betterment for the masses once the colonial yoke was removed. This made expectations upwardly mobile. But this upward mobility of expectations of material betterment was more than just a matter of the promises of politicians. To appreciate it fully we have to bear in mind that the nationalist movement was also a process of what one may call for the lack of a better term the internationalisation of the consciousness of the African masses. Colonialism in Africa was just a mode of articulation of imperialism. The nationalist movement, reflecting the objective reality of the colonial situation, had to phrase its ideology in terms of problems arising from the relationships between different socio-economic formations – relations of domination and subordination, of disparities in power, of unequal exchange, of the impoverishment of one region to the inordinate enrichment of another, and of free peoples and enslaved peoples. In short, the nationalist movement was inviting the African masses to revolt by making them think of their deprived societies in comparison to other societies, particularly the metropolitan countries. There was something strangely paradoxical about this comparison. While it aptly achieved the purpose it was calculated to achieve, namely to engender resentment against the metropolitan countries, it also implicitly held the metropolitan countries as paragons, or at any rate as acceptable models of what ought to be. The nationalist leaders were implying that they wanted to be free like the metropolitan countries, to be powerful like them, to be rich like them, to be developed like them, etc. In this way the nationalist movement was at once giving the African masses consciousness of a wider world, while nurturing their dissatisfaction with their lot and raising their expectations of betterment.

The ideology of development promoted so assiduously by both the African leaders and the metropolitan countries had a similar effect. When all the equivocations are done away with, the type of development which the bulk of African countries are seeking is in essence one that makes the industrialised Western countries the model of development, so that the African country engaged in the quest for development is really trying to fashion itself after the image of the West. However, the point of particular interest to us here is that the unflagging commitment to development implies both a strong dissatisfaction with what exists, as well as a strong expectation of betterment. These are the conditions which have caused what is popularly called the revolution in rising expectations and made the failure of development a serious liability to the ruling class.

It remains to bring one more element into this account of the implications of the failure of the development effort. In postcolonial Africa capitalism is the one thing which has been developing. This is partly because international and domestic social forces have conspired to push development along the line of least resistance. These social forces are associated with the class character of African societies, the dynamics of the class struggle in Africa, and the Western notions of development prevailing in Africa. As capitalism develops the basic contradiction in the relations of production develops also. What is of particular interest here is that the development of class contradiction appears to be quite out of proportion to what might be reasonably expected, given the stage of the development of productive forces in Africa. This is the cumulative effect of several factors. First, the smallness of the surplus in the impoverished economies of Africa has limited the ability of governments to provide the most elementary necessities, so that the gap between the mass demand for the basics and the supply capability of the ruling class has had to be bridged by repression, which tendentially sharpens the contraditions in production relations. Secondly, the appropriation and accumulation of capital by the ruling class was disproportionate to the development of productive forces. As a general rule the capitalist class in Africa engaged in very little productive activity. They tended to accrue their wealth through political corruption, by the use of state power for appropriation, and by acting as collecting and marketing agents and subcontractors of foreign capital. When capital accumulation goes on in this way, that is with little or no development of productive forces, it necessarily entails a very high intensity of exploitation. A higher intensity of exploitation calls for a higher level of repression, which tends to radicalise class contradictions. Thirdly there is the one-sided emphasis on the political. The nationalist leadership, marginalised economically, came to power by building a political base on mass support. When the nationalist leaders displaced the colonial rulers they proceeded to use political power to create an economic base. In office they have tended to use political power as the primary means of accumulating wealth. Unable to deliver the economic surplus to meet the demands of the masses, they have tended to frame political solutions to economic problems. The import of all this is the overpoliticisation of social life, which leads to the accelerated development of the contradictions in the relations of production. Fourthly and finally, there is the acceleration of the process of class formation. The nationalist leadership which succeeded the colonial regime was anxious to create a material base quickly, and had only political leverage to do it. Because of this and other reasons, which need not detain us here, capitalist accumulation tended to degenerate into primitive accumulation, thereby accelerating the process of proletarian-isation and accentuating class conflict. Also the policies which were popularly used in Africa to deal with the problems of underdevelopment tended to accelerate class formation. To illustrate this, the pursuit of indigenisation often meant easy opportunities for a small minority to get rich at public expense. The raising of revenue from primary export commodities ostensibly for development often amounted to the exploitation of peasant producers through the control of marketing, as well as government influence over the conditions of production. Policies such as import substitution, export promotion, and even measures such as import licensing, which were meant to conserve foreign exchange, were similarly abused to the benefit of the few and the acceleration of class formation. For instance, favoured entrepreneurs received heavy protection to allow them to produce inefficiently and profitably behind protective barriers, and were aided by all sorts of extravagant and unnecessary incentives. All these factors quickly advanced the development of class formation even when aspects of the development of capitalism remained rudimentary.

That then is the context in which the failure of the development effort is to be seen. It is a failure which poses grave dangers for the ruling class in Africa. The danger lies in the crisis of legitimacy which it has precipitated, and in the fact that it is generating revolutionary pressures in Africa by rapidly advancing the development of class contradictions. Let us now turn to the response to these problems.

Ideological containment

The struggle of the ruling class in Africa to contain the crisis of legitimacy and revolutionary pressures has taken rather predictable forms. To begin with it has tried to paper over class contradictions by promoting a new sense of common purpose. Since independence, African leaders have tended to adopt some variety of the following argument: 'Our national problems are quite clear and what to do about them is equally clear. We must deal with poverty, ignorance and disease, we must reduce our dependence, pursue development and become a going concern in the international system of states. And we must do this by relying essentially on our resources and in a way that reflects our own culture and our unique historical experience. The task to be done is very urgent and the resources with which to do it very limited. We cannot therefore afford wasteful divisiveness, ideological debates or tolerance of subversion of the effort so necessary to our survival'. This attempt to fabricate common cause and common commitment has not worked well. The reality of a fragmented and incoherent socio-economic formation and class contradiction has stood in the way of its plausibility.

The futility of this form of ideological containment appears to be fully recognised now and the African ruling class has realised that it has to do better than this. The new tendency is to come to terms with the reality that objective conditions in Africa favour progressive consciousness. African leaders now generally affect a radical or at least a populist stance. A reading of the more recent development plans reveals this tendency. They now generally reject growth without development, they generally profess commitment to the participative and distributive aspects of development; they tend to embrace ideas such as basic needs and integrated rural development. Most significantly there is much talk about socialism. There are not many African governments today which have not embraced some form of socialism, albeit qualified to the point of meaninglessness. The populism or radicalism is of course calculated for effect. No-one suggests that the ideas are taken very seriously in practice. Indeed, in general they provide a cover behind which the assiduous pursuit of capitalism proceeds apace. Nevertheless it is of immense significance that the African ruling class has opted almost uniformly for this type of ideological containment. That says something about the objective conditions prevailing in Africa. What it says is that objective conditions are creating strong revolutionary pressures and that the claims of progressive government are becoming irresistible. In taking a radical stance, however insincerely, African leaders are coming to terms with developments that they cannot stop. But this new form of ideological containment is itself pregnant with contradiction. The progressive ideas to which the ruling class pays lip-service in order to ride the tide of rising radical consciousness become fetters on them. These ideas become standards for the evaluation of regime performance – standards which must ultimately show them in a bad light because they cannot meet them. At the same time, by propagating these progressive ideas they are also aiding their own negation as a class.

Political containment

That is how the ruling classes in Africa have tried to deal with the problems of the level of ideology. How about the level of practical politics? What they have done in this sphere is to depoliticise the society and to discourage the expression of political dissent with very severe sanctions. It is in this context that the tendencies towards one-party systems and military interventions in politics are to be understood. The one-party system was the logical step for a ruling class which has apparently convinced itself that the problems of African socio-economic formations and the types of solutions they call for are clear, that ideological arguments and political rivalry are a criminal waste of time in the face of pressing problems.

Threatened by the crisis of legitimacy and revolutionary pressures from below, the ruling class used the pretext to mobilise violence to depoliticise the society; they imposed a common political creed, outlawed political organisations in competition with their own, reduced elections to a farce or dispensed with them altogether, discouraged any acknowledgement or expression of political differentiation, and as much as possible replaced politics with administration.

The one-party system eventually emerged as the classic form of the depoliticised African society. It allowed the ruling class to dispense with the substance of democratic participation while retaining its formal aspects. It is of course quite possible for democracy to be practised in the context of the one-party system. However, the experience of one-party systems in Africa does not demonstrate this possibility. The establishment of the one-party system in Africa involved the use of much coercion and even violence. It entailed one faction of the ruling class using coercion to make itself hegemonic, as well as using coercion to force the masses to acquiesce in the reduction of their political participation. And even after the establishment of the one-party system, the use of force continued to be necessary because the contradictions within the ruling class and the contradictions between the ruling class and the masses were so great that a one-party system which was so totally at odds with this reality could only be maintained by force. The threat of political instability engendered by pent-up resentment has not given the ruling class the confidence and security to practise democracy. The repression needed to establish and maintain the single-party system aided the development of the contradictions in society. Repression and the monopoly of political power increased the premium on the attainment of political power. The premium was already very high because of the use of political power to create an economic base and its use for the accumulation of capital. The premium on political power now became singularly high because political power had to be captured not only as a necessary condition for economic welfare but also as a necessary condition for avoiding brutalisation if not extermination.

The one-party system was not the only form which African politics assumed in the process of depoliticisation. In some places even the idea of a one-party system was too much politics; the government tried to govern without specialised political organisations or vehicles of mass mobilisation. In many cases African socio-economic formations eventually gravitated towards military regimes, a purer form of depoliticisation than the one-party system and the no-party system. It would be interesting to explore the reasons why this mode of depoliticisation prevails in a particular country and why a particular country changes from one mode of depoliticisation to another. However, that will take us too far afield. The point of immediate interest is that the African ruling class has had to embark on a course of depoliticisation, and that the process of effecting and maintaining a state of depoliticisation aggravates the tensions and develops the contradictions of the socio-economic formation.

It would be mistaken to regard depoliticisation as being just subjectively contingent, as being a measure which the African ruling class happened to adopt in order to deal with the dangers of legitimacy crisis and incipient revolutionary pressures from below. Depoliticisation was objectively necessary. In Africa there is convergence of a very small economic surplus and a very high degree of economic inequality. This is a state of affairs that does not permit political democracy or even liberalism; rather it makes political authoritarianism mandatory, for without it the existing property relations cannot be maintained in the face of the extreme deprivations of the masses.

This brings us back to the question of state power in the socio-economic formation. Depoliticisation expresses the unusually advanced development of state power. If state power had not been so developed, the immense coercion mobilised to effect depoliticisation would not have been available. But of course the necessity of depoliticisation and the implementation of the policy of depoliticisation further encouraged the growth of the coercive power of the state. The process of depoliticisation made the postcolonial state even more involved in the class struggle; it tried to pre-empt the political expression of contradictions within the ruling class as well as the contradictions between the ruling class and the subordinate classes. By getting the state involved in the class struggle the process of depoliticisation reinforced the blurring of the distinction between the ruling class and the state. In so far as the boundary between state and ruling class is blurred, the government, which is essentially the formal link between the state and ruling class, is, so to speak, dislocated, and collapses into the ruling class, so that it looks more like a tool or even an appendage of the ruling class.

By involving the state so intimately in the class struggle, and by increasing state power, the process of depoliticisation engenders very keen interest in the control of state power. The ensuing importance of controlling state power reinforces the authoritarianism of the hegemonic faction of the bourgeoisie. Under pressure of a seige mentality, this hegomonic faction is unwilling to accept liberal restraints on power which might give any other group leverage. As always when one competing political faction or class in political competition resorts to political extremism, others follow and a vicious circle is created.

All these effects in turn influence the process of accumulation. On balance their impact on accumulation is negative. The involvement of the state in the class struggle makes it more difficult for the government to affect the air of impartiality which elicits commitment to its development efforts from the subordinate classes. The bitter struggle for state power concentrates energy on politics and on survival, to the detriment of economic productivity. The interventionism of the state and the overpoliticisation of life encourages the rise of political power as a mode of surplus appropriation, a tendency that renders capitalism in Africa unproductive. It would appear that depoliticisation compounds the persistence of underdevelopment, the very factor that made it necessary in the first place.

Economic containment

It would seem superfluous to raise the issue of economic containment since we have already examined at considerable length the development policies and strategies of the African ruling class and have seen their inevitable failure to rescue Africa from underdevelopment and economic stagnation. The issue is pertinent nonetheless. What types of economic measures and orientations does the ruling class in Africa adopt in the face of the legitimacy crisis and the latent revolutionary pressures engendered by their past failures? We have already seen one answer to this question. The African ruling class has become remarkably eclectic and is trying to combine elements picked out of discredited development strategies tried in the past. This eclecticism of course underlines the fact that they are running out of ideas. Ideological exhaustion can only further impede the mobilisation of the masses for the battle against underdevelopment.

Whatever eclectic development strategies are adopted we can expect certain tendencies. First will be an ambivalence towards the struggle for self-reliance. This ambivalence is related to the alienation between the ruling class and the subordinate classes, caused by economic stagnation, the peculiar intensity of exploitation and the political disenfranchisement of the subordinate classes through the process of depoliticisation. Unable to capitalise on the energy of the masses, and yet under immense pressure to expand the surplus in order to meet urgent demands and to buy legitimacy, the African ruling class will find itself having to look abroad for help. It inevitably resorts to thinking of development in terms of the vertical relations between centre and periphery – the transfer of technology, better prices for primary commodities, commodity price stabilisation schemes, soft loans, and more foreign investment. In short, they would effectively be falling back on the factors which underline their exploitative dependence. We are already beginning to see this regress to dependence, for instance in Senegal, Ivory Coast, Kenya, Nigeria, Ghana, Sierra Leone, Zaire and Somalia. This regress does not of course help the struggle against underdevelopment, and the objective necessity of self-reliance will be increasingly obvious, hence the ambivalence.

There is a similar ambivalence towards capitalism. The involvement of the state in the class struggle has led to statism, which in the economic sphere has become manifest in various degrees of state capitalism or 'socialism'. The development of state capitalism was merely reinforced. It was already inherent in the monopolistic character of the colonial economy and had emerged into sharp relief in the postcolonial era as a result of the use of political power for surplus appropriation. Nevertheless, the involvement of the state in the class struggle in the postcolonial era has contributed immensely to the growth of state capitalism. Perhaps this should be restated as it comes dangerously close to a tautology. The more accurate position is that, for the most part, the involvement of the state in the class struggle – eg. nationalising enterprises to give the ruling class access to more surplus – is simultaneously the process of the development of statism and state capitalism. Be that as it may, the interesting thing is how the ruling class has rationalised the trend towards state capitalism by paying lip-service to the virtues of moderate socialism. Although capitalism is assiduously pursued in many parts of Africa, there seems to be an increasing reluctance to defend capitalist development. Even in those countries which are pursuing capitalist development, the ruling class feels obliged to refrain from justifying capitalism. That is part of the reason why there is talk about African socialism, communalism and the mixed economy. This stance is important and it reflects the fact that the objective conditions of the African socio-economic formations do not favour capitalism. To begin with, capitalism and imperialism are perceived as the major cause of the current underdevelopment of Africa. Capitalist development has tended to reinforce the exploitative dependence, which enables underdevelopment to persist. Most importantly, African conditions have revealed capitalism in its harshness and brutality: inequalities are too glaring and their brutal consequences all too obvious. In the face of the extremities of want and a meagre surplus, it is difficult to sell the idea that those who are in a position to accumulate should take what they can and leave the rest to suffer what they must. At the very least, it is embarrassing to propagate capitalism openly; if it must be propagated, it has to be done obliquely or by stealth. The dilemma is now clear. The African ruling class cannot afford to go socialist; nor can it afford to be capitalist.

This dilema only compounds the problems before the ruling class, as well as the problems of development. Earlier we pointed out that the African ruling class was running out of ideas for fashioning and inspiring a functional development strategy, limited as it is by the constraint of working with ideas compatible with the maintenance of the existing property relations. The hostility of objective conditions to capitalism causes not only ambivalence but even some loss of confidence in capitalism. These factors obscure any clarity of purpose and undermine the will and capability of the African ruling class to manage its capitalist system and to promote capitalist development.

Towards new syntheses

We have seen how the persistence of underdevelopment and economic stagnation has engendered a legitimacy crisis and revolutionary pressures, and how the ruling class has tried to deal with these problems by ideological, political and economic containment. It is clear from the preceding discussion that containment is unleashing forces which inhibit accumulation and the development of the productive forces; in doing so, it is reinforcing the very factors which caused the ruling class to resort to containment. How might this vicious circle be broken? What are the likely directions of movement of African socio-economic formations? These are very difficult questions to answer, especially as the answers have to make assumptions about a reality which is changing all the time. We cannot go fully into the answers to these questions here, but it is necessary to suggest how we might set about answering them.

In tackling this question it would be tempting to pay too much attention to what the African bourgeoisie might do or not do. That would be misleading, however. It is more useful to concentrate on the two groups whose real and potential power is essentially the most decisive on African socio-economic formations. These are the metropolitan bourgeoisie and the subordinate classes in Africa, and African workers and peasants.

Let us begin from the perspective of the metropolitan bourgeoisie. The power of the metropolitan bourgeoisie in the African socio-economic formation lies in the structural dependence of African economies brought about by colonialism and the framing of development strategies around the vertical links between Africa and the metropole. A concerted effort by the metropolitan bourgeoisie to transfer large quantities of resources to Africa, particularly technology and capital, could significantly increase the surplus available in Africa and stimulate a modest dependent capitalist development. This is really the option that the New International Economic Order is calling for.

The possibility of transferring resources on the requisite scale is highly problematic. The problems include the competition between imperialisms at the centre, which lead to immense expenditure on armaments. Also, nationalism and racism within the centre are unlikely to tolerate what must look like a reckless generosity towards real or potential enemies. The chances are that these difficulties will prove decisive in preventing the required transfer of resources to Africa and other parts of the third world.

To be sure, some effort will be made to transfer resources to the third world in the hope of stemming political radicalism and strengthening demand, making parts of the third world more inclined to cooperate in the strategic designs of the metropolitan powers. But the effort will fall far short of what is required. Of course the impact of this effort will be differential. There will be more interest in some African socio-economic formations than others, more willingness to transfer resources to some places than others. So it may be that here and there economic stagnation could be stemmed and some modest degree of dependent capitalist development could be achieved. The improvement will be necessarily marginal and it will come with serious problems: developing contradictions in the relations of production, encouraging further gross inequalities so that the marginal increase in per capita income has very limited or negligible effect on the level of welfare of the masses, and weakening the competitive position of the dependency, etc. In the final analysis these favoured socio-economic formations will be scarely distinct from the others, where it will be stagnation as usual.

Let us now turn to the subordinate classes, workers and peasants, the other possible source of change. The question of what the workers and peasants might do or can do is even more important than what the metropolitan bourgeoisie might do because the workers and peasants are the producers of value and the mainstay of the economy. Unfortunately, it is particularly hazardous to try to predict what the subordinate classes might do because there are so many variables to consider, so many uncertainties entering into the equation. The question usually asked is whether the subordinate classes can overturn the existing relations of production, thereby removing the contradiction between production (by the masses) and appropriation by the few, cutting the exploitative dependence on international capital which is against their objective interests, and paving the way to a real assault on underdevelopment through liberation of the energy of the masses and by gearing development efforts to their energy and needs. The revolutionary potential of African peasants and workers has been hotly debated for years, and a sizeable body of literature now exists on this question. Unhappily the debate has not been very illuminating and we shall not dwell on it here. Apart from problems of dogmatism, abstractness and hasty assumptions, the debate has been unfortunate in that it has encouraged us to think of the role of peasants and workers almost entirely in terms of the possibility of revolution. The possibility of revolution is of course the critical question. But it is not useful to limit our interest in the role of the subordinate classes in Africa to this question. We want to understand African socio-economic formations, what they are, how they are what they are, and how they might be other than what they are. There are aspects of the role of the subordinate classes which can increase this understanding without helping us significantly to answer the question of their revolutionary potential.

The subordinate classes exercise considerable influence on the character of African socio-economic formations by their latent radicalism. In most of Africa the class contradictions are all too visible in the different lifestyles and living conditions of the bourgeoisie and the subordinate classes. And the bourgeoisie is constantly reminded of the potential danger of the contradiction by occasional outbursts of violence, crimes against property, workers' militancy, and the subversion by workers and peasants of some 'development' policies. The assertiveness and starkness of the contradictions in production relations is such that the ruling class is increasingly preoccupied with coming to terms with it. It is the necessity of coming to terms with class contradictions that partly explains why the African ruling class has tended to resort to more radical anti-imperialist stances, state capitalism and mildly progressive changes in the sphere of distribution (such as less regressive tax policies) as opposed to the sphere of production.

These may be initially cosmetic or manageable changes, but they have a dynamic that makes them important in the development of African socio-economic formations. We have already taken note of the important implications of the move to state capitalism and of the dilemma of a ruling class which cannot afford to be either socialist or capitalist. The effects we have discussed are largely economic. It is useful to mention one important political effect. The advantage of appearing radical has affected intra-class power struggle within the ruling class. Quite often non-hegemonic factions of the African bourgeoisie try to win popular support by sounding more radical than the hegemonic faction, thus sparking off a scramble for the left – mainly verbal and symbolic rather than substantive, but nonetheless significant. Even the military has tended to defend its intervention in politics in terms of relatively progressive ideas. The mobilisation of essentially progressive ideas and progressive symbols to challenge and destabilise government, and to mobilise mass support and to seize state power, legitimises and diffuses progressive ideas essentially incompatible, at least in their logic, with the maintenance of existing relations of production. The diffusion of the elements of an ideology objectively expressing the interests of the subordinate classes, and the use of progressive ideas by factions of the ruling class to overthrow governments, contribute to the existence of what must be called a revolutionary situation. In most of Africa the legitimacy of the ruling class and the social order are in question, governmental instability is rampant, the ideology of the subordinate classes is becoming increasingly assertive, and the ruling class has little confidence in itself. One must conclude that a revolutionary situation exists in Africa.

Whether this revolutionary situation will yield to revolutions is another matter. The answer to this question has been attempted in my *Revolutionary Pressures in Africa* and will not be repeated here. For the limited purposes of this work, it is more useful to see what can be learned from the present reality, the reality being that there are several African governments who have come to power in the name of socialist revolution, or who have proclaimed socialism as the basis of their rule. Some distinctions are helpful. There are those like Mozambique, Guinea-Bissau and Angola where there was a revolutionary struggle led by a party with a sophisticated political organisation and an essentially Marxist-Leninist ideology. It is in these places that the claim of socialism is most convincing: very concrete steps have been taken to effect the transition to socialism in both the spheres of distribution and production. But as the leadership in these places readily admit, it is still very much socialism from the top, serious contradictions remain and the class struggle goes on. In the other places, such as Tanzania, Ethiopia and Benin, where socialism has been formally embraced by a leadership which was not involved in a revolutionary colonial struggle and did not before coming to power belong to a disciplined socialist party, evidence of socialist transformation is far less tangible. Socialist transformation has tended to be confined to the sphere of distribution and has barely touched the sphere of production, which is what really counts. Perhaps the transition to socialism has gone as far as might be expected in these formations. It is unlikely that a petit-bourgeois leadership already well-established in power will, so to speak, commit suicide as a class. Nevertheless it would be dangerous to be dogmatic about the limits of socialist development in these places. The very impressive changes achieved in the sphere of distribution have created a momentum for more socialism, which the leadership has had to curb, in some cases, like Tanzania, quite successfully. Nevertheless it is entirely possible for this momentum to counteract the reactionary tendencies of the leadership and to propel the system towards more socialism. This may well be the case in Ethiopia.

The problem of transition to socialism is extraordinarily complex and should not be confused with the problem of making a socialist revolution. Unfortunately, much of the writing on socialism in the third world, including Africa, is very concerned with the question of the possibility of socialist revolution but pays hardly any attention to the problem of the transition to socialism. This particular emphasis is unfortunate, for a socialist revolution is only part of a very complicated and hazardous process of the transition to socialism. Associated with this misplacement of emphasis is a tendency to discuss the problem of realising socialism as a matter of commitment and taking the right action. In the case of the African socio-economic formations whose leaders have opted for socialism, scholarly assessment has focused on leaders' intentions, policies and actions, as if intentions and actions tell the whole story. Not enough attention has been paid to objective forces. We appear to have forgotten Marx's admonition that 'no social order is ever destroyed before all the productive forces for which it is sufficient have been developed, and new superior relations of production never replace older ones before the material conditions for their existence has matured within the framework of the old society'. One of the pertinent objective forces posing problems for the transition to socialism is the state of the development of productive forces. The point here is not so much the problem it poses for socialist revolution as the problem it poses for the transition to socialism. The state of the development of productive forces in Africa threatens to turn socialism into caricature, even with the best of intentions: for instance, it tends to encourage political authoritarianism and reduce socialism to the management and redistribution of poverty.

Let us now return to our original question. We were considering socialist revolution as a way for African socio-economic formations to overcome economic stagnation and liquidate underdevelopment. The question arises for two reasons: first, because the subordinate classes in Africa are one of two social groups (the other being the metropolitan bourgeoisie) who have real or potential power to influence African socio-economic formations decisively; second, because underdevelopment is organically related to class contradictions in Africa and the exploitative dependence of Africa on international capital.

It is clear enough that underdevelopment will persist if the existing capitalist relations of production are maintained, and if the dependence of Africa on international capital continues. One has to conclude from this that the overturning of the existing relations of production is necessary for overcoming underdevelopment. Having said that we must avoid the common error of seeing socialist revolution as the panacea for all the problems of Africa, including underdevelopment. For one thing there is the dilemma of the state of the development of productive forces which will tend to distort socialism and greatly limit what can be achieved under socialist regimes. Of course in the long run the transition to socialism in Africa should further the development of productive forces. But the problem is how to get to the point when this can happen on a significant scale – when the initial dilemma of socialist regimes can be solved. This dilemma is that the state of the development of productive forces impedes the transition to socialism. To this should be added the difficulties arising from the pressures of the international system. The transition to socialism is not pursued in the context of a closed socio-economic system, but rather in the context of an international system which exerts very strong pressures on the domestic system. For instance, international capital is apt to subvert (by destabilisation, economic sanctions and other means)

African socio-economic formations seeking to go socialist. That makes things difficult enough. Worse, they also face pressures from 'friendly' industrialised progressive socio-economic formations who would normally be expected to be sympathetic and supportive. These pressures include being asked to play, at great cost to themselves, roles which further the strategic and other interests of the advanced 'socialist partner', and to adopt an approach to socialism which is out of tune with the historical realities of the African socio-economic formation. In the face of such difficulties we can only expect very limited success in the struggle against underdevelopment, even where a socialist revolution has occurred.

Conclusion

The indications are that for the vast majority of African socio-economic formations there will be neither significant capitalist development nor socialist development. The present state of economic stagnation will continue, deepening class contradictions and causing governmental instability but not necessarily sparking off revolution in the foreseeable future. In the event of such protracted stagnation, the politics of anxiety will become institutionalised; increasingly, the ruling class will display signs of paranoia while the subordinate classes become frustrated, demoralised and available for induction into extremist, though not necessarily radical, movements. Since the defensive radicalism of the ruling class has almost gone as far as it can be pushed, the ruling class will tend increasingly to 'psychologise' failures which lie in the economic sphere. To conceal class contradiction and boost morale, the ruling class will increasingly appeal to loyalty, patriotism, discipline and dislike for outsiders. Enemies of society will be found all too ubiquitously and will be dealt with summarily. Fascism – that is the reality staring us in the face in most of Africa. The fascist option cannot really be called a resolution of the contradictions. It is only a 'stalemate' which may be very protracted but nevertheless transitional. In the long run objective conditions are more likely to move Africa towards socialism.

Bibliography

AKE, C., *Revolutionary Pressures in Africa*, London, 1978.
AKE, C., 'Ideology and Objective Conditions', in J. Barkan ed., *Politics and Public Policy in Kenya and Tanzania*, New York, 1979.
COLLIER, R., 'Parties, Coups and Authoritarian Rule', *Comparative Political Studies*, 11, 1, 1978.
GUTKIND, P., 'Political Consciousness of the Urban Poor in Ibadan', *International Journal of Sociology*, Summer, 1977.
MOHAN, J., 'Varieties of African Socialism', *Socialist Register*, 1966.
OGANOVA, A., 'The Development of a Common Class Interest Among The Urban Proletariat in Tropical Africa', *International Journal of Sociology*, Summer, 1977.

Index

Abidjan, 78; economic dominance of, 89
Aborigines Protection Society (1909), 77
African, Caribbean and Pacific countries (ACP), 164, 165, 166; see also EEC
African Common Market, 169
African Monetary Fund, 169
African Progress Union (1919), 77
African Regional Conference on Integrated Rural Development, 155
agriculture, 98–100; output, 100–1; Tanzania, 117, 118; see also primary products
Amin, Samir, 26
Anglo-German Agreement (1886), 48
Anglophone countries (trade distribution), 59
Angola, 154
Angola Diamond Co., 48
Arrighi, Giovanni, 26
Arusha Declaration (1967), 94, 116
asbestos cement products, 148
Asian businesses (Kenya), 124
Azikiwe, Nnamdi, 80

Bakary, Djibo, 74
balance of payments, 35, 39
Bank of West Africa (British), 34, 50
banks, colonial, 55
Banque de l'Afrique Occidentale, 34, 50
Banque du Sénégal, 34
Barclays Bank, 50
barter trade, 33; and terms of trade, 69
Basel Mission, 52, 54
Belgium (Mozambique coal concessions), 48–9
Benin, Republic of, 111
Berlin Conference, 48
Bismark, German Chancellor, 29
Bokassa, Emperor, 139
boom (post-1945), 71
Bo School (Sierra Leone), 74
bourgeoisie, African, 15, 16, 61, 71–7, 128–9, 139; and tribalism, 2; and nationalist movements, 80; and state capitalism, 96, 125; contradictions within, 140; metropolitan, 185

Brandt Commission Report (1980), 172
Brett, E. A., 46
Britain, 123
British East Africa Co., 48
British South Africa Co., 48
Brown, M. B., 26

Cabinda, 48
Cabral, Amilcar, 76
Cameroons, Southern, 63
capital:
    definitions, 15–16
    metropolitan, and primary production, 38
    formation, Francophone Africa, 56
capitalism:
    definitions, 16–19, 128
capitalist development (postcolonial), 139–40, 178, 179
capitalist penetration, 32, 49–50
capitalist sphere (colonial economy), 60, 61, 62, 125; and precapitalist sphere, 61–2
Capitalists:
    indigenous, 39, 138, 184
    and the peasants, 62, 65
cash crops v. food crops, 117, 118
Chautemps, Félix, 84
Chelarams, K., 93
Chilivumbo, A., 159, 160
chrome, 40
Chunya goldfield, 52
Civil Servants' Association (1907), 77
class:
    divisions, 36, 61, 126, 181, 182, 184
    differentiation, 74, 122
    contradictions, 120, 125
    ruling, 127, 128, 129
    subordinate, 185–6
coal:
    deposits, 49, 71
    miners' strike, 71
cobalt, 40
cocoa, 44, 45, 52, 54; drying process, 63; see also Ghana
coffee, 76
Coffee Plantations Registration Ordinance (1918), 76
Colonial Development Advisory Committee, 46
colonial economy, see economy

191